Isaac Smith Homans

The Banker's Common Place Book

Isaac Smith Homans

The Banker's Common Place Book

ISBN/EAN: 9783337111984

Printed in Europe, USA, Canada, Australia, Japan

Cover: Foto ©Suzi / pixelio.de

More available books at **www.hansebooks.com**

THE

BANKER'S

COMMON-PLACE BOOK:

CONTAINING

I.—A TREATISE ON BANKING. BY A. B. JOHNSON, ESQ., OF UTICA, N. Y.
II.—TEN MINUTES' ADVICE ON KEEPING A BANKER. BY J. W. GILBART, ESQ.
III.—BYLES ON THE FOREIGN LAW OF BILLS OF EXCHANGE.
IV.—REMARKS ON BILLS OF EXCHANGE. BY JOHN RAMSEY M'CULLOCH, ESQ.
V.—FORMS OF BILLS OF EXCHANGE, IN EIGHT EUROPEAN LANGUAGES.
VI.—FORMS OF NOTICE OF PROTEST, WITH REMARKS.
VII.—FINANCIAL AND COMMERCIAL MAXIMS. BY AMERICAN AND FOREIGN AUTHORS.
VIII.—A CHAPTER ON YOUNG MEN.
IX.—THE CURIOSITIES OF NUMBERS.
X.—DECISIONS ON BANKING, BY THE SUPREME COURT OF MASSACHUSETTS.
XI.—ON THE DUTIES AND MISDOINGS OF BANK DIRECTORS. BY A. B. JOHNSON.
XII.—SUGGESTIONS TO YOUNG CASHIERS ON THE DUTIES OF THEIR PROFESSION. PRIZE ESSAY.
XIII.—A NUMISMATIC DICTIONARY; OR, AN ACCOUNT OF COINS OF ALL COUNTRIES.

"*While a banker adheres with regularity to known forms of business and settled principles, Providence is a guarantee for his success; but when he deviates from these, Providence is almost equally a guarantee of disaster, both personal and official.*"

NEW YORK: 23 MURRAY ST. 1870.

PUBLISHED AT THE OFFICE OF THE BANKER'S MAGAZINE.
Price, $1.50.

PREFACE.

The following treatise on Banking, written by, perhaps, the oldest practical banker in America, was published originally in the June number of the Bankers' Magazine, for 1849. It was extensively noticed by the daily press in many parts of our Union, and its information on the subject of banking was deemed so useful to every class of persons, that several of the papers in the State of New York recommended that a copy of the treatise should be placed in every school district library in the State. No doubt the procurement of bank loans would be facilitated by a knowledge that bank loans are not properly accorded as personal favors, or distributed by the caprice of bankers, (though such erroneous opinions are not uncommon,) but depend on principles which the treatise discusses, and which can be conformed to by persons who desire to become borrowers.

The Bankers' Magazine, of London, quoted largely from the work, and with much commendation; and bankers everywhere who have seen it seem to unite in its praise. The first edition is now out of print, except as it exists in the third volume of the Bankers' Magazine, bound up with the other matter of the volume, and some copies of which are still for sale by the editor and at several of his agencies in different cities But as inquiries for the treatise are numerous, from different places, and an order for a copy of the work has just been received from Paris, the editor has republished it, carefully revised by the author, and accompanied it with several other articles from other sources; but making, in the whole, a volume that cannot fail of being useful to bankers, and to readers of every kind who desire a knowledge of what has heretofore been deemed the occult science of Banking.

CONTENTS.

I. A TREATISE ON BANKING, THE DUTIES OF A BANKER, AND HIS PERSONAL REQUISITES THEREFOR. By A. B. JOHNSON, Esq., President of the Ontario Branch Bank, Utica; Author of "A Treatise on Language, or the Relation which Words bear to Things," "Religion in its Relation to the Present Life," etc.

PART FIRST.—THE BANK.

		Page
I.	Of Discount or Interest	7
II.	Difference among Banks as to the Allowable Rate of Interest	7
III.	The Profits to a Bank from its Bank Notes and Deposits	8
IV.	Bank Dividends	9
V.	Benefits to the Public from the use of Bank Notes	9
VI.	Relative Utility to the Public of the Safety Fund and Free Banks	10
VII.	Loss to the Public from Insolvent Bank Notes	11
VIII.	The Safety Fund System of New York	12
IX.	Relative Lucrativeness to Bank Owners of the Safety Fund and Free Banks	12
X.	Free Banking in New York	13
XI.	Relative Effects on City and Country Capitalists of the Safety Fund and Free Bank Systems	14
XII.	Relative Effects on City and Country Commerce of the Safety Fund and Free Bank Systems	14
XIII.	Different Legal Privileges accorded to different Safety Fund Banks	15
XIV.	Difference in the Productiveness of Different Magnitudes of Bank Capital	15
XV.	The Currency	16
XVI.	The Currency of the State is a sort of Measure of the Business of the State	16
XVII.	The Business of the State is a sort of Guarantee to Banks for the Permanence of a given amount of Currency	17
XVIII.	A Surplusage of Currency can never exist long	17
XIX.	The Extinguishment of Bank Circulation and Deposits, and the Extinguishment of Debts due to Banks, preserve a pretty uniform equality	18
XX.	Specie Payments.—Specie Suspensions	18, 19
XXI.	Suspension of Specie Payments by a single Solvent Bank	19
XXII.	Legal Tender	9
XXIII.	Receivables and Treasury Notes	20
XXIV.	A National Currency	20
XXV.	Expansions of the Bank Note Currency	21
XXVI.	The Spirit of Speculation is Contagious	22
XXVII	Expansion of Bank Deposits	22

		Page
XXVIII.	Contraction of the Currency	22
XXIX.	Periodical Contractions	23
XXX.	Pressure Contraction	23
XXXI.	Panic	24
XXXII.	The Pressure in the Interior	24
XXXIII.	The Pressure and Panic Terminate	25
XXXIV.	The Sale of Exchange	25
XXXV	Collections within the State	26
XXXVI	Collections out of the State	26

PART SECOND. — THE BANKER.

I.	The Objects of Banking	28
II.	The Pecuniary Prosperity of his Bank should constitute the Pecuniary Object of the Banker	29
III.	Specie Suspensions are never necessary to Banks	29
IV.	The Interests of Debtors and Dealers should be subordinate to the Interests of the Bank	30
V.	Security	30
VI.	Moral Security	31
VII.	Security founded on the Morality of the Debtor	31
VIII.	Security founded on the Habits of a Debtor	31
IX.	Security founded on the Nature of a Man's Business	31
X.	Security founded on the Application of the Loan	32
XI.	Security founded on the Character of the Paper that is to be Discounted	32
XII.	Acceptances in advance of Consignments	32
XIII.	Assimilated Notes and Acceptances	32
XIV.	Kiting. — Dummies. — Void Notes and Drafts	33
XV.	Of Gains	34
XVI.	When to be Moderate	34
XVII.	The kind of Paper that a Banker should prefer	34
XVIII.	Selection of Loans founded on Incidental Circulation and Deposits	35
XIX.	Selection of Loans founded on the Place of their Repayment	36
XX.	Selection of Loans founded on the Sale of Exchange	37
XXI.	Selection of Loans founded on the Commission for their Collection	37
XXII.	Selection of Loans founded on the Time they are to endure	38
XXIII.	Time Estimated with reference to the Prospective Wants of a Bank	38
XXIV.	Time with reference to Panics and Pressures	39
XXV.	A Banker should acquaint himself with the Pecuniary Circumstances of his Dealers	39
XXVI.	A Banker should, as far as is practicable, know the Signatures of his Dealers	40
XXVII.	A Banker should know the Residence of Endorsers	41
XXVIII.	A Banker should know the Pecuniary Condition of his Bank	42
XXIX.	Prospective Resources	42
XXX.	Provision for the Future	42
XXXI.	General Supervision	43
XXXII.	Over-drafts	43
XXXIII.	Enforcement of Payments	43
XXXIV.	Adherence to Good Principles	44
XXXV.	A Banker should beware of Persuasion, and of undue Pertinacity in Applicants	44

		Page
XXXVI.	A Banker should beware of Speculators..................	44
XXXVII.	A Banker should keep independent of his Debtors........	45
XXXVIII.	Economy..	45

PART THIRD—THE MAN.

I.	He should be wary of Recommendations...................	47
II.	He should be governed by his own Judgment...............	47
III.	Final Remarks.—Contingent Expenses.—Dividends...........	48

TEN MINUTES' ADVICE ON KEEPING A BANKER. By J. W. GILBART, Esq...... 49

CONTENTS OF PART SECOND.

I.	The Law of Bills of Exchange. By J. BARNARD BYLES...................	60
II.	Laws and Customs respecting Bills and Notes. By JOHN RAMSAY McCULLOCH..	83
III.	Forms of Bills of Exchange ordinarily used in the French, German, Dutch, Italian, Spanish, Portuguese, Swedish, and Danish languages..........	93
IV.	Forms of Notice of Protest used in New York, Boston, Philadelphia, Richmond, Auburn, &c., with Remarks......................................	96
V.	Banking, Financial, and Commercial Maxims...........................	101
VI.	A Chapter on Young Men	114
VII.	The Curiosity of Figures..	119
VIII.	Decisions of the Supreme Judicial Court of Massachusetts on Banks, Cashiers, Notaries, Stockholders, Bills, and Notes....................	119
IX.	On the Duties, Omissions and Misdoings, of Bank Directors. By A. B. JOHNSON, of Utica...	138
X.	Suggestions to Young Cashiers on the Duties of their Profession. Prize Essay. By LORENZO SABINE.......................................	148
XI.	A Numismatic Dictionary, or Names of Coins of all Nations...........	166

A TREATISE ON BANKING

BY A. B. JOHNSON.

PART FIRST.—THE BANK.

Of Discount or Interest. — Banking consists, principally, in lending money at the legal rate of interest, and, sometimes, under. The loans are called discounts because the interest is paid in advance and deducted from the amount of the note. But if a bank were to deduct seven dollars from a hundred dollar note payable a year after date, the bank would receive seven dollars for a loan of only ninety-three dollars. To avoid such a result, which is, probably, an excess, beyond the legal rate of seven per cent. interest, the bank deducts from the note as much ess than seven dollars, as will prevent any illegal excess of interest. The bank pays ninety-three dollars and forty-six cents for the note, because that sum, if placed on interest for a year, will become a hundred dollars; just the amount of the note. Formerly all the banks of our state would have deducted seven dollars from the note; and such a mode of computation has been adjudged in England to be legal, and has been twice thus adjudged by our Supreme Court. But several years ago, in a case before the Court of Errors, the then Chancellor stated, incidentally, that he deemed such a computation usurious. Since then, all the banks in the state, except some, or all, in the city of New York, have, from timidity or caution, adopted the modified calculation, as above exemplified, even when calculating interest on notes that are to mature in two or three months. If, however, the original mode of calculating is defensible at law, (some eminent lawyers insist it is defensible,) the legality ought to be established by adjudication or legislation, for the benefit of the banks who refrain from that mode of computing discount, and for the safety of uch as hazard the computation.

Difference among Banks as to the Allowable Rate of Discount. — All the safety fund banks of our state are restricted, in the computation of interest, to six per cent. the year on notes and drafts that will become payable in sixty days or less, from the time of the discount; but what are termed free banks are permitted to take seven per cent. In the early periods of banking, when banks were located in only large commercial cities, nearly all loans were of the above short description; and as no mode of computing six per cent. discount will make the interest exceed the legal rate of seven per cent., banks took the whole of such discount in advance; hence, probably, arose the practice of deducting, in advance, the seven per cent., also, on loans that exceeded sixty days in duration; — the question of usury being either unthought of, or deemed inapplicable to such transactions. So, probably, originated the practice of computing sixty days as the sixth part of a year in all calculations of bank discounts. The computation resulted in no usury while applied to six per cent. loans, but, subsequently, when, from habit or inadvertence, sixty days were called by banks the sixth part of a year, in seven per cent. calculations, and ninety days were called the fourth part of a year, all the banks of the State about twenty-five years ago suddenly discovered, by an accidental decision of the Supreme Court, that nearly all the bank securities then existing were void in law; and at least one bank lost largely by the discovery.

The Profits to a Bank from its Bank Notes and Deposits. — A bank which should possess a capital limited to a hundred thousand dollars, could lend only a hundred thousand dollars, if it possessed neither bank notes of its own creation, nor deposits of other persons' money; hence, such a bank could gain but six per cent. the year on its capital, if its loans were made on securities that would mature in sixty days, or but seven per cent. if its loans were made on longer securities. But from this six or seven per cent. would have to be deducted, the salaries of the bank's officers, the rent of its banking house, its stationery, fuel, taxes, &c., so as to leave of its income, to be divided among its stockholders, not more than from three to five per cent. the year, — a dividend smaller than the productiveness of capital in other occupations, and, consequently, destructive to the continuance of banking.

By means, however, of lending bank notes of its own creation, such a bank may be able to lend much more than the amount of its capital; and increase its profits accordingly. And if the borrowers or other persons, will deposit with the bank a portion of their money, the bank can lend, also, some part of these deposits, and thereby enlarge further the profits of the bank. The effect is alike, therefore, of circulation and deposits; and the nature of them is similar; — circulation is deposits inside out, while deposits are circulation outside in. Both also must be paid by the bank on demand, and the bank knows no when the payment of either may be demanded; but so long as any bank possesses, daily, a sufficiency of money to pay all the deposits and bank notes whose payment is daily demanded, the bank feels at liberty to lend on interest the excess. From the last December official returns, on oath, sent to the Comptroller, by the one hundred and eighty-four banks of our state, their aggregate capital, including accumulated profits, and deducting the money invested in banking houses, a little exceeds forty-seven millions of dollars, which is all loaned on interest; and in addition thereto, some more than forty-five millions of their bank notes and deposits; hence, we discover the amount of benefit which banks derive practically from their bank notes and deposits.

Bank Dividends.— The benefit derived from circulation and deposits, though large in the aggregate, as appears above, still barely suffices to make bank capital desirable property. In January, of the year eighteen hundred and thirty-five, the then bank commissioners reported to the Legislature, that "the average dividends of all the banks, during the last three years, had been $7\frac{81}{100}$ per cent. the year on the invested capital." The present public statements required periodically from the banks, omit the amount of dividend which the banks pay; but no reason exists for supposing that banking is more profitable than it was at the former period; or even quite so profitable, as more competition exists than existed then.

Some small banks, that are favorably located, and conducted with great economy, pay annually ten per cent. in dividends, and a few pay more; but a bank that pays eight per cent. the year will contrast favorably with the general average of banks; while the ruin which occasionally overwhelms banks, absorbing their whole capitals, evinces that banking is so hazardous, that the excess, if any, of bank dividends over seven per cent. the year, the legal rate of interest, is, even in prosperous banks, rarely more than an equivalent for the hazards incident to banking; this, too, after we include, in the annual dividend, the exemption from taxation that pertains to the owners of bank capital; the taxes being all paid by the bank. We are yet to learn whether banking will continue to be desirable by capitalists, when it shall, next year, become burthened with the additional liability contemplated by our State's new constitution;— the addition doubling the existing liability of bank stockholders, and adding no new remuneration to the invested capital. The morality, and, perhaps, the constitutionality of the law, may well be questioned, of thus adding ex post facto liabilities to preëxisting bank stockholders; for though bank charters reserve to the legislature a power to alter charters, the proposed alteration relates not to the charters, but to the ownership of bank stock.

Benefits to the Public from the Use of Bank Notes. — We shall, however, possess but an inadequate appreciation of the nature of bank notes and deposits, if we estimate them by only their lucrativeness to banks. To so insufficient an estimate we probably owe the prejudice which exists

against banks, and certainly bank notes wou 1 be intolerable, if the pub
.ic sustained, without an equivalent, the hazards incident to papei
money. By the published bank reports of December last, the banks
have loaned to the public, on private and public securities, ninety-two
millions and a half of dollars, while the banks could have loaned only
about forty-seven millions had the banks not been assisted by the use
of bank notes and deposits. The excess is some more than forty-
five millions of dollars. Twenty-three millions of this is composed
of bank notes; the residue is composed of deposits. But as we desire to
estimate, impartially, the merits of paper money, we will assume that
the amount of bank notes loaned was only twenty millions of dollars;
and that the remaining three millions of them was represented by
specie, which the bank notes had taken out of circulation and placed in
the vaults of the banks. This is probably accurate, for though the
banks possessed, last December, nearly seven millions of dollars in
specie, yet we may well assume that a rateable portion of it belonged to
the deposits.

Assuming, then, that the ability to create bank notes nan caused the
banks to increase their loans twenty millions of dollars, the public are
benefited by the bank notes to the extent that the use of twenty millions
of money exceeds in productiveness the interest that the banks charge
therefor. That the productiveness is more than the bank interest, is
demonstrable from the competition that exists for loans. They are usually deemed favors by borrowers who can give for them the most undoubted security.

Nor is the benefit which accrues from the employment of paper money
confined to the borrower. It is shared variously by every person
amongst whom the bank notes are circulated; for whoever receives
money receives it in exchange for his labor or property that he values
less than the money for which he exchanges it. Conceive now the ra-
pidity with which money passes from one person to another, (its use
being too costly to permit any person to retain it long in inactivity,) and
you may approximate, remotely, to the number of persons who, during
any one year, must be benefited by the twenty millions of dollars; and
if you can aggregate during any such year the benefits to the borrowers, and the innumerable participants as above, you will obtain a
glimpse (greatly inadequate it must be) of the merits of bank notes
irrespective of their use to banks as a means of banking profits.

Relative Utility to the Public of the Safety Fund and Free Banks.— Nor
must we omit, in our calculations as above, that the twenty millions of
loans produced by the use of bank notes, can exist by no other means.
Any legal prohibition of bank notes would compel banks to reduce their
loans to an amount equal to the extinguished bank notes. In this con-

nection, we may contrast, with possibly some utility, the two systems of banking which are struggling for mastery in our State; if the struggle be not already over by a tacit decision in favor of what are termed the free banks. The free banks can issue no bank notes without pledging with the Comptroller an equal amount of the public stocks of this State; whilst the safety fund banks can create bank notes at no greater expense than the cost of paper and printing. The free banks, therefore, take out of circulation, for the purchase of public stocks, as much money as they subsequently are able to return in bank notes.* That this theoretical view is not essentially different from the actual result will appear by the last December bank reports. Ninety free banks exist in the State, excluding the free banks of New York, Brooklyn, Albany and Troy. These ninety banks own an aggregate capital of six millions and a half of dollars. The capital was taken from the community in which the banks are situated, and the banks have returned it back in "loans and discounts;" and only one million two hundred thousand dollars in addition. The same district of country is occupied by fifty-one safety fund banks, who own an aggregate capital of eight millions seven hundred thousand dollars. This sum has likewise been returned in "loans and discounts," with seven million two hundred thousand dollars in addition. If, then, the above safety fund banks should be converted into free banks, the loans to the public would, on the above principles, have to be diminished some more than five millions of dollars, a diminution which exceeds one fifth part of the whole existing "loans and discounts" of both the safety fund and free banks in the district of country embraced in the above calculation; — namely, the whole of the State, with the exception of New York, Brooklyn, Albany and Troy. The country, thus abridged in its means of active business, would receive no equivalent therefor in any shape, except an imagined greater security against insolvent bank notes.

Loss to the Public from Insolvent Bank Notes. — Legislation on the subject of bank notes has looked only to the evils of loss from insolvent banks. This evil will be terminated when no bank notes can be created except on an equivalent pledge of public stocks; but the legislature ought to inquire whether the remedy is not worse than the disease. Possibly, if the disease be estimated by practical results rather than by declamation, (and declamation is much our wont in this particular,) each man may find, on reflection, that his loss from insolvent bank notes has been small, even without setting off against it the amount that he has been benefited by solvent bank notes. The laboring

---

* Free banks can now issue bank notes on a pledge in part of real estate; and notes thus issued are not obnoxious to the above difficulty, as the real estate remains in the possession of the mortgagors subject to its accustomed uses to society.

poor are the persons for whom, in this matter, commiseration is usually most eloquent; but no class of society is benefited more directly by an exuberant currency than manual laborers, and no class hazards so little by its dangers. From the danger which attends the creation of paper money, (the danger from owning bank stock,) the laboring poor are necessarily exempt. The only danger to which a poor laborer is exposed is the casual possession of an insolvent bank note. This loss we fallaciously magnify by saying, that the loss of a dollar, when it constitutes the whole property of a man, is relatively as great a loss to him as the loss of a thousand dollars is to a man a thousand times richer. The fallacy of the argument becomes manifest when we estimate the respective losses by the respective power of the parties to reinstate themselves as they stood before the loss. The laboring man accomplishes this by a day's labor, while the richer man may labor a year and not accomplish a like result.

The Safety Fund.—But while we speak in favor of the safety fund banks, we would not be understood as speaking favorably of the safety fund principle which punishes honest bankers for the frauds of the dishonest. It is, also, vicious in its tendency, for it promises indemnity against bank insolvency, and thereby prevents the scrutiny of the public into the conduct of bankers; permitting extravagance, improvidence and dishonesty, to unmolestedly effect their ravages. The solvent banks who are liable to the safety fund have paid thereto nearly two millions of dollars for losses, and are still to pay, annually, during the continuance of their charters, the half of one per cent. on their respective capitals. Of this immense loss, about one million and a half of dollars accrued from banks in Buffalo, of whom in particular, and of all the broken banks in a great degree, may be affirmed, that if they had been unaided by the credit of the safety fund, they never would have been trusted sufficiently to much injure any person. And could the money abstracted by their agency from the safety fund be traced to the real beneficiaries, it would be found in the possession, not of innocent sufferers, but mostly of accessories to the frauds and mismanagements by which the losses to the safety fund were produced

Relative Lucrativeness to Bank Owners of the Safety Fund and Free Banks.—Having thus shown how our existing two systems of banking act respectively on society, we will examine how they compare in profits to the stockholders. We will assume that the free banks can issue no bank notes except on an equivalent pledge of State six per cent. stocks; and that the State stocks can be purchased at par. The legal and attainable interest of money is seven per cent.; hence the free banks lose one per cent. the year on the amount of all their bank notes. Some persons may say that the difference is not merely the excess of legal interest over the six per cent. received on the State stock, but the excess of what the hundred dollars, which is invested in State stocks, would have earned in banking—say eight per cent.; and thus that the loss in procuring bank notes is one per cent. the year in the interest, and an additional one per cent. in privation of productiveness; making the real loss two per cent. the year on the amount of bank notes. We will, however, adopt the first mode of computation, and call the loss only one per cent., when the stocks can be purchased at par.

But the stocks cannot be thus purchased. They are selling at a premium of ten per cent., which makes the loss of interest one dollar and seventy cents the year on every hundred dollars of bank notes, without allowing for the ultimate loss of ten per cent. on the stock, when it comes to be paid off at par by the State. We shall not, therefore, be extravagant in assuming that the free banks lose one and three quarters per cent. the year on the amount of their bank notes; while the safety fund banks create bank notes without any loss, except the half per cent. the year paid on their aggregate capitals to the safety fund, and now a total loss. This reduces the comparative disadvantage of the free banks to one and a quarter per cent. the year on the amount of their capital invested in bank notes. By the published bank reports of last December, all the free banks of the State (excluding those of New York city) possessed an aggregate capital of a little more than seven millions and a half of dollars, while the bank notes were equal to that sum with the exception of about four hundred thousand dollars; so that the free banks out of the city of New York were (so far as our hypothesis is applicable to them) banking at a disadvantage, as compared with the safety fund banks, of one and a quarter per cent. the year on nearly their whole capitals.

Free Banking in New York. — The free banks in the city of New York are differently circumstanced. Their aggregated capital, in December 1848, was $7,148,710, while their bank notes amounted to only $1,745,250. In the city, therefore, the free banks lose annually 1¾ per cent. on their bank notes say - - - - - - - $30,510
And gain, by exemption from the safety fund, half per cent.
  the year on their capitals, say - - - - -   35,743

Leaving an annual balance in favor of free banking in the
  city of New York, - - - - - - - - $5,203
besides the further benefit of being able to charge seven per cent. the year interest on loans of sixty days and under, while the safety fund banks can charge only six per cent. This source of benefit is enjoyed also by the country free banks, and, to the extent of its availability, will

mitigate the assumed loss of free banking in the country. In large cities like New York, the difference between six per cent. and seven, on short loans, must produce a gain to the free banks of at least a quarter of one per cent. on the whole of their bank capital, and, possibly, much more, for such paper is abundant in cities. If, therefore, we credit the free banks of New York city with the above advantage, in addition to the advantage already shown to exist in their favor, we shall see that in the city free banking is more lucrative than safety fund banking; burdened as the latter is with a safety fund tax of a half of one per cent.

If, however, the free banks of the city employ a smaller amount of bank notes in loans than they would employ if they could create bank notes without expense, as the safety fund banks create them, a consequent loss to the city free banks must be estimated before we can settle accurately the relative lucrativeness in the city of the two systems of banking; but banking in the city is so largely transacted on deposits, that the amount of the above supposable loss is, probably, much too small to counteract the preponderance of benefit which belongs there to the free banks.

Relative Effects on City and Country Capitalists of the Safety Fund and Free Bank Systems. — To bank stockholders, therefore, the free bank system is rather more lucrative in New York city than the safety fund system with its existing burdens; while, in other parts of the State, the free bank system is less lucrative by about one per cent. the year on the invested capital than the safety fund system. City capitalists, therefore, possess, in the business of banking, an advantage over country capitalists.

Relative Effects on City and Country Commerce of the Safety Fund and Free Bank Systems. — Let us now inquire what portion belongs to the country and what to the city of the public loss which will result, as we have shown, when no bank notes can be created except on an equivalent pledge of public stocks. By the bank statement of last December, the bank loans founded on bank notes are about three dollars in the country to every one dollar in the city; so, whatever injury may result from the extinguishment of safety fund bank notes, the injury will fall on the country in the proportion of three dollars on the country to every one dollar of injury on the city. The customers of the city banks live near the banks, and, consequently, employ but few bank notes; — checks founded on deposits being substituted in the city, for bank notes, in nearly all business transactions. In the country, the bank borrowers employ the borrowed money at places remote from the ding bank, and must use bank notes. The country therefore, and

.he city are interested in very different degrees by all laws which abridge the free issue of bank notes; but should the legislature prohibit bank deposits, except on a pledge by banks of State stocks, the law would embarrass the business of the city beyond its embarrassment to the country, in just about the same proportion as such a law, in relation to bank notes, embarrasses the business of the country beyond its embarrassment to the city.

Different Legal Privileges accorded to Different Safety Fund Banks. — Originally, every safety fund bank was permitted to issue bank notes to three times the amount of its capital, but in cities, where large banks are needed, business is transacted principally by means of deposits; hence a New York two million bank soon found that its ability to issue six millions in bank notes was a useless privilege. But in the country where banks are small, in accordance with the small pecuniary ability of country capitalists, and the smallness of inland dealings, business is transacted principally with bank notes; hence a hundred thousand dollar country bank found that it could, occasionally, employ more than all its allowable issue of bank notes. From this development of practice, the legislature abrogated the useless ratable equality that existed in the allowable issue of bank notes, and permitted a two million bank to create only twelve hundred thousand dollars of bank notes, while a hundred thousand dollar bank was permitted to issue a hundred and fifty thousand dollars in bank notes. The bank note issues of intermediate magnitudes of capital were graduated by the above proportions. The advantage is still largely on the side of the two million bank, for the legal limit is much above its wants, while the limit on the small bank is often a practical abridgment of its business. The two existing two million banks of New York had together, last December, only four hundred and sixty thousand dollars of bank notes in circulation; and as nothing but their own wishes prevented them from issuing more, we must infer that they desired no greater issue.

Difference in the Productiveness of Different Magnitudes of Bank Capital. — The existing graduation of bank notes to capital, as above explained, is, practically, more favorable to the two million bank than to the hundred thousand dollar bank; still, when we compare the proportionate gains of the two banks, a preponderance exists usually in favor of the hundred thousand dollar bank. Different locations afford, no doubt, different degrees of facility for the production of gain in banking, as in other operations; yet, independent of that and every other accidental difference, some magnitudes of capital seem in every place to be naturally more lucrative than other magnitudes in the same place.

To investigate the source of the above differences, and to determine what magnitude of capital yields inherently the largest annual per centage of gain, would involve us more deeply into the philosophy of banking than is necessary to our present design; and we have introduced the subject only to excite attention to it, should any person wish to investigate it further.

The Currency. — On the ninth of December, 1848, the one hundred and eighty-four banks of our State owed individual depositors $29,205,332
Their bank notes in circulation amounted to - - - 23,206,289

Making the aggregate of indebtedness payable on demand, $52,411,621
Of which aggregate the banks had loaned on public and
private securities, - - - - - - - 45,209,372

Being the whole, with the exception of - - - $7,202,249
This seems bold, but if the money has been so loaned that it can be recalled by the banks respectively, as fast as they are respectively called on to pay the deposite and bank notes, the apparent boldness will subside. The banks possess another reliance. They have loaned not only the above deposits and bank notes, - - - - $45,209,372
But also the capitals of the said banks, say - - - 47,333,879

Making a total of loans on public and private securities of $92,543,251
The banks are therefore safe if they can recall enough daily, out of the above enlarged aggregate, to meet the daily returning bank notes, and the daily withdrawn deposits. This theoretical ability of the banks is strengthened by experience, which shows that the aggregate amount of bank deposits and bank note circulation varies but comparatively little from day to day, and even from month to month, and from year to year. Bank notes are continually being returned to banks for payment, but they are continually paid out again as money · so deposits are continually being drawn out by depositors, but they are continually returned as new deposits.

The Currency of the State is a sort of Measure of the Business of the State. — The small variation in our State from month to month, in the aggregate amount of bank circulation and deposits, evinces that the commerce of the State employs a given amount of circulation and deposits. They constitute the currency of the State, for usually the other items of currency (specie and foreign bank notes) are small in comparative amount. Commerce cannot ordinarily expand without an expansion of the currency, nor can either contract without a contraction of the other. And we may all have experienced, that business is more usually contracted from inability to obtain currency, than currency is contracted from diminution of business. A proof of this is the expansion, apparently illimitable, that gradually occurs in business whenever banks become able to expand the currency.

The Business of the State is a sort of Guarantee to Banks for the Permanence of a given amount of Currency. — The connection which thus exists between business and currency constitutes a practical guarantee to the banks that their bank notes will not all be suddenly returned for payment, nor all deposits be withdrawn. But for this guarantee no banker would dare to issue bank notes beyond the amount of his specie in bank, or to lend any portion of the money that he holds in deposit. If we examine the magnitude of the currency of our State when money is said to be scarce, and compare it with the magnitude that exists when money is said to be abundant, the difference will be small, and thereby shows that the guarantee above alluded to is potent. The currency will occasionally suffer a diminution that may distress bankers but the great bulk of it must be as permanent as the business operations of men.

A Surplusage of Currency can never exist long. — Neither bank notes nor bank deposits can exist long in excess, for some persons are paying interest for them to the banks : — for example, the public, last December, owed the banks more than forty millions of dollars, beyond the aggregate of all the deposits and bank notes ; consequently, an extinguishment of this indebtedness furnishes a use for all existing bank notes and deposits, a use equal to say seven per cent. the year on the whole sum ; hence, the extinguishment of the currency, by the payment of bank debts, becomes a sort of safety valve through which the currency vanishes during any diminution of existing business pursuits " Dust thou art, and unto dust shalt thou return," is not more applicable to the human body with reference to the earth, than to bank currency with reference to bank loans. The currency originates with bank loans, and by the repayment of the loans the currency becomes extinguished. We accordingly find that when business is technically dull — that is, when men cannot use currency at a sufficient profit to pay the banks seven per cent. interest thereon for short loans, the aggregate of bank debts diminishes daily by voluntary payments from bank debtors. At such times the Bank of England reduces its rate of interest ; for though no existing business may justify the payment of seven per cent. the year, on short loans, for the use of currency, business may exist that will justify the payment of six per cent., or five, or four. By thus periodically graduating the rate of bank interest, by the contemporaneous

2*

profitableness of the employment of currency, the Bank of England keeps its aggregate amount of loans as high as it desires.*

The Extinguishment of Bank Circulation and Deposits, and the Extinguishment of Debts due to Banks, preserve a pretty Uniform Equality. — The daily payments to all the banks of the State come naturally to be about equal in amount to the aggregate daily redemptions of bank notes and bank deposits. In the production of this equality the banks sometimes act compulsorily on the public; sometimes the public act compulsorily on the banks. When bank debtors pay voluntarily their bank loans, they compulsorily extinguish bank notes or bank deposits to the extent of the loans paid; but when banks exact a reduction of bank oans, the banks compel the extinguishment of bank notes and deposits o the extent of the reduction. Both calculations assume that the bank oans are paid not with specie, but with bank notes or deposits, for specie constitutes too small a portion of the currency of the State to vary much the general calculation.

Specie Payments. — The last December bank reports show that the banks of the State owe, in circulation and deposits, nearly fifty-two millions and a half of dollars, payable on demand in specie; while the specie in all the banks is not quite seven millions of dollars. To an inexperienced observer, nothing seems wanting to the destruction of banks thus circumstanced, but some casual run on them for specie. Indeed, a sort of vulgar error exists in relation to the importance of specie to the currency of bank notes, and even to the ultimate value of both bank notes and bank deposits. Bad indeed, and fallacious indeed would be both these, if their currency or value depended on the amount of specie owned by the banks at any given moment. Of the fifty-two millions in bank notes and deposits due from the banks last December, the true basis of their value was the ninety-two millions and a half in

---

* Borrowers may often be found for money when the loan is to continue for several months; while no borrowers may be willing to take money on loans for short periods. The Bank of England accordingly extends the duration of its loans, as well as reduces its rates of interest, when borrowers are not sufficiently numerous. But loans for short periods are alone desirable to banks, for a bank knows not when its currency may return for redemption, and hence cannot safely loan for long periods. The duration of bank loans comes naturally to be graduated by the time that ordinarily intervenes between the issue of currency by banks, and its return for redemption and extinction. The period of return varies with different employments of currency, and in different localities, but the period is rarely so long as to enable banks to extend the duration of loans beyond a few months, especially with the facilities which exist now everywhere for the return of bank notes to the bank that issued them.

debts due to the banks, which, with the seven millions in specie, made together ninety-nine millions and a half of dollars, wherewith to pay the fifty-two millions of deposits and bank notes. For all purposes of solvency, the banks, therefore, possessed ninety-nine millions and a half of specie, — seven millions of it in the vaults of the banks, and ninety-two millions and a half in the pockets of the people.

Specie Suspensions. — But as the fifty-two millions due from the banks in deposits and bank notes are payable on demand, while the ninety-two millions due to the banks are payable in daily portions, the whole not collectable under some months, the banks may be called on for payments faster than the bank debts will become payable, and a suspension of specie payments may ensue, notwithstanding the assistance which the banks will derive from the possession of seven millions in specie at the commencement of the struggle. Our State has experienced three such suspensions, but no abatement of avidity by the public was produced thereby, in the desire to procure bank notes and bank deposits. They continued as valuable as ever for the purposes of currency, and were less valuable than specie only when specie was wanted for some other purpose than for currency within our State.

Suspension of Specie Payments by a Single Solvent Bank. — The inherent value of bank notes and bank deposits, independently of their convertibility on demand into specie, is best seen when a single solvent bank suspends specie payments. Within a circuit of country occupied by the debtors of the bank, its notes and deposits will continue to be current as long as the debts daily becoming due to the bank continue to be equal in amount to the bank notes and deposits that will be daily seeking redemption. Suppose, however, that the debt which you may owe the bank will not become payable under four months, still notes and deposits to the amount of your debt will possess a value to you equal to specie, less the interest for the four months; hence, if the bank possesses good debts equal in amount to its notes and deposits, such notes and deposits can, intrinsically, depreciate in value only to the amount of such interest; nor will the deposits and notes depreciate intrinsically to that extent, if the bank shall be sufficiently solvent to eventually pay its notes and deposits with interest superadded, according to the requirement of law.

Legal Tender. — The Bank of England suspended specie payments continuously during twenty years, and its notes and deposits retained the value of specie, except where gold and silver were needed for other purposes than domestic currency. Some persons attribute the result to an act of Parliament, by which costs could not be recovered in a legal prosecution against a debtor who tendered payment in notes of the Bank of England. No law, however, can confer a value on insolvent paper money, except as the law may act on preëxisting contracts. The law may, indeed, forbid you from refusing to receive the money on new contracts, but you will enter into none. The experiment was tried during our revolutionary war, and it was tried subsequently by France, but prices for all salable property increased continually, as the supposed actual value of the paper decreased.

Receivables and Treasury Notes. — During our specie suspension of the year 1814, the value of paper money was well illustrated by the origination of a new species of bank note, which, instead of promising to pay, promised to receive the note in all bank payments. The notes were called receivables, and they circulated as readily as specie in the vicinity of the issuing bank, so long as the bank restricted the emission within the amount needed by the bank debtors of the vicinity. The same principle is apparent in the treasury notes emitted occasionally by the Federal Government, and bearing no interest. The notes are receivable for duties, and in all other governmental payments, and this receivability confers a specie value as currency on such notes, to the amount of several millions of dollars scattered over the Union. Occasionally the notes accumulate in New York faster than they can be used in governmental payments, and then they sell at a discount which is graduated in degree by the time that will elapse before the notes will be needed in payments to government. The currency of such treasury notes, despite their inconvertibility into specie, is often attributable to the known solvency of the government; but no considerations are necessary to the currency of the notes, but a consciousness that the notes will immediately, or shortly, supply a use for which specie will otherwise be needed.

A National Currency. — In a national bank, like the Bank of England, possessing a capital of many millions of pounds sterling, invested in short loans to bankers and merchants, and the recipient of all the governmental moneys that accrue from taxes, duties, excise, &c., any notes would circulate as specie that the banks would receive. The notes which the Bank of England now issues being payable on demand in specie, the bank is compelled to subordinate the amount of its bank note currency, and, consequently, the amount of its daily loans, to the accidental fluctuations that occur in the demand for specie; how disastrously soever the subordination may affect the internal commerce of the kingdom. In place of its present notes, were the bank to substitute a currency like the receivables of which we have been speaking, gold and silver could be exported or imported according to the requirements of commerce without any consequent derangement of business. Such a currency would be as expansible, at all times, as the business requirements of the country; and without losing, intrinsically, its ultimate specie value, since every debtor of the bank would be holden to pay his debt in specie, to the extent that he could not procure the notes of the bank. The ultimate value of the present currency is connected with specie, by means of an ability to compel the bank to pay specie on its notes; but, in the other currency, the ultimate value would be connected with specie, by means of the bank's ability to compel its debtors to pay specie on their bank debts. The responsibility of procuring specie rests now on the bank; the responsibility in the other system would rest on the bank's debtors. We cannot, however, avoid seeing that the bank might issue so large an amount of such notes that an excess might be occasionally produced beyond the quantity that could be kept at par value. The depreciation might be illimitable in its degree, should the bank augment illimitably the excess of currency. Possibly, therefore, the power to create such a currency cannot be safely committed to any institution; and evils less radical result from the existing system of paper money, notwithstanding its sudden contractions on a foreign demand for specie, than would result from any different system.

Expansions of the Bank Note Currency. — Having thus considered the nature of paper money, we will proceed to consider the principles by which its volume is regulated, when a power exists, as in safety fund banks, to expand at will the currency within a given limit.* When country products sell at unusually high prices, the purchase of them employs a greater amount of money than when the articles sell at low prices. High prices proceed, usually, from some extraordinary demand for the appreciated articles, and the extraordinary demand increases the number of the purchasers, and the frequency of sales and resales; all consequences which augment the amount of money that purchasers of

* This expansibility to meet the wants of commerce makes the safety fund banks more useful than the free banks. As relates to deposits, both banks possess an equal expansibility. The expansibility of a bank note currency renders such a currency better, as a commercial instrument, than a currency wholly of specie, whose unexpansibility would constitute a great practical check on competition and on enterprise generally. A specie currency is not, however, wholly unexpansible. We experienced this in the late famine in Ireland. Specie was sent from England to purchase our breadstuffs, but an expansibility from such a source is slow; and it can occur in only emergencies of international commerce, not in emergencies of domestic commerce. The effect of paper money on prices during times of speculation, we will not discuss, the discussion being not necessary to our design; but the discussion is essential to a proper understanding of the utility of paper money.

produce borrow from the banks. Besides, as the price augments of any article, the area enlarges over which purchasers extend their operations, creating thereby new applicants for bank currency.

The Spirit of Speculation is Contagious. — Every marketable article is subject to an increased action like the above, and after speculation is aroused, it becomes contagious, so that speculators multiply fast; and though the original purchasers may be limited to wheat, all other species of grain soon become added thereto, and other articles of a different nature. In the year eighteen hundred and thirty-seven, every man and woman became infected with a desire for the unoccupied lands of the United States, and millions of dollars in bank notes were borrowed from banks and sent to Michigan, Ohio, Illinois, and other places where the coveted lands were situated. City and village lots anywhere soon were purchased with like avidity; and the purchases undergoing an incessant activity of sale and resale, vast amounts of new currency were created for the occasion.

Expansion of Bank Deposits. — The operations which produce in the country an expansion of the bank note currency, produce in cities an expansion of bank deposits. These became accordingly, in 1837, as unusually expanded in amount as bank notes. Banks readily encourage expansions, because bank profits are thereby augmented; nearly every dollar of the increased bank notes and deposits being represented by some loan made on interest by the banks.

Contraction of the Currency. — The currency of the State is subject to an incessant ebb and flow, as respects the amount of the aggregate, and as respects each bank's particular share thereof. Our State possesses one hundred and eighty-four banks, and as each bank is a sort of independent sovereignty, each guards vigilantly its own interests, by endeavoring to obtain for itself as many deposits as it can, and as large a share as it can of the aggregate bank note circulation of the State; hence, when bank A receives in payments or deposits notes or checks of bank B, they are speedily sent to bank B for redemption. By this process, bank notes and bank deposits circulate through the State, as blood circulates through the human body. Every bank is a heart, from which is continually flowing its bank notes by means of borrowers and depositors, who act as arteries to distribute the bank notes through all the business ramifications of the State; while every other bank is a vein, that is incessantly absorbing the said bank notes, and returning them to the bank from which they originally emanated. Some of the notes of every bank are returned to it through the agency of brokers, who, like separate and peculiar absorbents, soak up, by purchases at a smal' discount, bank notes which have been casually carried out of their proper sphere of action, and thereby become a sort of merchandise more or less depreciated in value, as the notes have wandered from home, and lost their properties as currency.

Periodical Contractions. — To carry further the analogy between the circulatory systems of banks and of the human body, banks are, as well as men, subject to an occasional rush of blood to the head. The disease is prevalent with banks in the spring and fall. Country merchants resort then to New York for their mercantile supplies, and take thither country bank notes which they have accumulated from their customers and debtors. Every merchant draws also from his depositing bank all his deposits, and borrows from the banks to the extent that loans are attainable. When he arrives at New York, any part of his money that is current at the city banks soon flows thither; while the part which is uncurrent flows to the brokers; and brokers and banks, with the utmost speed* of railroads and steamboats, send the country money home for redemption.

Pressure Contraction. — The contraction just referred to is almost peculiar to inland banks, but the Atlantic banks are subject to a contraction that rarely affects extensively the interior. This contraction is consequent to a demand for specie on the Atlantic banks, whether the specie is to be exported to Europe, or paid into the sub-treasury, or to be used for any other purpose. In December, 1848, the banks of New York city possessed less than six millions of dollars in specie; while they were liable to be called on for rather more than twenty-seven millions in payment of bank notes and deposits, besides some nine millions in payment of debts due banks and other corporations. To be thus liable was not peculiar to that period. The position then may be esteemed something better than a fair average of the usual condition of the city banks. Nor is the position bad, as the banks possess a claim on their debtors to the amount of forty millions and a half of dollars in discounted notes payable daily, and nearly all becoming due within three months; besides some seven or eight millions of dollars in other securities.

But the banks are liable primarily, and if specie is demanded from them to the extent of even half a million of dollars, the banks become sensitive and severally endeavor to strengthen themselves by refusing

* Speedy redemptions are desired by brokers as a means of saving interest on the money which they employ. The country money that is received by the New York banks is paid by the country banks as soon as it is received in New York, for the New York banks take no country money except of banks that keep money with them wherewith to redeem.

to lend, and by exacting payments from their debtors. Now, as all the current money of the city is composed of the bank notes of the city banks, and of deposits in the said banks, all the loans that bank A can call in will be paid in some of the aforesaid currency; consequently, so far as the payments strengthen bank A, they impoverish bank C, D and E. But C, D and E, were too poor already, and were severally endeavoring to strengthen themselves, the same as bank A was endeavoring to strengthen itself; hence C, D and E, will call on their debtors more stringently than before, and their efforts will impoverish A in the same way as the efforts of A impoverished them.

Panic. — The struggle just described must, as it proceeds, increase in intensity with a sort of compound progression; and as each bank, in recalling its loans, looks only to its own safety, each bank is practically impoverishing the others to the extent of its power. But the consequences of the struggle are not confined to the banks. The currency (bank notes and deposits) being thus suddenly diminished in amount, by the payment of bank debts, enough is not left to transact the usual business in the community. Money is said to become scarce. Property on sale cannot be readily sold, and, with the diminution in the number of competing purchasers, prices languish and fall. Many persons, who have depended on borrowing, to meet accruing engagements, are unable to borrow, and are compelled to suspend payments. In this category will be some merchants who have lived expensively in the most costly parts of the city, and been deemed rich; though actually long insolvent and kept from bankruptcy by only an ability to pay old debts by contracting new ones. Still they have been deemed as safe as other debtors, and men begin to query whose solvency may not follow next; especially as every failure involves other failures of indorsers and creditors. A new element, panic, is introduced into the pressure; and persons who have money to lend keep it unemployed until the storm subsides; and thus the last resource of embarrassment, the resource technically termed "the street," where notes can ordinarily be sold at a usurious discount, is closed against the needy, except at rates of discount so enhanced by avarice and fear, as to engulf nearly the whole principal of any proposed loan, and thus to defeat the motive for the sacrifice.

The very day-laborers, journeymen-mechanics, and market-people, will sometimes become infected with the panic, and add to the general trouble by a petty run on the banks for specie, in liquidation of small deposits, or the payment of small bank notes.

The Pressure reaches the Interior. — While pressure and panic thus ravage the metropolis, the banks of the interior, who at first are mere spectators of the struggle, begin to partake of the metropolitan distress.

While money is plenty in the city, a portion of its currency consists of the notes of country banks, which are employed in ordinary occupations to avoid the expense attendant on their transmission home for payment; but when the pressure enhances the value of money, country bank notes are sold to the brokers in unusual quantities, and transmitted home for redemption. Nor is this the only intimation to country banks of the commotion in the city. The merchants of the country who are indebted to the city, are strongly importuned by the city creditors to make speedy or even anticipated payments; and debts already due can receive no further postponements. While country banks are weakened to the extent that these requirements are complied with, the resources of the country banks are often sadly diminished, in these moments of unusual need, by the return unpaid of many New York acceptances, on whose payment the country banks have relied for funds. The country banks can now no longer furnish loans, but begin to require payment from their debtors; and thus bring on, in the country, a mutual struggle of bank A against bank B, in the way we have represented the struggle in the city.

The Pressure and Panic Terminate.— Every pressure in New York will not rage to the extent we have described, nor will every city pressure extend into the country; but when a pressure is commenced, it rarely is arrested, till business is greatly diminished, and comparatively but little currency is required to conduct it. Exportable produce in the mean time becomes so reduced in price that it may be exported more advantageously than specie, in the liquidation of foreign balances. Importers have also abridged their foreign orders in accordance with the diminished prospects of a profitable trade. Specie is no longer in demand. The banks cease from urging the payment of bank debts, and gradually begin to resume the process of lending. Business men foresee that money will soon become abundant. They wish to purchase while prices remain at the panic and pressure standard. All entertain the same views. Competition revives, prices advance, the banks lend freely to indemnify themselves in profits for the late period of abstinence. A new expansion is begun, to end, at some future day, in another contraction, another pressure, and, perhaps, another panic.

The Sale of Exchange. — Notes of the New York city banks are, in all parts of the State, equal in value to specie, by reason that persons in all parts are debtors to the city. Indeed, so much of the money of the State is required for uses in the city, that country banks can generally satisfy any demand for specie by a payment of the demand in bank notes of that city, or in a check upon some New York bank; so that the burden of maintaining specie payments in our State rests wholly

3

on the banks of New York. Their currency is the standard in our State of par value, and by it we graduate the currencies of all other places in the State and out ; just as the longitude of places is estimated with reference to the distance east or west from Washington. Even during the various suspensions which we have experienced of specie payments, the currency of New York city banks has continued to be the standard of par value ; and when the city currency has been less valuable than specie, the specie has been deemed above par, instead of the currency being deemed below par. People are often willing to allow a country bank a premium of half of one per cent., and sometimes more, for a draft of the bank on New York; especially, as every country bank will receive, in payment of the draft, notes of remote banks, on which the holder could not obtain the specie without much travel and expense. The draft can be transmitted by mail, and its transmission, by any mode of conveyance, is, from the legal nature of negotiable paper, less hazardous than the transmission of bank notes ; to say nothing of the exemption, produced by the draft, from the expense which attends the transportation of specie in large amounts. The selling of drafts on New York becomes, therefore, one of the regular sources of profit to country banks, as well as of convenience to men of business ; and every country bank keeps funds there, and keeps funds in Albany, Boston, or other places, for the purpose of selling drafts thereon at a premium, when the business of its vicinity makes drafts on such places desirable.

Collections within the State. — The principle which makes a merchant at Buffalo purchase, at a premium of one per cent., a draft on New York, will make a merchant of New York sell, at a discount of one per cent., a draft which he may own payable at Buffalo. Banks, accordingly, charge a discount, varying in magnitude of rate, according to distance, and other circumstances, when they give money to any person on drafts payable at remote banks. The charge is intended to remunerate the bank for its expense and trouble in procuring the payment of such drafts. The discount is, however, usually given, not on drafts payable at sight, but on notes and drafts payable at some future period ; the bank charging interest for the unexpired time, and discount for collecting the money at a distant place.

Collections out of the State. — The collections just described are usually but a small source of profits. Some banks refuse the business wholly, but the banks in New York are said to transact such business largely, with paper payable in Philadelphia, Baltimore, Boston, and other large cities of the Union and of Europe ; a description of paper which the commerce of New York makes abundant in that city. In loaning money on such paper, banks allow nothing to the holder when the rate of exchange happens to be in favor of the place where the paper is payable; but this rule is not applied to European drafts, on which the difference of exchange is usually large. In paper on Philadelphia and other large cities of our Union, the rate of exchange is generally in favor of New York; hence the banks of New York, in lending money on such paper, rarely receive any benefit from the rate of exchange, except as they may charge a per centage for collection in addition to the interest on the money loaned. The charge for difference of exchange between any two commercial cities will vary naturally at different periods; but the multitude of collecting agencies which exist keep down the charge at all times to the lowest limit of reasonable remuneration. Still the business constitutes one of the phases of banking, and it completes the summary that we have proposed to make of banking operations.

PART SECOND—THE BANKER.

The Objects of Banking.—Correct sentiments beget correct conduct a banker ought, therefore, to apprehend correctly the objects of banking. They consist in making pecuniary gains for the stockholders, by legal operations. The business is eminently beneficial to society; but some bankers have deemed the good of society so much more worthy of regard than the private good of stockholders, that they have supposed all loans should be dispensed with direct reference to the beneficial effect of the loans on society, irrespective, in some degree, of the pecuniary interests of the dispensing bank. Such a banker will lend to builders, that houses or ships may be multiplied; to manufacturers, that useful fabrics may be increased; and to merchants, that goods may be seasonably replenished. He deems himself, ex-officio. the patron of all interests that concern his neighborhood, and regulates his loans to these interests by the urgency of their necessities, rather than by the pecuniary profits of the operations to the bank, or the ability of the bank to sustain such demands. The late Bank of the United States is a remarkable illustration of these errors. Its manager seemed to believe that his duties comprehended the equalization of foreign and domestic exchanges, the regulation of the price of cotton, the upholding of State credit, and the control, in some particulars, of Congress and the President:—all vicious perversions of banking to an imagined paramount end. When we perform well the direct duties of our station, we need not curiously trouble ourselves to effect, indirectly, some remote duty Results belong to Providence, and by the natural catenation of events, (a system admirably adapted to our restricted foresight,) a man can usually in no way so efficiently promote the general welfare, as by vigilantly guarding the peculiar interest committed to his care. If, for instance, his bank is situated in a region dependent for its prosperity on the business of lumbering, the dealers in lumber will naturally constitute his most profitable customers: hence, in promoting his own interest out of their wants, he will, legitimately, benefit them as well as himself; and benefit them more permanently than by a vicious subordination of his interests to theirs. Men will not engage permanently in any business that is not pecuniarily beneficial to them personally; hence, a banker becomes recreant to even the manufacturing and other interests that he would protect, if he so manage his bank as to make its stockholders unwilling to continue the employment of their capital in banking. This principle, also, is illustrated by the late United States Bank, for the stupendous temporary injuries which its mismanagement inflicted on society are a smaller evil than the permanent barrier its mismanagement has probably produced against the creation of any similar institution.

The Pecuniary Prosperity of his Bank should constitute the Primary Object of the Banker. — From the foregoing remarks we infer, that the honor and pecuniary prosperity of his bank should constitute the paramount motive of every banking operation. A violation of this principle produced, in the year eighteen hundred and thirty-seven, a suspension of specie payments, which was visited on bank stockholders by a legislative prohibition of dividends, and visited on banks and bankers by a general obloquy. The banks suspended that the debtors of the bank might not suspend: or worse, the banks suspended that the debtors might be spared the pecuniary loss that would have resulted from paying their bank debts. A conduct so suicidal was probably fostered by the pernicious union, in one person, of bank director and bank debtor; a union from which our banks are never wholly exempt; nor are they always exempt from the same union still more pernicious, in bank presidents and cashiers. With this inherent defect in the organization of our banks, we can the more readily understand why, in 1837, the banks assumed dishonor to shield their debtors, and why the dishonor was continued for some more than a year in our State, and longer in others; and would have continued longer in ours, but from a refusal of its further tolerance by the legislature.

The said defect produced each of the three specie suspensions which the banks of our State have suffered. As a prelude to each suspension, the Atlantic cities held enthusiastic public meetings, in which suspension was recommended to the banks; and the recommendation enforced by the assurance that the meetings would sustain the banks in assuming a suspended position: — What a farce! What a "thimble-rig!" Such meetings were composed of bank debtors, (many of them being bank directors,) and meant, substantially, — suspend payments that you may leave in our possession the money that we owe you; — assume dishonor that we may remain honorable.

Specie Suspensions are never necessary to Banks. — Every suspension of specie payments might have been prevented, had the bankers performed their duty to their respective banks, by prudence in the quality of their loans, and vigor in the enforcement of payments. No proof of this can be more convincing than the successfully sustained refusal of the

Union Bank of New York to unite in the specie suspension of the year eighteen hundred and thirteen. All the banks, also, of New England preserved specie payments. We admit that, had all the banks of the Union refused to suspend payments in 1813, 1819 and 1837, business would have severely suffered; but this is a consideration for the legislature, and not for the banks. They are creations of the law, and should obey their creator. In England, during its struggle with Napoleon, the government prohibited specie payments by the Bank of England, when the suspension was deemed publicly useful. The suspension continued for twenty years, but the bank incurred thereby no disgrace, for it obeyed the law.

The Interests of Debtors and Dealers should be subordinated to the Interests of the Bank. — The subordination of the honor and interests of a bank to the avarice or necessities of its managers, or dealers of any description, is productive, not of suspensions only, but of every disaster which usually befalls banks; and unless such a subordination can be prevented by the officer who acts specially as banker, no man who respects himself should continue in the position, when he discovers that such a subordination is in progress. The owner of a steam engine regulates its business by the capacity of his engine, but should he regulate it by the necessities of his customers, he would probably burst his boiler. A shipowner regulates his freight by the tonnage of his ship; a contrary course would sink it. So every bank possesses a definite capacity for expansion by which bank dealers can regulate their business; but, when a bank regulates its expansion by the wants of its dealers, or the persuasions of friendship, it will probably explode, or be otherwise unprofitable to its stockholders.

Security. — Banks charge for the use of money no more than the use is worth. Nothing is added for risk, and thereby money-lending differs from all other business that involves hazard. A great disproportion exists also between the amount hazarded by any loan, and the amount gained. The loan of a thousand dollars for sixty days involves the possible loss of a thousand dollars, without the possibility of a greater gain than some ten dollars. Banks, therefore, never regularly lend money without receiving the security of more than one person who is deemed safe for the debt; and a good banker will err on the side of excessive security, rather than accept security whose sufficiency may reasonably be questioned. In the country, two endorsers are usually required on every note that is discounted; but in cities, where discounts are made for shorter periods than in the country, one endorser is more usual than two.

Moral Security. — Independently of the wealth of the endorser, the banks derive from him a security founded on the natural desire of every borrower to protect his friends, should insolvency occur to the borrower during the pendency of the bank loan. An endorser will, also, usually foresee earlier than the bank when mischances threaten the borrower, and when appeals for protection should be made. To derive these benefits from endorsers, they should be disconnected in business from the borrower, so as not to be involved in his calamities; hence, such disconnection is always one of the circumstances from which a banker judges of the sufficiency of any proffered endorser. Relationship of either consanguinity or affinity, between a debtor and his sureties, sharpens usually the desire of the debtor to protect his endorser; while again such relationship facilitates the concealment of a common pecuniary interest in enterprises, and facilitates collusions against the bank in times of disaster, that may more than counterbalance the benefits expected by the bank from the relationship.

Security founded on the Morality of a Debtor. — The more lax the morality is of a borrower, the less will he probably feel the obligation to protect his endorsers; and the more lax the morality is of an endorser, the more will he struggle against the surrender of his property to pay an unprotected endorsement. As a general result, however, debts are rarely collectable from the property of an endorser, unless his property very greatly overbalances the amount of his endorsement. Instances are continually occurring where an endorser who is become liable for a bad debt, which his property could pay, and leave him a surplus, will ruin himself in successfully preventing the application of his property to the debt in question. Hence, when a debt is contracted wholly on the property of the endorser, the debt will not be safe unless it is small in comparison with the wealth of the endorser.

Security founded on the Habits of a Debtor. — Men who are prone to extravagance in their domestic or personal expenditures rarely possess the amount of property they are reputed to possess. Men expend to be thought rich more frequently than they expend by reason of being rich. The rich are usually more inclined to parsimony than expenditure. Any way, persons who practise parsimony are in the way of becoming rich, whatever may be their present poverty; while persons who are profuse in expenditures are in the way of becoming poor, though they may possess a present opulence.

Security founded on the Nature of a Man's Business. — A man who transacts a regular business in a regular way is not liable to sudden fluctuations in his pecuniary solvency; but when a man's business is novel, and its results are untried, — or when its results are frequently disastrous, the banker who grants him loans assumes some of the hazards and uncertainties of the business.

Security founded on the Application of the Loan. — When money is to be invested in the purchase of merchandise, cattle, flour, or other property in the regular course of the borrower's business, the investment yields to the borrower a means of repayment; nothing is hazarded but ordinary integrity, and ordinary exemption from disasters; but when the borrowed money is to pay some preëxisting debt, none of the foregoing securities apply, and, possibly, you are merely taking a thorn out of another person's side, to place it in your own.

Security founded on the Character of the Paper that is to be Discounted. — Notes which a man receives, on the sale of property in his ordinary business, are termed business notes. The owner, having received them as money, had satisfied himself of their safety; hence, when they are offered to a banker by a prudent man of business, they possess an inherent evidence of value. They were given also for property that will, in the ordinary course of business, furnish the means by which the notes may be paid; and thus they possess an additional ingredient of safety. Kindred to such notes are drafts which a man draws on a consignee to whom property has been forwarded for sale. If the consignee be a prudent man, (the consignor must deem him prudent or he would not trust to him the property,) he will not accept unless the property forwarded is equivalent in value to the amount of the acceptance. The property, therefore, will pay the acceptance, and while the property remains unsold, it constitutes an equitable pledge for ultimate payment. A country banker, however, will usually be benefited, in a long course of business, by never loaning on city names without a reliable country endorser or maker, or both; for nothing is usually more unreliable than the reputed solvency of the merchants of large cities.

Acceptances in Advance of Consignments. — A factor will sometimes accept in confidence that the drawer will supply him with funds in time to pay the acceptance. This will not constitute a worse security than an ordinary accommodation endorsement; but the transaction lacks the reliability and security that are consequent to the acceptor's possession of consignments in advance of his acceptance, and so far as the nature of the acceptance is concealed, the ostensible character of the paper will give it a fictitious security.

Assimilated Notes and Acceptances. — Notes and acceptances are often assimilated to the foregoing character to facilitate the procurement of loans. Two merchants will exchange notes, and offer each other's notes at different banks, as business paper. Such notes are peculiarly hazardous by reason that the insolvency of either of the parties will usually produce the insolvency of the other. Acceptances are exchanged in the same way, and possess the same element of danger.

Kiting. — Sometimes a country merchant will draw on a merchant of New York, and obtain thereon a discount at some country bank. The draft will have some months to run before it will become payable; but when it is payable, the New York merchant will obtain the means of payment by drawing on the country merchant, payable some months thereafter, and getting a discount thereon in New York. Such transactions are termed "kiting." They are practised on notes as well as on drafts; and by persons residing in the same place as well as at distant places. When practised by persons who live at a distance from each other, the operation is usually very expensive, by incidental charges of exchange and collection. Bankers should suspect the solvency of parties who resort to expedients so commercially disreputable. The real character of the transactions is rarely avowed by the parties inculpated in the practices; but a vigilant banker will soon suspect the operations, and not touch them, unless the security can be made very ample.

Dummies. — A country produce dealer, or manufacturer, will some times place in New York an agent on whom to draw; or he may connect his operations with some person there of no capital, whom he will use as an acceptor. Such acceptances are no better than the note of the country dealer. They constitute, moreover, a hazardous class of paper, as you may rely somewhat on an assumed capital in the acceptors. Such methods are rarely practised except by persons who want to extend their operations beyond a limit to which a real consignee would restrict them. No prudential limit exists with the dummy acceptor, hence, the drawer is able to carry his operations to an extent unlimited, except by his own will, or his ability to find lenders; and men thus predisposed, and supplied with the requisite machinery, usually extend their speculatious till they are overwhelmed in ruin.

Void Notes and Drafts. — Notes and drafts are often made to be sold at a usurious discount, by parties ostensibly solvent, but who are struggling to purchase a transient respite from bankruptcy, or to amend their fortunes by desperate enterprises. Banks are, therefore, usually reluctant to discount paper offered by brokers and other persons who are known to practise usury; for such paper is, by existing laws, void as against makers and endorsers, in the hands of even an unconscious holder. In New York the defence of usury is said to be so discreditable that few men will avail themselves of it. In the country people feel less fastidious in this respect, and any debt which can certainly be avoided by means of usury would be very apt to be uncollectable.

Of Gains. — But the avoidance of loss is only a negation of evil. To make gains is the proper business of a banker, and as the principal source of legitimate gain is lending money, the bank must lend to the extent of its ability — erring on the side of repletion, rather than of inanition ; for a banker knows not how far his bank can bear extension till he tries ; — hence, if timidity, indolence, or apathy, limits his loans in advance of necessity, he may injure the community by unnecessarily withholding pecuniary assistance, and injure the stockholders by unnecessarily abridging the profits. A banker must not, however, extend his loans regardless of the future, but, like a skilful mariner, he should see an approaching storm while it is an incipient breeze, and meanwhile carry all the sail that will not jeopard the safety of his charge : — governing his discounts, at all times, more by the condition of his funds, and his own prospective resources, than by any reputed scarcity or abundance of money in other places and in other banks.

When to be Moderate. — If a banker can make reasonably good profits on his capital without much expansion, he may keep more restricted in his loans than a banker should who is less favorably circumstanced. Every banker must, however, remember, that to be strong in funds and rich in profits are natural incompatibilities ; hence, the more money a banker wishes to make, the poorer in funds he must consent to become. In banking operations, as in most other, wisdom lies in a medium between extremes ; and if a banker can keep funds enough for practical safety, he had better forego excess of funds, and receive an equivalent in gains. Physicians say that the human body can bear excess of food better than deficiency. The excess can be discharged by cutaneous eruptions, as we see sometimes in over-fed infants ; but deficiency of nourishment will not relieve itself ; so in banking, a repletion of loans, if they are undoubtedly solvent, prompt and short, will soon of themselves work a relief to the bank ; but a paucity of loans cannot, by any process of its own, cure the scant profits of the stockholders. Banks are rarely injured, therefore, by an excess of discounts. When banks fail, their disaster proceeds from the quality of their loans, not from the quantity.

The Kind of Paper that a Banker should Prefer. — No banker should keep his funds inactive when no better excuse exists therefor than that the business he can obtain is not so lucrative as the business of some other place, or as his own business was at some other period. The legal rate of interest is so high, that the voluntary forbearance of its reception for even a short period, is ordinarily a greater evil than the reception of any common description of solvent loans. Any way, a banker who keeps his funds inactive, to await the offer of loans more lucrative than simply the interest of money, should be well assured that the future loans will be sufficiently lucrative to compensate for the forbearance. But no disadvantages of position must be deemed a sufficient apology for the assumption of hazardous loans. When no safe business offers, no business should be transacted by a banker who entertains a proper respect for himself, or a proper feeling for his stockholders. Gains may be impossible, but losses are measurably avoidable. If any location presents the alternative of no business, or great hazards, a banker is accountable for the choice which he may make between the two alternatives; and he is accountable no further.

Selection of Loans founded on Incidental Circulation and Deposits. — But ordinarily every banker is presented with more business than he can assume, and he is enabled to select the more profitable and reject the .ess profitable. In speaking of the profits of banking we mean gains that proceed from some other source than the interest allowed by law for the use of the money. These gains are derived most largely from circulation and deposits; hence the loans are advantageous to a bank, in proportion as they increase the circulation or deposits of the bank. Money is sometimes borrowed to pay debts to a neighboring bank, or to a person who keeps his money deposited in a neighboring bank. Such loans yield no profit to the lender except the interest on the loan; hence they are not so profitable as loans to borrowers who will take bank notes of the lending bank, and circulate them over the country in the purchase of agricultural products. While the notes remain in circulation, the bank is receiving interest on them from the borrower, — interest not for the loan of money, but for the loan by the bank of its promises to pay money when demanded. So, on a loan made by a bank to one of its depositing customers, the bank receives interest only on its promise to pay the borrowed money when the borrower shall from time to time draw for the same. And when a deposit is thus drawn from a bank, the draft is not necessarily paid in money, but in bank notes which may obtain a circulation. This advantage is a usual attendant of the deposits of some customers, and makes their accounts doubly beneficial to a bank. Whether a depositor asks for more loans than his deposit account entitles him to receive, is a question whose solution depends on whether the bank can lend all its money to better depositing customers, or more profitably use it in loans for circulation. A banker should, however, estimate liberally the merits which pertain to a steady customer; not deciding on any proposed loan by the amount of the proposer's deposit at the time of the proposal, but his antecedent deposits, which were doubtless made in reliance on the bank for a fair reciprocity of benefits. Competition for profitable customers exists among banks as eagerly as competition among borrowers for bank loans; hence liberality to customers by a banker is as much a dictate of interest as of justice.

Selection of Loans founded on the Place of their Repayment. — Notes and drafts discounted by country banks, and payable in New York, Albany, Troy, and some other eastern places, are payable in a currency whose value is enhanced some half of one per cent. by the rate of exchange, which exists in favor of the east, and against the west. As country banks never allow any premium in the reception of such paper, the benefit of the exchange is a strong inducement to a country banker for preferring loans thus payable to loans payable at his own counter. Borrowers will often take advantage of this predilection, and make notes payable artificially at New York, as a means of obtaining a loan of a country banker. Notes thus made are rarely paid at maturity; hence, so far as a banker relies on their payment, and founds his business calculations thereon, they are hurtful. To the extent that he colludes with the maker and supplies him with funds by which any such note can be paid at New York, at a loss to the maker of the difference in the rate of exchange, the transaction is unlawful; and banking is not exempt from the ordinary fatality which ever in a long course of business makes honesty the best policy. To gain unlawfully must also be a poor recommendation to a banker, with any thoughtful stockholder; for if a man will collude to make dishonest gains for his stockholders, what security can the stockholders possess that he will not collude against them, to make dishonest gains for himself? A country banker may properly discount a note payable in New York when the maker's business will make New York the most convenient place of payment, though the borrower's residence may be in the country: such is often the case with drovers, lumbermen, and some manufacturers. Transactions of this circuitous nature must, however, be spontaneous on the part of the borrower; for a note is usurious if, in addition to the receipt of legal interest, the banker superadds, as a condition of the loan, that it must be paid at a distant city, and consequently in a currency more valuable than that the lender received. But when such loans are legal, and possess the best commercial character for punctuality and security, they are not always so advantageous to the country bank as notes payable at the country bank, and connected with the circulation of bank notes or with deposits. The force of this remark can perhaps be better seen in what follows.

Selection of Loans founded on the Sale of Exchange. — Banks can usually make as many loans as they desire to borrowers who will use the loan in purchasing from the bank a draft on New York or other eastern city, whereby the bank will obtain a premium on the sale of the draft, in addition to the interest on the loan. The operation becomes peculiarly advantageous to the bank when the loan is itself payable in New York, for while the borrower pays, in such a transaction, a half of one per cent. to the bank for a bank draft on New York, he subsequently repays in New York the borrowed money without receiving any return premium from the bank. But how lucrative soever such a transaction seems, banks can rarely transact profitably much of such business. Should the entire capital of a safety fund bank of three hundred thousand dollars be employed in discounting drafts on New York payable at three months from the time of discount, and should the bank pay therefor sight drafts on New York, charging for them a premium of a half of one per cent., the bank could not pay its stockholders above six per cent. the year in bank dividends. To pay that much, the bank would have to earn nine per cent. the year on its capital, as follows:

Dividend of six per cent. the year on $300,000 is - - $18,000 00
Half per cent. to be paid to the safety fund, - - - 1,500 00
Salaries, taxes, stationery, and other contingencies during
the year, at the lowest calculation for such a capital, - 7,500 00

Making a total which is equal to 9 per ct. on $300,000, $27,000 00
Being just what such a bank would earn during the year, if it transacted no other business than the discount of drafts as above supposed. The calculation shows that the sale of exchange must be deferred to business which brings with it circulation or deposits. They are the only sources of large profits, as well as the great instruments of legitimate banking. Brokers can deal in exchange as well as banks, and banks should make loans predicated on the sale of exchange, for only so much as can be thus sold without impairing the ability of the bank to lend money for circulation, &c. The ability of a bank to lend for circulation is impaired by the sale of exchange, because such sales take the funds with which country banks redeem their bank notes; and no banker is willing to issue bank notes for circulation except in proportion to the amount which he possesses of redeeming funds.

Selection of Loans founded on a Commission for their Collection. — Banks often make loans that are payable at places where the currency that will be received in payment, is worth less to the lending bank than a payment at its own counter. But banks turn to a profit this disadvantage, by charging, in addition to the interest, a commission for collecting payment of the loans. Notes payable as above are given extensively by country merchants to the persons of whom they purchase goods, and the commission charged by banks for collecting the payment of such notes varies according to distance, and the facilities which exist for making the collections; but whether a bank can make money by such collections, depends on the arrangements it is able to make; for instance, a bank at Buffalo may receive one per cent. for collecting a note payable at Utica, while a bank at Utica may receive one per cent. for collecting a note payable at Buffalo; hence, if the two banks can exchange this paper with each other, each bank will be paid at its own counter, and gain the one per cent., without any inconvenience except the trouble of corresponding with each other, and the expense of postage. Every good banker endeavors to acquire correspondents of the character indicated, for in banking, as in other business, competition keeps down profits; so that much gain is impracticable except as a result of good management.

Selection of Loans founded on the Time they are to Endure. — As every loan is usually attended with some advantage to the bank, in the ways we have explained, beyond the interest paid by the borrower, the sooner the loan is to be repaid to the bank, the more frequently will the bank be able to reloan the money, and obtain a repetition of the incidental advantages. Loans, however, that are not longer to run than sixty days must be discounted at the rate of six per cent. the year interest, instead of seven, by all safety fund banks; hence, when a safety fund banker makes such loans, the incidental benefits must be sufficient to countervail this loss of interest, or longer paper will be more profitable.

Time Estimated with reference to the Prospective Wants of a Bank. — As country banks are subject every spring and fall to a revulsion of their bank notes, every judicious banker will endeavor to so select the loans which he makes during a year, that large amounts of them will become payable at the precise periods of the spring and fall when funds will be most needed. This is imitating the conduct of Pharaoh, who, during the years of plenty, accumulated provisions for the periods of apprehended famine. Many months of every year are months of plenty with every well-conducted bank. The paper which is selected for the future contingency will be useful in proportion to its reliability; and paper payable in New York, or other eastern cities, will be more useful than any other. No rule of banking is more practically valuable than the foregoing.

Time with reference to Panics and Pressures. — As banking is liable to panics and pressures which may arise without being preceded by any long premonitory symptoms, a banker must invest his funds in short loans, which measurably accomplish the feat that is proverbially impossible, "to have a cake and eat it at the same time :"— that is, by means of short loans, the bank keeps its funds always available within a short period, and yet keeps them always loaned out on interest. The banks of large cities are able to make loans payable on demand, or in a few days' notice; while country banks possess no such opportunities, but are able usually to deposit their spare funds in some banks of Albany or New York, subject to a repayment on demand, or on short notice; and in the mean time to receive on the deposit an interest of some four or five per cent. Such arrangements are peculiarly beneficial to country banks, as every country bank is compelled, by existing laws, to keep in New York or Albany an agency for the redemption of its bank notes; and hence must keep funds in one of those cities. Experience, however, has painfully demonstrated, in a recent bank failure, that the convenience of an interest paying depository is not exempt from danger. The legislature, in compelling country banks to incur this danger, has looked solely to the convenience of the public, and possibly estimated too lightly or disregarded the hazard to the banks.

A Banker should acquaint himself with the Pecuniary Circumstances of his Dealers. — What is every person's business is proverbially nobody's; hence the safety of banks depends less on boards of directors than on some single person to whom the bank is specially confided, and to whom we have alluded under the name of *the banker*. He is to be always present, and always responsible, in his feelings and in public estimation, for the prosperity of the bank; and for these services he ought to be well compensated, pecuniarily, so as to stimulate his faculties to their best efforts. We mistake human nature when we expect great efforts from any man, and supply no proper motive therefor. The banker we have described will acquaint himself with the pecuniary circumstances of the dealers of his bank, and of their endorsers, and of all persons who, though not present debtors or endorsers, may probably become such Persons enough will hasten to inform a banker when any of his debtors are become declared insolvents; but such shutting of the stable door after the horse is stolen is not the information that is useful to a banker. The information which is useful must be made while the person in question retains a reputation for solvency; and the information will be valuable in proportion as "it scents any coming mischief in the far-off gale." To acquire information, some country bankers obtain extracts from the assessment rolls of the towns within the circuit of their dealings; such extracts including only the men of reliable property. Other bankers keep a book, composed by themselves, of names accumulated, from day to day, of persons whose pecuniary position may interest their bank. Such a book may assume the form of an extensive alphabet, and the persons therein may be registered under the name of the town in which they reside. By this arrangement, when a banker is brought in contact with a person who resides, say, in Oswego, he can, by looking in his book under the head of Oswego, see the names of his debtors, and obtain such information in relation to them as the person from Oswego can supply; and which information he can record against each name respectively. The information thus acquired may be revised by other informants, as opportunities may offer; and the banker must give to the whole such an interpretation as his judgment shall dictate. The record will be improved by noting the name of the person from whom the information is received, and the date of its reception; for the information will be reliable in proportion somewhat to its recentness, and to the character of the informant. In large cities, where discounts are rarely made except to persons of the city, who are personally known to some of the directors, such a record may be useless; but in country banking, the borrowers and their endorsers are generally residents of remote places, and unknown, personally, in the locality of the bank. A country banker, who should insist on a personal acquaintance with his dealers and their endorsers, will find his business restricted to a circle too small for the employment of his capital. In vain will such a banker insist that he ought not to make loans to persons of whom he possesses no knowledge; the answer will be that he should acquire the knowledge. It is indispensable to his bank. He is bound to know a sufficient number of persons to enable his bank to employ its capital advantageously. Every note, therefore, that he rejects for want of knowledge, is ostensibly a slight reproach on him, in cases where he has not a sufficiency of known borrowers; while every note that he rejects or accepts by means of his knowledge of the parties is a tribute to his industry and vigilance.

A Banker should, as far as is practicable, know the Signatures of his Dealers. — The preceding remarks will show why country banks are specially liable to loss from forgeries. Moreover, many of the makers and endorsers who deal with country banks write poorly, and their signatures bear but little internal evidence of genuineness, even when you are partially acquainted with the parties; for the same person will write differently at different times, and especially with different pens and different qualities of ink; and he varies these continually. Still, the greater the danger, the greater is the caution which the banker must exercise. He must bring to the difficulty all the scrutiny of which the case is susceptible, or he will not stand excused for consequent losses.

A comparison of any proffered signature with one that is genuine, though encumbered with difficulties as above explained, is a guide that should not be neglected; and it is often the best that can be resorted to. Some bankers, therefore, keep a book in which every person who frequents the bank inserts his name. The signatures should be placed alphabetically, to facilitate a future reference to them. The endorsers may never visit the bank; but, when a note is paid, the names of the endorsers may, with the consent of the maker, be cut from the note, and pasted into the book, in their proper order. In no very long time, a mass of autographs may be thus collected. Some names on notes may not be deserving of such preservation; and in this particular, as in all others, the banker must exercise his judgment.

A Banker should know the Residence of Endorsers. — The law in relation to endorsers renders them liable only on due notice of the non-payment of the endorsed note. This avenue of loss is felt but seldom in large cities; but in the country it produces constant danger. A country banker, therefore, must know where endorsers reside, and usually the information can be obtained most readily when each note is discounted, and from the person who brings it for discount. The information can be written on the note under the name of the endorser, and it will serve as a direction to the notary public, should the note be protested for non-payment. The laws of our State required, formerly, that the notice of non-payment should be forwarded by mail to the post-office nearest to the residence of the endorser. This imposed on the banker a knowledge of postal locations that added much to the difficulty of his position. The law has since meliorated the difficulty by rendering a notice sufficient if directed to the town in which an endorser resides. When a banker desires to avail himself of this law, he had better comply literally with its conditions, and direct the notice " to the town of A," — thus showing that your letter is not sent to A, but to the town of A; — leaving the particular post-office in the town (some towns have more than one) to the discretion of the postmaster, for whose errors you are not accountable: — for instance, two or more post-offices are located in the town of Whitestown, and one of them is at a place called Whitestown; hence, if you direct a notice "Whitestown," you designate a post-office, and it may not be the one which the endorser frequents. In such a case the notice would probably be deemed defective, and the debt would not be recoverable against an endorser thus notified; but should you direct "to the town of Whitestown," you designate no post-office, and as you have performed all that the law requires, the endorser will be holden for the debt, in whatever part of the town he may reside.

4*

A Banker must know the Pecuniary Position of his Bank. — As a banker will lend to the extent of his ability, that he may make for his bank all the gains in his power, he must be well acquainted with the present pecuniary means and liabilities of his bank. He can keep on his table a summary showing the precise amount of his funds, and where they are situated, and of what they are composed; also, an aggregate of his various liabilities. Such a summary, when corrected daily, or more frequently if necessary, will constitute a chart by which he will be able to judge whether he can lend, or whether he must retrench existing loans. The funds that will be adequate to any given amount of liability, a banker must learn by experience, embarrassed as he will be by a want of uniformity in the results of his experience, at different periods. Every bank must be liable, momentarily, to demands for payment of its bank notes and deposits, beyond its present funds. Practically, however, if a banker has funds enough, day by day, to meet the requirements of the day, he has funds enough. " Sufficient for the day is the evil thereof," is a proverb peculiarly applicable in banking.

Prospective Resources. — But a banker must not be satisfied by knowing that his funds of to-day will be sufficient for the wants of the day. He must possess a reasonable assurance that the same will be his position " to-morrow, and to-morrow, to the end of time." To gain this assurance, he ought to keep also before him one or more lists in detail of his prospective resources; showing what notes and acceptances will be payable to the bank daily for some weeks or months ahead, and where they are payable. With such lists, and a knowledge of the reality of the paper thus going onward to maturity, he will be able to judge whether his prospective resources will need the aid of his existing unemployed funds; or whether he may loan them, and even extend his liabilities in anticipation of a prospective surplusage of resources.

Provision for the Future. — By means of such lists as we have just described, should a banker discover that his existing resources will be small during, say, the month of June, he can aid the defect by discounting in the preceding May, April or March, paper that will mature in June. By thus regulating, prospectively, his future resources, he can be always provided with funds. And that a banker may, at all times, be master of his resources, he should never promise prospective loans, or make loans with any promise of their renewal. The more he keeps uncommitted, the better will he be able to accommodate himself to future exigencies. Banking is subject to sufficient uncertainties, without unnecessarily aggravating them by prospective agreements. A banker may be unable to fulfil such pledges, and be thus compelled to falsify his promises; or he may be able to fulfil them only at a sacrifice of the interests of his bank, and thus be placed in the unwholesome dilemma of injuring his personal character, or of preventing the injury by only a sacrifice of the interests of his bank.

General Supervision. — A banker is compelled to employ officers to whom he must intrust his vaults and their contents. Robberies are often committed by persons thus intrusted, and some such robberies have remained long concealed. The banker cannot be responsible for all such occurrences; still, vigilance can accomplish much in the way of security against mischances, and the banker is responsible for the exercise of all practicable vigilance. Robberies and frauds possess usually some discoverable concomitants. No man plunders to accumulate property that is not to be used. Its use, therefore, which can rarely be wholly concealed, is a clue which a vigilant eye can trace to the plunderer. Nearly every plunderer is a prodigal, and may thereby be detected; nearly every plunderer is needy, and should therefore be suspected. The banker should know human nature, and be able to trace effects to their causes, and to deduce effects from causes. To this extent he is answerable for the safety of his bank. The sentinel whose post happens to be surprised by an enemy may escape punishment as a criminal, but he can rarely gain commendation for vigilance, or escape censure for carelessness.

Over Drafts. — To permit over drafts is to make loans without endorsers, and without the payment of interest. It is, moreover, to empower a dealer to control your resources. No mode of lending money can be more inconsistent with all safe banking; and it should never be permitted. Still, every man who keeps a bank account can draw checks for an amount exceeding his balance in bank; nor can the banker personally supervise the payment of checks. A vigilant banker will, however, provide vigilant subordinate officers: "The eye of the master maketh diligent," say the Scriptures. An intelligent and careful teller will soon learn whom he must watch; but after all precautions an overdraft may be perpetrated, and, whether by accident or design, the bookkeeper should forthwith report to the banker the occurrence, and he must act thereon as his judgment shall deem proper.

Enforcement of Payments. — No system of banking can escape the casualty of doubtful debts. Usually the most favorable time to coerce payments is when they first become payable. Then the debtor has expected to pay, and if he is then in default, no certain dependence can be made on his subsequent promises. He is also usually less offended by a legal enforcement of payments when they are promptly enforced, and when he knows the creditor is disappointed by the default, than he is after the default has been tacitly acquiesced in by a long forbearance of coercive measures. Additional security, when necessary, can also be more readily obtained at the time of the default, than it can after the debtor has become reconciled by time to his dishonorable position. His credit is better now than it will be subsequently, and he can more readily now than subsequently obtain responsible endorsers. In relation to the extension of time on receiving additional security on a weak debt, any extension that is productive of security is a less banking evil than insecurity ; just as any protraction of disease that results in health is a less physical evil than death.

Adherence to Good Principles. — A banker will be often subjected to importunity by persons who will desire a deviation from the usual modes of banking. They will propose a relaxation of good rules, and allege therefor some pressing emergency ; but if the relaxation involves any insecurity, any violation of law, or of official duty, the banker should never submit, even when the result may promise unusual lucrativeness to his bank. While a banker adheres with regularity to known forms of business and settled principles, Providence is a guarantee for his success ; but when he deviates from these, Providence is almost equally a guarantee of disaster both personal and official.

A Banker should beware of Persuasion, and of undue Pertinacity in Applicants. — Banking is a business, and should be reciprocally beneficial to the borrower and the lender. When a borrower's business cannot yield the requisite reciprocity of benefit, he will often attempt to mend the defect by pertinacity of application, and by persuasions addressed to the directors of a bank personally, as well as to the banker ; and by servility and sycophancy. Such conduct is a strong symptom of some latent defect in the applicant's pecuniary position, and the appliances should strengthen a banker in his refusal of loans, rather than facilitate their acquisition. Loans thus obtained rarely result favorably to the lender.

A Bank should beware of Speculators. — No man is safe when engaged in a speculation, especially when the price of the article that he purchases is above the usual cost of its production. The speculator's intellect soon loses its control over him, and he will be controlled by his feelings, and they are unnaturally excited. He becomes a monomaniac in the particular concern with which he is engaged. He will increase his purchases beyond all moderation, and at prices which he himself, when he commenced his purchases, would have deemed ruinous. Many banks are destroyed by such speculators. A bank will loan to them till its safety seems to require that the speculation must be upheld against a falling market; and the effort is made till the continued decline in prices ruins both speculators and sustaining bank.

A Banker should keep independent of his Debtors. — When a debtor arrives at a certain magnitude of indebtedness he becomes the master of his creditor, who is somewhat in the position of Jonah when swallowed by the whale. The debtor can say to a bank thus circumstanced, that to stop discounting for him will ruin him, and that his ruin will involve a loss of the existing debt. No prudent banker will be placed in such a position, but should any banker lapse into so sad an error, he will rarely mend his position by yielding to the proposed necessity for further loans. He had better brave the existing evil than yield to an argument which, if already too potent to be disregarded, will acquire additional strength by every further discount, and render his inevitable fall more disastrous to his stockholders, and more disreputable to himself.

Economy. — We will close our summary of a banker's duties with a few remarks on his contingent expenses. The more a banker can reduce their amount, the more easily will he make reasonable dividends of profit among his stockholders, without an undue expansion of loans and consequent anxiety to himself. The income of a bank is an aggregate of only petty accumulations. The unnecessary expenditure of every hundred dollars the year, will nullify the interest on four ninety day loans of fifteen hundred dollars each — loans often withheld from meritorious claimants. The economy of which we speak is not any unjust abridgment of proper remunerative salaries to faithful officers and servants, who should, however, labor diligently and perseveringly in their vocations, as men labor in other employments; so that the bank may economize in the number of its agents, instead of economizing in the magnitude of their salaries. A hundred dollars, or a thousand, when contrasted with the capital of a bank, may seem a small matter, and probably bank expenditures are often incurred under such a contrast; but the true contrast lies between the expenditure and the net per centage of a bank's gains. A bank whose net income will not exceed the legal rate of interest possesses no fund from which to squander. And banks often expend an unduly large part of their capital in architecture to ornament the city of their location, or to rival some neighboring institution, whose extravagance ought to be shunned, not followed. No person has yet shown why banks should be built like palaces, while the owners of the banks are to a good extent poor, and live humbly. The custom is perhaps founded on the delusion of deeming a great capital identical with great wealth. When several men for any purposes of gain, unite their several small capitals, they may well need a larger building and more agents than each man would require were he unassociated; but that the association can afford an organization increased in splendor as much as in magnitude, is a fallacy somewhat analogous to the blunder of the Irishman, who, hearing that his friend intended to walk forty miles during a day, said that he would walk with him, and then they could walk eighty miles.

PART THIRD.—THE MAN

HAVING completed our summary of banking, and the duties consequent thereon of a banker, we will subjoin a few suggestions personal to the man who has to perform the duties.

He should be wary of recommendations. — When solicited by a neighbor or a friend, few men possess vigor enough, or conscientiousness enough, to refuse a recommendation, or to state therein all they suspect or apprehend. They will studiously endeavor not to make themselves pecuniarily responsible by any palpable misrepresentation; hence they will so qualify the recommendation that it will admit of a construction consistent with truth; but the qualification will be so enigmatical or subtle that the banker will not interpret it as the recommender will show subsequently it ought to have been interpreted. Besides, the man who merely recommends a loan acts under circumstances that are much less favorable to caution than the man who is to lend. When we are in the act of making a loan, our organization presents the danger with a vividness that is not excited by the act of recommending. To speculatively believe that we will suffer the extraction of a tooth, is a wholly different matter from sitting down and submitting to the operation. Suicide would be far more common than it is, if a man could feel, when the act was to be performed, as he feels when he only prospectively resolves on performing it. This preservative process of nature no banker should disregard by substituting any man's recommendation for the scrutiny of his own feelings and judgment at the time when the loan is to be consummated; though he may well give to recommendations all the respect which his knowledge of the recommender may properly deserve.

He should be governed by his own judgment. — By acting according to the dictates of his own judgment, a man strengthens his own judgment as he proceeds; while a man who subordinates his judgment to other men's is continually debilitating his own. Nothing also is more fallacious than the principle on which we ordinarily defer to the decision of a multitude of counsellors. If fifty men pull together at a cable, the pull will combine the strength of one man multiplied by fifty; but if fifty men deliberate on any subject, the result is not the wisdom of one man multiplied by fifty, but at most the wisdom of the wisest man of the assemblage; just as fifty men, when they look at any object, can see only what can be seen by the sharpest single vision of the group; they cannot combine their vision and make thereof a lens as powerful as the sight of one man multiplied by fifty. A banker may, therefore, well resort to other men for information, but he may differ from them all, and still be right; any way, if he perform the dictates of his own judgment, he performs all that duty requires; if he act otherwise, he performs less than his duty. Let the counsel of your own heart stand, says the Bible; and, by way of encouragement, it adds, that a man can see more of what concerns himself, than seven watchmen on a high tower.

Finally.— As virtue's strongest guarantee is an exemption from all motive to commit evil, a banker must avoid all engagements that may make him needy. If he wants to be *more* than a banker, he should cease from being a banker. Should he discover in himself a growing tendency to irritability, which his position is apt to engender, let him resist it as injurious to his bank and his peace; and if he should find himself popular, let him examine whether it proceeds from the due discharge of his duties. A country banker was some few years ago dismissed from a bank which he had almost ruined, and was immediately tendered an honorary public dinner by the citizens of his village, into whose favor his misdeeds had unwisely ingratiated him. The service of massive plate that was given to a president of the late United States Bank was in reward of compliances which soon after involved in disaster every commercial interest of our country. Could we trace actions to their source, these mistakes of popular gratitude would never occur. The moroseness that we abhor proceeds often from a sensitiveness that is annoyed at being unable to oblige; while the amiability that is applauded proceeds from an imbecility that knows not how to refuse.

A banker should possess a sufficiency of legal knowledge to make him suspect what may be defects in proffered securities, so as to submit his doubts to authorized counsellors. He must, in all things, be eminently practical. Every man can tell an obviously insufficient security, and an obviously abundant security; but neither of these constitute any large portion of the loans that are offered to a banker. Security practically sufficient for the occasion is all that a banker can obtain for the greater number of the loans he must make. If he must err in his judgment of securities, he had better reject fifty good loans than make one bad debt; but he must endeavor not to err on the extreme of caution or the extreme of temerity; and his tact in these particulars will, more than any other, constitute the criterion of his merits as a banker.

TEN MINUTES' ADVICE ABOUT KEEPING A BANKER.

BY J. W. GILBART, F. R. S,

GENERAL MANAGER OF THE LONDON AND WESTMINSTER BANK

1. A BANKER is a person who has an open shop, with proper counters, clerks, and books, for receiving other people's money, in order to keep it safe, and return it upon demand.

2. The building or shop in which this business is carried on is usually called in London a "Banking-house," but in Scotland, and in the country parts of England, it is called a "Bank." The word "bank" is also employed to denote the partnership or company who carry on the business of banking. Thus we say, the Bank of Scotland, the London and Westminster Bank, the Bank of Messrs. Coutts & Co.

3. When a company of this kind does not consist of more than six partners, it is called a "Private Bank;" but when the company consists of several hundred partners, it is called in Scotland a "Public Bank" and in England a "Joint-stock Bank."

4. A private bank is usually managed by one or more of the partners, and all the partners are styled bankers. A public bank is managed by a principal officer, who is usually styled a manager. In England, a bank manager is not commonly called a banker; but in Scotland, all managers of banks and managers of branch banks are called bankers. So mind, when I use the word "banker," you may apply it either to a private banker or to a bank manager, whichever you please, as my observations will be as applicable to one as to the other. A banker is a man who carries on the business of banking; and, whether he carries it or

upon his own account, or as the agent of a public company, it appears to me to make no difference as to his claims to be called a banker.

5. It is the business of all these banks to receive other people's money, and return it upon demand. And when any person puts money into one of these banks, he is said to open an account with the bank; and when he has thus opened an account, and continues to put in and draw out money, he is said to have a current account, or, in London phraseology, "to keep a banker."

6. In Scotland, almost every man has an account of some sort with a bank. The rich man in trade has an account because of the facility of conducting his operations; the rich man out of trade has an account because he gets interest upon his lodgments, and he keeps his money in the bank until he has an opportunity of investing it elsewhere at a better rate of interest. The middle class of people have an account because of the convenience of it, and because they obtain the discount of their bills, and perhaps loans, on giving two sureties, which are called cash credits. The poorer classes lodge their small savings in the bank, because of the security, and because they get interest on the sums which are lodged.

7. But in London the practice of keeping an account with a bank is by no means so common as in Scotland. The London banks are banks only for the rich. The bankers require that every person opening an account shall always have a sum to his credit; and if the sum thus kept is not what they deem sufficient, they will close the account. Hence the middle class of people in London have no banker at all, and the poorer class lodge their money in the savings banks, where they get interest, which they would not get from the London banker. It should also be stated that, besides keeping a sufficient balance, a party opening an account with a London banker is expected to give a certain sum every year to the clerks. This is called Christmas money and the object is merely to enable the banker to pay a less salary to his clerks at the expense of his customers.

8. But within a few years, public or joint-stock banks have been established in London. These banks, or at least some of them, will allow you to open an account without promising to keep a large balance, or even any balance at all, provided you pay a small sum annually as a commission. The sum is fixed when you open the account, and it is about the same that you would be expected to give as Christmas money to the clerks of a private bank. Hence, people of moderate incomes, and those who can employ the whole of their capital in their business, are now able to keep a banker. These banks, too, give interest on deposits, whether the sums be large or small, as I shall hereafter explain.

9. The first public or joint-stock bank established in London was the London and the Westminster Bank. This bank is in Lothbury, and it

has branch establishments at No. 1, St. James' square; No. 214, High-Holborn; No. 3, Wellington street, Borough; No. 87, High street, White-chapel; and No. 4, Stratford place, Oxford street. The success of this bank has led to the formation of several others. You will observe that all banks which have branches conduct their business on the same terms at the branches as they do at the central office.

10. Since, then, the Scotch system of banking is established in London, why should not the keeping of a banker be as general in London as in Scotland? I have stated that, under the old system, those chiefly who were denied banking facilities were the middle class of people. Now, these people may be subdivided into two classes — those who are engaged in trade, and those who are not. I shall address myself, in the first place, to the former class.

11. Now, I ask you, why don't you keep a banker? You say you have been in business several years, and have never kept one. Of course, if no banker would take your account, you could not do otherwise; but now there are bankers willing to take your account. But you say you can do without a banker. Of course you can. The question is, not whether by possibility you can do without a banker, but whether you cannot do better with one? But you reply, it would not be worth any banker's while to take your account. That is for his consideration, not for yours. The question for you to decide is, not whether your keeping a banker would be of use to him, but whether it would be of use to yourself. I shall point out to you some of the advantages.

12. In the first place, by keeping a banker, your money will be lodged in a place of security. You have now £50 or £100, or perhaps sometimes £200, that you keep in your own house; you take it up into your bedroom at night, and when you go out on a Sunday you carry it in your pocket. Now, you may lose this money out of your pocket — the till may be robbed by your servants — or your house may be broken open by thieves — or your premises may take fire and the money may be burned. But, even should you escape loss, you cannot escape anxiety. When you have a little more money than usual, you have fears and apprehensions lest some accident should occur. Now, you will avoid all this trouble by keeping a banker.

13. The banker will not only take care of your money, but also of anything else you commit to his charge. You can get a small tin box, with your name painted on it, and into this box you can put your will, the lease of your house, policies of insurance, and any deeds or other documents that require particular care. You can send this box to your banker, who will take care of it for you; and you can have it back whenever you like, and as often as you like. If your premises are insured, it is clearly improper to keep the policy on the premises; for

if the house be burned, the policy will be burned too; and where then is your evidence of claim upon the insurance office?

14. Another advantage is the saving of time. When you receive money you will send it in a lump to the bank; and when you pay away money you will draw checks upon the bank. Now, to draw a check takes up much less time than counting out the money that you have to pay, and perhaps sending out for change because you have not the exact sum. Besides, you sometimes hold bills which, when due, you have to send for payment; now, you can lodge these with your banker, who will present them for you. And, when you accept bills, you will make them payable at your banker's, instead of making them payable at your own house. Now, in all these cases there is a great saving of time; and, besides, your bills, from being made payable at the bank, will be considered more respectable.

15. Another advantage of keeping a banker is, that it will be a check upon your accounts. I need not speak to you, as a trader, of the importance of correct accounts. Your banker's book will be an authentic record of your cash transactions. If you make a mistake in your trade books, the banker's book will often lead to a detection of the error. If you have paid a sum of money, and the party denies having received it, you can refer to your banker's account, and produce your check, which is as good as a receipt. By means of a banker's account, you could trace your receipts and payments, even after a number of years had elapsed; and hence, disputed accounts could be readily adjusted, and error, arising from forgetfulness or oversight, be speedily rectified.

16. I could mention several other reasons why you should keep a banker.* But what I have said will be enough to induce you to make a trial; and when you have once opened an account, you will find so much convenience from it, that you will require no further reasons to induce you to continue it. If it should not answer your expectations, you can, whenever you please, close it again.

17. Now, then, as you have made up your mind to keep a banker, the next thing is to determine at what bank you will open your account. On this point I must leave you to make your own choice. All the public banks issue prospectuses, containing a list of their directors, the amount of their paid-up capital, the names of the bankers who superintend their respective establishments, and their rules for transacting business. You can get a prospectus from each bank, compare them

---

* The reasons assigned here have a reference chiefly to London banking. The operations of country banking are familiarly described in "The Anatomy and Philosophy of Banking; or, the true Character and Value of Banks briefly explained to the Middle Classes of Society By James Strachan." (Groombridge.)

together, and please your own fancy. But if you have no other grounds for preference, I advise you to open your account with the BANK or BRANCH BANK that is NEAREST TO YOUR OWN PLACE OF BUSINESS. You will often have to go or send to the bank, and if it be a great way off, much time will be lost, and you will at times be induced to forego some of the advantages of keeping a banker rather than send to so great a distance. On this account, let your banker be your neighbor. Recollect, time is money.

18. There is no difficulty in opening an account. You will enter the bank, and ask for the manager. Explain to him what you want to do. He will give you every information you may require, and you will receive, without charge, a small account-book, called a Pass-book, and a book of checks. I advise you to keep these two books, when not in use, under your own lock and key.

19. You now require no further advice from me, as your banker will give you the most ample information respecting the way of conducting your account. Nevertheless, I may mention a point or two for your own government: — Do not depend entirely upon your banker's Pass-book, but keep also an account in a book of your own. Debit your banker with all cash you may pay into the bank, and credit him for all the checks you may draw at the time you draw them. Send your Pass-book frequently to be made up at the bank, and, when it returns, always compare it with your account-book. This will correct any mistake in the Pass-book. Besides, some of your checks may not be presented for payment until several days after they are drawn, and if, in the mean time, you take the balance of the banker's Pass-book, you will seem to have more ready cash than you actually possess, and this may lead you into unpleasant mistakes.

20. When you lodge any money at the bank, always place the total amount of the cash, and your name, at full length, upon the outside of the parcel, or on a slip of paper. The cashier will then see at once if he agrees with your amount. This will save time, and prevent mistakes.

21. Be always open and straightforward with your banker. Do not represent yourself to be a richer man than you are; do not discount with your banker any bills that are not likely to be PUNCTUALLY paid when due; and, should any be unpaid and returned to you, pay them yourself IMMEDIATELY. Do not attempt to OVERDRAW your account; that is, do not draw checks upon your banker for more money than you have in his hands, without first asking his consent; and if you make him any promises, be sure that they be strictly performed. If you fail ONCE, the banker will hesitate before he trusts you again.

22. Should you be dissatisfied with anything connected with your account, make your complaint to the BANKER himself, and not to the

clerks. Let all your communications be made in PERSON, rather than by LETTER. But do not stay long at one interview. Make no observations about the weather or the news of the day. Proceed at once to the business you are come about, and, when it is settled, retire. This will save your banker's time, and give him a favorable impression of your character as a man of business.

23. If you are in partnership, besides opening an account with your banker in the names of the firm, you should open a private account for yourself, that your personal affairs may be kept separate from those of the partnership. Or, if you are in an extensive way of business, and have a large family, it is advisable that you open a separate account with your banker, in the name of your wife, that your trade payments and your household expenses may not be mixed up together in the same account. This is a good way of ascertaining the exact amount of your family expenditure.

24. If you are appointed executor or assignee to an estate, or become treasurer to a public institution or charitable society, open a separate account with your banker for this office, and do not mix other people's moneys with your own. This will prevent mistakes and confusion in your accounts. These separate accounts may be kept still more distinct by being opened with another banker, or at another branch of the same bank.

25. There are a good many of the middle class of people who are not in trade, and I must now address them. Perhaps you are a clergyman, or a medical man, or you are in a public office, or are living on your rents or dividends. At all events, whatever you may be, I conclude you are not living beyond your means. If you are, I have not a word to say to you about keeping a banker; you will soon, most likely, be within the keeping of a jailor.

26. Several of the reasons I have given to the trader will also apply to you; but there is one that applies with much greater force — the tendency to insure accurate accounts. As you are not a man of business, I shall not advise you to keep an account of your receipts and expenditures. I know you will do no such thing. Should you ever commence to do so, you will get tired before the end of the year, and throw the book aside. Now, if you keep a banker, he will keep your accounts for you; his Pass-book will show you the state of your accounts. All the money you receive you must send to the bank, and all your payments must be made by checks upon the bank. If you want pocket-money, draw a check for £5 or £20, payable to cash, but by no means disburse any money but through your banker. Your book will be balanced every half year. You will then see the total amount of your receipts during the half-year, and your various payments to the butcher, the baker, the tailor, &c., &c. The names to which the checks are made

payable will show for what purpose they were given, and you snould write these names in a plain hand, that the clerks may copy them correctly in the Pass-book. Now, if you look through your book once every half year in this way, you will probably see occasion to introduce some useful reforms into your domestic expenditure. But if you are too lazy to do this, hand the book to your wife, and she will do it for you.

27. I shall now address another class of people. Perhaps you are a clerk, or a warehouseman, or a shopman, or a domestic servant. Well, you have no occasion to keep a banker; that is, you have no occasion to open a current account. But you have got a little money which you would like to put into some safe place, and upon which you would like to receive interest. Well, now, listen to me.

28. If the sum be under £10, or if the sum be above £10, and you are not likely to want it soon, put it into the savings bank; and you will receive interest for it at the rate of about £3 for every £100 for a year. But mind, you can only put money into the savings bank at certain hours in the week, when the bank is open, and you cannot put in more than £30 in any one year, nor more than £150 altogether, and you will receive no interest for the fractional parts of a month, and you cannot draw out any money without giving notice beforehand.

29. If, then, your money is more than £10, and you have already lodged £30 this year in the savings bank, or £150 altogether, or if you will have occasion to draw out your money without giving notice, then lodge it in one of the public banks. These banks are open every weekday from nine o'clock in the morning till four in the evening; they will take lodgments of money to any amount, and interest will be allowed from the day it is lodged until the day it is drawn out; and if the sum is under £1,000 no notice is required. For all sums lodged on interest, the bankers give receipts called deposit receipts.

30. When you go to the bank to lodge upon interest any sum under £1,000, you need not inquire for the manager. Hand your money to any clerk you may see standing inside of the counter, and ask for a deposit receipt. You will be requested (the first time you go) to write your name and address in a book which is kept for that purpose, and then the deposit receipt will be given to you without any delay.

31. Mind, this deposit receipt is not transferable; that is, you cannot lend it or give it to anybody else. When you want the money, you must take it yourself to the bank, and ask the cashier to pay you the amount. You will then be requested to write your name on the back of the deposit receipt; the cashier will see that the signature corresponds with the signature you wrote in the book when you lodged the money, and will then pay you the amount, and keep the receipt.

32. Although you cannot lodge upon a deposit receipt a less sum in the first instance than £10, yet, having lodged that sum, you can make

any additions to it you please. Thus, if you wish to lodge £5 more, you can take your £5 note and your deposit receipt for £10 to the bank, and get a new receipt for £15. If, after having lodged £10, you wish to lodge £10 more, you can get a separate receipt for the second £10, or have a new receipt for £20, whichever you please; and observe, whenever any addition is made to a former receipt, the old receipt is cancelled and the interest due upon it is either paid to you in money, or added to the amount of the new receipt, as may be most agreeable to yourself.

33. The interest allowed you at the bank will at present be at the rate of 2 per cent.; that is to say, after the rate of £2 upon every £100 for a year.

34. Upon sums above £1,000 the interest allowed is sometimes more and sometimes less than 2 per cent., according to the value of money; that is, according to the rate at which the bankers can employ it again; and a few days' notice is usually required before the money is withdrawn; but, upon sums under £1,000, the rate of interest varies less frequently, and they are always repayable upon demand.

35. You will be surprised to find how the desire of lodging money in a bank will grow upon you. When you had the money in your pocket, you were anxious to find reasons for spending it. When you have placed it in the bank, you will be anxious to find reasons for not spending it. All habits are formed or strengthened by repeated acts. The more money you lodge in the bank, the more you will desire to lodge. You will go on making additions, until, at last, you will probably have acquired a sum that shall lay the foundation of your advance to a higher station in society.

ALPHABETICAL INDEX

TO THE SUBJECTS CONTAINED IN

A TREATISE ON BANKING, BY A. B. JOHNSON," AND "TEN MINUTES ADVICE ON KEEPING A BANKER, BY J. W. GILBART."

	Page
Acceptances in advance of Consignments,	32
Banker (the). duties and requisites of,	28
———— his primary objects in the prosperity of his Bank,	29
———— should acquaint himself with the circumstances of his dealers,	39
———— should know the signatures of his dealers,	40
———— should know the residences of endorsers,	41
———— should know the pecuniary position of his Bank,	42
———— prospective resources of,	42
———— should never promise prospective loans,	42
———— should be wary of recommendations,	47
———— his adherence to good principles,	44
———— should beware of persuasion and of speculators,	44
———— should keep independent of his debtors,	45
———— should be governed by his own judgment,	47
———— description of, by J. W. Gilbart,	49
Banks. Profits from Bank Notes and Deposits,	8
———. Relative utility of Safety Fund and Free,	10
———— of New York, aggregate Capital,	8
———, large and small, relative productiveness of,	15
———, on the gains of,	34
———, the general supervision of,	43
———, general use of, in Scotland,	50
Bank Dividends, average rate for three years,	9
———— Notes, benefits to the public from the use of,	9
————————, loss to the public from insolvent,	11
———— Circulation, Deposits, and Loans. equally extinguished,	18
————————, not wholly redeemable in specie,	18
————————, increased by spirit of speculation,	22
———— Suspensions, how produced,	19
———— Loans to be regulated by prospective wants,	38
———— Circulation and Deposits expand together,	22
———, prospective resources of,	42
———— Loans, regulated by habits, &c., of the borrower,	31
Banking, objects of,	28
————, economy in, recommended,	45
———— in London,	50
Business of the State diminished by a contracted currency,	17
————————, a guarantee for currency,	17
Capital, always withdrawn during a panic,	21
City and Country Commerce, as affected by the Banks,	14
Collections within the State,	26
———— out of the State,	26
Country Banks, how affected by the city pressure,	24

ALPHABETICAL INDEX.

	Page
Currency of the State of New York,	16
———, a measure of the business of the State,	16
———, not contracted by business, diminished,	17
———, excess of, cannot last long,	17
———, National, receivable for taxes, duties, &c.,	20
———, expansions of, how produced,	21
———, contractions of,	22
———, periodical,	23
Customers should be straight-forward with their bankers,	53
Debtors. Security founded on the morality of,	31
———. Security founded on the habits of,	31
———. Security founded on the business of,	32
Dividends. Insufficient to make bank capital desirable property,	9
Dummies, paper of should be avoided,	33
Economy in Banking recommended,	45
——— in the use of a Bank by traders,	51
Exchange, profits on the sale of, by Banks,	25
Endorsers, two usually required in the country,	30
Extravagance of borrowers, to be considered,	31
Free Banks in New York, policy of,	14
Interest. Laws of, in New York,	7
Interests of debtors subordinate to those of the Bank,	30
Kiting, sometimes resorted to by borrowers,	33
Legal Tender, how affected by statutes,	20
Loans, founded on incidental circulation,	35
———, founded on the place of repayment,	36
———, founded on sale of exchange,	37
———, founded on a commission for their collection,	37
———, founded on the time they are to endure,	38, 39
London, banking in,	50
Moderation, to be observed in the business of Banks,	34
Moral Security should be considered, in loans,	31
Morality of a Debtor, security founded on,	31
New York Safety Fund Banking System,	12
——— and Free Banks, compared,	12, 14
New York Safety Fund Banks, Legal Privileges of,	15
Offerings for Discount, character of,	32
Overdrafts, equivalent to loans without endorsers,	43
Partnership Accounts, should be kept separate from individual accounts,	51
Pressures upon Banks, periodical,	23
———, increase with a compound progression,	24
———, commence in large cities,	24
———, of the interior,	24
———, termination of, succeeded by expansion,	25
———, loans, with reference to,	39
Redemptions, speedy, desired by Brokers,	23
Risks on Loans, not charged for,	30
Specie Shipments productive of pressure,	23
Suspended paper, payment of should be enforced,	43
Suspension of specie payments, how produced,	18
———, never necessary,	29
Treasury Notes and Receivables,	20
Usurious Notes and Drafts,	33

SECOND PART.

                                                                                       Pag;

I. EXTRACTS FROM THE LAW OF BILLS OF EXCHANGE. By John Barnard Byles, author of a "Treatise on the Law of Bills of Exchange, Promissory Notes, Bank Notes, Bankers' Cash Notes and Checks," 60

II. REMARKS ON BILLS OF EXCHANGE. By John Ramsey McCulloch, author of "The Dictionary of Commerce," &c., . . 83

III. FORMS OF BILLS OF EXCHANGE IN THE FRENCH, GERMAN, DUTCH, ITALIAN, SPANISH, PORTUGUESE, AND SWEDISH LANGUAGES, ... 93

IV. FORMS OF NOTICE OF PROTEST; WITH REMARKS, ... 96

V. SYNOPSIS OF THE BANK LAWS OF MASSACHUSETTS, IN FORCE JANUARY, 1851. — 1. BANKS. — 2. BANK NOTES. — 3. CASHIERS AND OTHER OFFICERS. — 4. DIRECTORS. — 5. FORGERY. — 6. INTEREST. — 7. PROMISSORY NOTES. — 8. STOCKHOLDERS. — 9. NOTARIES PUBLIC. — 10. BANK COMMISSIONERS. — 11. MISCELLANEOUS. — 12. DECISIONS OF THE SUPREME JUDICIAL COURT OF MASSACHUSETTS IN REFERENCE TO BANKS, &c., 10

THE LAW OF BILLS OF EXCHANGE.
BY JOHN BARNARD BYLES,
AUTHOR OF A TREATISE ON BILLS OF EXCHANGE.

I.—HISTORY OF BILLS OF EXCHANGE.

THERE is no vestige of the existence of Bills of Exchange among the ancients, and the precise period of their introduction is somewhat controverted. It is, however, certain that they were in use in the fourteenth century, though we find in our English law-books no decision relating to them earlier than the reign of James the First.

It is probable that a bill of exchange was, in its original, nothing more than a letter of credit from a merchant in one country, to his debtor, a merchant in another, requesting him to pay the debt to a third person, who carried the letter, and happened to be travelling to the place where the debtor resided. It was discovered, by experience, that this mode of making payments was extremely convenient to all parties: — to the creditor, for he could thus receive his debt without trouble, risk, or expense — to the debtor, for the facility of payment was an equal accommodation to him, and perhaps drew after it facility of credit — to the bearer of the letter, who found himself in funds in a foreign country, without the danger and incumbrance of carrying specie. At first, perhaps, the letter contained many other things beside the order to give credit. But it was found that the original bearer might often with advantage transfer it to another. The letter was then disencumbered of all other matter; it was opened and not sealed, and the page on which it was written gradually shrunk to the slip now in use. The assignee was, perhaps, desirous to know beforehand whether the party to whom it was addressed would pay it, and sometimes showed it to him for that purpose; his promise to pay was the origin of acceptances. These letters or bills, the representatives of debts due in a foreign country, were sometimes more, sometimes less, in demand; they became, by degrees, articles of traffic; and the present complicated and abstruse practice and theory of exchange was gradually formed.

Upon their introduction into our own country, other conveniences, as great as in international transactions, were found to attend them. They offered an easy and most effectual expedient for eluding the stubborn rule of the common law, that a debt is not assignable; furnishing the assignee with an assignment binding on the original creditor, capable of being ratified by the debtor, perhaps guaranteed by a series of responsible sureties, and assignable still further, *ad infinitum*. Not only did these simple instruments transfer value from place to place, at home or abroad, and balance the accounts of distant cities without the transmission of money; not only did they assign debts in the most convenient, extensive, and effectual manner; but the value of a debt was improved by being authenticated in a bill of exchange, for it was thus reduced to a certain amount, which the debtor, having accepted, could not afterwards unsettle; evidence of the original demand was rendered unnecessary, and the bill afforded a plainer and more indisputable title to the whole debt. A creditor, too, by assigning to a man of property a bill at a long date, given him by his debtor, could obtain, for a trifling discount, his money in advance. Credit to the buyer was thus rendered consistent with ready money to the seller, and the reconciliation of the apparent inconsistency was brought about by a further benefit to a third person, for it was effected by advantageously employing the surplus and idle funds of the capitalist. At the first introduction of bills of exchange, however, the English courts of law regarded them with a jealous and evil eye, allowing them only between merchants; but their obvious advantages soon compelled the judges to sanction their use by all persons; and of late years the policy of the Bench has been industriously to remove every impediment, and add all possible facilities to these wheels of the vast commercial system.

The advantages of a bill of exchange, in reducing a debt to a certainty, curtailing the evidence necessary to enforce payment, and affording the means of procuring ready money by discount, often induced creditors to draw a bill for the sake of acceptance; though there might be no intention of transferring the debt. Such a transaction pointed out the way to a shorter mode of effecting the same purpose by means of a promissory note. Promissory notes soon circulated like bills of exchange, and became as common as bills themselves. Notes for small sums, payable to bearer on demand, were found to answer most purposes of the ordinary circulating medium, and have, at length, in all civilized countries, supplanted a great portion of the gold and silver previously in circulation. Great, however, as was the saving, and numerous the advantages arising from the substitution, it was discovered by experience that the dangers and inconveniences of an unlimited issue of paper money were at least as great. The legislature have, therefore, found it necessary to place the issue of negotiable notes for small sums under the restrictions which have been pointed out elsewhere; and experience has proved that the only mode of preserving paper money on a level with gold, is to compel the utterers to exchange it for gold, at the option of the holder. And peradventure, even then, unless the State controls the issue of paper, on principles imperfectly understood at present, the value of the whole circulating medium may decline together, as compared with other commodities or the currency of foreign countries, and the precious metals may in consequence leave the kingdom. This consequence does not appear to have been foreseen by the late Mr. Ricardo.

During the suspension of cash payments and the circulation of one pound notes, nearly every payment in this country was made in paper. And some idea may be formed of the immense amount of property even now afloat in bills and notes, when it is considered that all payments for our immense exports and imports, almost every remittance to and from every quarter of the world, nearly every payment of large amount between distant places in the kingdom, and a large proportion of payments in the same place, are made through the intervention of bills; not to mention the amount of common promissory notes, at long and short dates, and the notes of the Bank of England and country banks. It will not, perhaps, be an unreasonable inference that the bills and notes of all kinds, issued and circulated in the United Kingdom in the space of a single year, amount to many hundred millions, and that this species of property is now, in aggregate value, inferior only to the land or funded debt of the kingdom.

This deduction is fully supported by the returns of the Stamp Office. The net produce of the stamps on bills of exchange and promissory notes in Great Britain alone, for the year ending on the 5th January, 1828, was £578,654 4s. 5d. Now, supposing that the gross amount received for stamps amounted to £600,000, — an estimate, in all probability, considerably below the truth, — and that the stamp is, upon an average, 4s. per cent. on the value of the instrument, (for, though it is more on small, it is less on large sums,) the value of the bills and notes stamped in a single year will be *three hundred millions.* The amount circulated must be considerably more, for in this calculation are not included any bills drawn abroad, or in Ireland, and a further allowance is to be made for instruments of more than twelve months' date, and for all reissuable notes. I presume the above return includes the composition in lieu of stamp duties paid by the governor and company of the Bank of England. The weekly average amount of Bank of England notes and bank post bills in circulation for the year preceding April 6, 1828, was £21,549,318 10s.; in 1818-9, about eighteen millions sterling.

Simple as a bill or note may in form appear, the rights and liabilities of the different parties to those instruments have given rise to an infinity of legal questions and multitudes of decisions. A striking proof of what the experience of all ages had already made abundantly manifest — that law is, in its own nature, necessarily voluminous; that its complexity and bulk constitute the price that must be paid for the reign of certainty, order, and uniformity; and that any attempt to regulate multiform combinations of circumstances, by a few general rules, however skilfully constructed, must be abortive.

In France this subject has been briefly but most luminously treated by M. Pothier, a learned civilian of the last century, whose work, as well as his other performances, and in particular the *Traité des Obligations*, evinces a profound acquaintance with the principles of jurisprudence, and extraordinary acumen and sagacity in their application; the result of the laborious exercise of his talents on the Roman law. There cannot be a greater proof of the surpassing merit of his works, than that, after the lapse of more than half a century, and a stupendous revolution in all the institutions of his country, many parts of his writings have been incorporated, word for word, in the new code of France. The *Traité du Contrat de Change* is often cited in the English Courts of Law. "The authority of Pothier," says the present learned Chief Justice of the Common Pleas, " is as high as can be had, next to the decision of a Court of Justice in this country; his writings are considered, by Sir William Jones, as equal, in point of luminous method, apposite examples, and a clear, manly style, to the works of Lyttleton on the Laws of England."

In Great Britain, the growth of the law on bills and notes has been almost proportionate to the increase of those instruments; insomuch that within the last sixty years the reported decisions upon them, in law, equity and bankruptcy, would fill many volumes. Numerous have been the attempts to reduce the mass of authorities to the shape of a regular treatise; but amongst all these, two only (by Englishmen) are now in common use in the profession,*—the treatise of Mr. Chitty, and the summary of Mr. Justice Bayley.

Mr. Chitty's treatise is a laborious and full collection of almost all the cases, by an eminent counsel, the extent of whose legal acquirements, and the readiness of their application, can only be appreciated by those who have been in the habit of personal intercourse with him. But the size of the book is an objection with many, and a cloud of authorities will sometimes obscure the most luminous arrangement.

* To which we may add, *Story on Bills*, a work now in high repute in both Great Britain and the United States.—*American Editor.*

II.—OF PRESENTMENT FOR ACCEPTANCE.

Advisable in all Cases. — Necessary where Bill is drawn at or after sight When to be made. — At what Hour. — Excused by putting Bill in Circulation. — Or by other reasonable Cause. — To whom it should be made. — What Time may be given to the Drawee. — Consequence of Negligence in Party presenting. — Proper Course for Holder when Drawee cannot be found, or is Dead. — Pleading.

It is in all cases advisable for the holder of an unaccepted bill to present it for acceptance without delay; for, in case of acceptance, the holder obtains the additional security of the acceptor, and, if acceptance be refused, the antecedent parties become liable immediately. It is advisable, too, on account of the drawer, for, by receiving early advice of dishonor, he may be better able to get his effects out of the drawee's hands.

But presentment for acceptance is not necessary in the case of a bill payable at a certain period after date. It is said, however, that it is incumbent on a holder who is a mere agent, and on the payee, when expressly directed by the drawer so to do, to present the bill for acceptance as soon as possible; and that, for loss arising from the neglect, the payee must be responsible, and the agent must answer to his principal.

Presentment for acceptance is necessary, if the bill be drawn payable at sight, or at a certain period after sight. Till such presentment there is no right of action against any party; and unless it be made within a reasonable time, the holder loses his remedy against the antecedent parties.

What is a reasonable time, depends on the circumstances of each particular case, and is a mixed question of law and fact; although reasonable time in general, and reasonable time for giving notice of dishonor in particular, is clearly a question of law. Plaintiff, on Friday, the 9th, at Windsor, twenty miles from London, received a bill on London, at one month after sight, for £100. There was no post on Saturday. It was presented on the Tuesday. The jury thought it was presented within a reasonable time, and the Court concurred.

A bill drawn by bankers in the country on their correspondents

London, payable after sight, was endorsed to the traveller of he plaintiffs. He transmitted it to the plaintiffs after the interval of a week, and they, two days afterwards, transmitted it for acceptance. Before it was presented to the drawees, the drawer had become bankrupt; the drawees, consequently, refused to accept. Had the bill been sent by the traveller to the plaintiffs, his employers, as soon as he received it, they would have been able to get it accepted before the bankruptcy. "This is," says Lord Tenterden, "a mixed question of law and fact; and, in expressing my own opinion, I do not wish at all to withdraw the case from the jury. Whatever strictness may be required with respect to common bills of exchange, payable after sight, it does not seem unreasonable to treat bills of this nature, drawn by bankers on their correspondents, as not requiring immediate presentment, but as being retainable by the holders for the purpose of using them, within a moderate time, (for indefinite delay, of course, cannot be allowed,) as part of the circulating medium of the country." The jury concurred with his lordship, that the delay was not unreasonable. Where the purchaser of a bill on Rio Janeiro, at sixty days' sight, the exchange being against him, kept it nearly five months, and the drawee failed before presentment, it was held that the delay was not unreasonable. "The bill," says Tindal, C. J., "must be forwarded within a reasonable time under all the circumstances of the case, and there must be no unreasonable or improper delay. Whether there has been, in any particular case, reasonable diligence used, or whether unreasonable delay has occurred, is a mixed question of law and fact, to be decided by the jury acting under the direction of the judge, upon the particular circumstances of each case."

But where a bill, payable after sight, was drawn in duplicate on the 12th of August, in Newfoundland, and not presented for acceptance in London till November 16th, and no circumstances were proved to excuse the delay, it was held unreasonable, the Court laying some stress on the fact that the bill was drawn in sets.

Presentment should be made during the usual hours of business.

The holder may, however, put the bill into circulation without presenting it. "If a bill, drawn at three days' sight," says Mr. Justice Buller, "be kept out in circulation for a year, I cannot say that there would be laches; but if, instead of putting it into circulation, the holder were to lock it up for any length of time, I should say that he would be guilty of laches." "But this cannot mean," says Tindal, C. J., "that keeping it in hand for any time, however short, would make him guilty of laches. It never can be required of him, instantly on receipt of it, under all disadvantages, to put it into circulation. To hold the purchaser bound by such an obligation, would impede, if not altogether destroy, the market for buying and selling *foreign bills*, to the great injury, no less than to the inconvenience, of the drawer himself." Two bills, one for £100 and the other for £500, were drawn from Lisbon, on May 12th, at thirty days after sight, endorsed to G. at Paris, and by G. to R. at Genoa, and by R. endorsed over. They were not presented for acceptance till 22d of August. The jury found, and the Court concurred, that the bills were, under the circumstances, presented within a reasonable time.

Illness, or other reasonable cause, not attributable to the misconduct of the holder, will excuse. But the holder must present, though the drawer have desired the drawee not to accept.

The presentment must be made either to the drawee himself, or to his authorized agent. The holder's servant called at the drawee's residence, and showed the bill to some person in the drawee's tan-yard, who refused to accept it; but the witness did not know the drawee's person, nor could he swear that the person to whom he offered the bill was he, or represented himself to be so. Lord Ellenborough: "The evidence here offered proves no demand on the drawee, and is, therefore, insufficient."

When the bill is presented, it is reasonable that the drawee should be allowed some time to deliberate whether he will accept or no. It seems that he may demand twenty-four hours for this purpose, (and that the holder will be justified in leaving the bill with him for that period ;) at least, if the post do not go out in the interim, or unless, in the interim, he either accepts, or declares his resolution not to accept. If more than twenty-four hours be given, the holder ought to inform the antecedent parties of it.

If the owner of a bill, who leaves it for acceptance, by his negligence enables a stranger to give such a description of it as to obtain it from the drawee, without negligence on his part, the owner cannot maintain trover for it against the drawee.

In case the bill is directed to the drawee at a particular place, it is to be considered as dishonored if the drawee has absconded. But, if he have merely changed his residence, or if the bill is not directed to him at any particular place, it is incumbent on the holder to use due diligence to find him out. And due diligence is a question of fact for the jury. If the drawee be dead, the holder should inquire after his personal representative, and, provided he lives within a reasonable distance, present the bill to him.

In an action against the drawer on non-acceptance, it is not sufficient to allege mere non acceptance; presentment for acceptance must be alleged.

III.—OF PRESENTMENT FOR PAYMENT.

How made. — In case of Bankruptcy or Insolvency. — Unnecessary to charge a Guarantee. — In case of Drawee's death. — Of Holder's death. — When to be made. — Time, how computed. — Months. — Days. — Bills and Notes at Sight. — Usance. — Old and New Style. — Days of Grace. — What in different Countries. — How reckoned. — Sundays and Holidays, how reckoned. — On what Instruments Days of Grace allowed. — When Presentment of Bills payable on Demand is to be made. — Of a common Bill of Exchange payable on Demand. — Of a Check. — Of a common Promissory Note payable on Demand. — Of a Bank Note. — Of other Bankers' Paper. — When no time of Payment is specified. — At what Hour. — Where, when a Bill is made payable at a particular place. — Pleading. — When a Note is made so payable. — Consequence of not duly Presenting. — Presentment not necessary to charge Acceptor. — When Neglect to Present excused. — Of Bill seized under extent. — By circulating. — By the Absconding of the Drawee. — By Absence of Effects in the Drawee's hands. — Not by declaration of Acceptor that he will not pay. — Advantage from Neglect, how waived. — Pleading. — Evidence of Presentment.

A PERSONAL demand on the drawee or acceptor is not necessary. It is sufficient if payment be demanded, at his usual residence or place of business, of his wife or other agent; for it is the duty of an acceptor, if he is not himself present, to leave provision for the payment. And it is sufficient if payment be demanded of an agent who has been authorized to pay, or has usually paid, bills for the drawee. Thus, where a country bank note was made payable both at Tunbridge and in London, presentment in London was held sufficient, though it was proved, that, had it been presented at Tunbridge, the nearest place, it would have been paid.

The bankruptcy or insolvency of the drawee is no excuse for a neglect to present for payment; for many means may remain of obtaining payment, by the assistance of friends or otherwise. It has been held in the King's Bench, that the shutting up of a bank, when any demand there made would have been inaudible, is substantially a refusal by the bankers to pay their notes, to all the world. But it was decided in the same case, on error in the Exchequer Chamber, that an allegation in the declaration, that the makers became insolvent, and ceased, and wholly declined, and refused, then and thenceforth, to pay at the place specified, any of their notes, is insufficient, not being an allegation of presentment. But it is conceived, notwithstanding the observations of the Court in the last case, that it cannot be necessary for the holders of the notes of a bank which had notoriously stopped payment, to go through the empty form of carrying notes up to the bank doors, and then carrying them home again.

A presentment for payment is now decided not to be necessary in order to charge a man who guarantees the due payment of a bill or note. And it had before been held that where a party was guarantee for the vendee of goods, who had accepted a bill for the amount, and then became bankrupt, the notorious insolvency of the vendee was sufficient so far to excuse the drawer as to enable him to charge the guarantee, unless it could have been shown that the bill would have been paid, if duly presented, though it would have been otherwise in an action of the bill.

If the drawee has shut up his house, the holder must inquire after him, and attempt to find him out.

If the drawee be dead, presentment must be made to his personal representative; and, if he have none, then at his house.

If the holder die, presentment should be made by his personal representatives.

In treating of the *time when* presentment is to be made, it will be necessary to consider, first, how, on the various sorts of bills, time is computed, and then on what bills, and to what extent, days of grace are allowed.

In acts of Parliament, in deeds, and in legal proceedings, the word *month* is taken to mean a lunar, and not a calendar, month; unless there be something in the context to indicate the latter sense: but in matters ecclesiastical, and by the custom of trade, in bills and notes, a month is deemed to be a calendar or solar month. The inequality in the length of the respective months may sometimes occasion a difficulty; but it is said to be a rule not to extend the time at which the bill falls due beyond the month in which it would have fallen due, had that month been of the length of thirty-one days. Thus, if a bill at one month be drawn on the 31st of January, it will be due on the 28th of February, and, with the days of grace, payable on the 3d of March.

When a bill is drawn at a certain number of days after date, or after sight, those days are reckoned exclusively of the day on which the bill is drawn or accepted, and exclusively of the day on which it falls due.

We have already observed, that on a *bill* the words "after sight" are equivalent to "after acceptance;" for sight must appear in a legal way

If a *note* be made payable at sight, it must be presented, before action brought against the maker.

Usance is the period which in early times it was usual to appoint between different countries for the payment of bills. — When usance is a month, half usance is always fifteen days, notwithstanding the unequal length of the months. An usance between London, Aleppo, Altona, and Amsterdam, Antwerp, Brabant, Bruges, Flanders, Geneva, Germany, Hamburg, Holland and the Netherlands, Lisle, Middleburg, Paris or Amsterdam, Rotterdam and Rouen, is one calendar month; between London and the Spanish or Portuguese towns, two calendar months; between London and Genoa, Venice, or places in Italy, it is three calendar months.

It is said that all the countries with which the English are in the habit of negotiating bills computed their time by the new style, with the single exception of Russia. In the case of bills drawn in a place using one style, and payable in a place using another, if drawn payable at a certain period after date, they fall due as they would have done in the country in which they were drawn. Thus, a bill drawn Feb. 1, in London, on St. Petersburg, at one month, would be payable without the days of grace, on March 1, in our calendar; and, as it was drawn on Jan. 21, old style, it would fall due on Feb. 21, in the Russian calendar. But, if the bill were drawn payable at a day certain, or at a certain period after sight, the time must then be reckoned according to the style of the place on which it is drawn.

Days of grace are so called, because they were formerly allowed the drawee as a favor; but the laws of commercial countries have long since recognized them as a right. The number of these days varies in different places. Mr. Kyd gives the following table, which, however, has been altered in many places since his day, by the substitution of the French code, and other circumstances : —

"Great Britain, Ireland, Bergamo and Vienna, three days.

"Frankfort, out of the fair-time, four days.

"Leipsic, Naumberg and Augsburg, five days.

"Venice, Amsterdam, Rotterdam, Middleburg, Antwerp, Cologne, Breslau, Nuremburg and Portugal, six days.

"Dantzic, Koningsberg and France, ten days.

"Hamburg and Stockholm, twelve days.

"Naples, eight; Spain, fourteen; Rome, fifteen; and Genoa, thirty days.

"Leghorn, Milan and some other places in Italy, no fixed number.

"Sundays and holidays are included in the respite days, at London, Naples, Amsterdam, Rotterdam, Antwerp, Middleburg, Dantzic, Koningsberg and France; but not at Venice, Cologne, Breslau and Nurem berg. At Hamburg, the day on which the bill falls due makes one of the days of grace; but it is not so elsewhere."

Three days of grace are allowed in North America, at Berlin, and in Scotland.

At Rio de Janeiro, Bahia and other parts of Brazil, fifteen days.

At St. Petersburg, ten days on bills after date; three days on bills at sight, ten days on bills received and presented after they are due.

At Trieste and Vienna, three days on bills after date.

The three days' grace allowed in this country are reckoned exclusive of the day on which the bill falls due, and inclusive of the last day of grace.

Where there are no days of grace, and the bill falls due on a Sunday, Christmas-day, Good Friday, public fast or thanksgiving day, or where the last of the days of grace happens on such a day, the bill becomes payable on the day preceding; and, if not then paid, must be treated as dishonored.

A presentment for payment before the expiration of the days of grace is premature, and will not enable the holder to charge the antecedent parties.

Days of grace are allowed on promissory notes, as well as on bills. They are allowed, whether the bill or note be made payable on a certain event, or at a certain day, or at a certain number of years, months, weeks or days, after date or after sight, or at usance, or by instalments. But they are not allowed on bills or notes payable on demand. Whether days of grace are allowed on bills payable *at sight*, seems yet undecided. The weight of authority has been considered to incline in favor of such an allowance.

If days of grace are to be allowed on bills payable at sight, the time when they should be presented has already been considered, in the Chapter on *Presentment for Acceptance*. If not, then they stand on the same footing as bills payable indefinitely, and bills payable on demand.

We have already seen that the time which bills payable *after* sight have to run is computed from the date of the acceptance; a note payable at a certain period after sight is payable at that period after presentment for sight. So, if, some time after a refusal to accept, a bill, payable after sight, be accepted, *supra protest*, the time is calculated, not from the date of the exhibition of the bill to the drawee, but from the date of the acceptance, *supra protest*.

Bills and notes payable on demand, and checks, must be presented within a reasonable time. What is a reasonable time seems to be a law. And such a decision is conformable with the principles of law. " Reasonable time," says Lord Coke, " shall be adjudged by the discretion of the Justices before whom the cause dependeth; and so it is of reasonable fines, customs and services, upon the true state of the case depending before them; for reasonableness in these cases belongeth to the knowledge of the law, and, therefore, to be decided by the justices *Quam longum esse debet non definitur in jure, sed pendet ex discretione justiciariorum.* And, this, being said of time, the like may be said of things incertaine, which ought to be reasonable; for nothing that is contrary to reason is consonant to law." Besides, the opinions of jurors have been so various that there can be no certainty on the subject, unless it be held to be a question of law. Yet we have seen that what is a reasonable time within which to present for acceptance a bill drawn payable after sight has been held a question of fact to the jury, and the same point has been ruled as to the time of presentment for payment of a note payable on demand.

A man taking a bill or note payable on demand, or a check, is not bound, laying aside all other business, to present or transmit it for payment the very first opportunity. It has long since been decided, in numerous cases, that, though the party by whom the bill or note is to be paid live in the same place, it is not necessary to present the instrument for payment till the morning next after the day on which it was received. And later cases have established, that the holder of a check has the whole of the banking hours of the next day within which to present it for payment.

Negotiable instruments payable on demand may be distributed into several classes, and the time within which they ought to be presented for payment, and the consequences of a failure to make due presentment are not precisely the same in every class.

Negotiable instruments payable on demand are common commercial bills of exchange, checks, common promissory notes, bank notes, and bankers' cash notes and bankers' bills.

It is conceived that a common bill of exchange payable on demand ought, if the parties live in the same place, to be presented the next day after the payee has received it. If the bill must be sent by post to be presented, it ought to be posted on the day next after the day on which it was received, and that the person who receives it by post, that he may present it, should do so on the day next following the day on which he receives it.

Such, also, are the general rules regulating the presentment of bankers' checks, which are really bills of exchange; but as checks on bankers are now extremely common, it has been thought convenient to discuss the presentment of checks more in detail in the chapter relating to checks.

A common promissory note payable on demand differs from a bill payable on demand, or a check, in this respect; the bill and check are evidently intended to be presented and paid immediately, and the drawer may have good reasons for desiring to withdraw his funds from the control of the drawee without delay; but a common promissory note payable on demand is very often originally intended as a continuing security, and afterwards endorsed as such. Indeed, it is not uncommon for the payee, and afterwards the endorsee, to receive from the maker interest periodically for many years on such a note. And sometimes the note is expressly made payable with interest, which clearly indicates the intention of the parties to be, that though the holder may demand payment immediately, yet he is not bound to do so. It is, therefore, conceived that a common promissory note, payable on demand, especially if made payable with interest, is not necessarily to be presented the next day after it has been received, in order to charge the endorser; and that, when the endorser defends himself on the ground of delay in presenting the note, it will be a question for a jury, whether, under all the circumstances, the delay of presentment was or was not unreasonable.

Bank notes and bankers' cash notes differ again from other promissory notes in this, that they are intended to pass from hand to hand, and are issued that they may circulate as money, returning to the bank as seldom as possible; but they are not intended as a continuing security in the hands of any one holder. Therefore, a man who takes bank notes, or bankers' cash notes in payment must present them or forward them for presentment the day after he receives them, in order to enable him, in the event of the bank failing, to sue the person from whom they were received on the consideration that was given for them. But, as it would be inconsistent with the very nature and design of such notes, that every man who takes them should present them for payment, it is sufficient to exonerate the taker from the charge of laches, if he circulated them within the time within which he ought otherwise to have presented them.

IV.—OF PAYMENT.

To whom it should be made.— *Of Crossed Checks.* — *To a wrongful Holder* — *Effect of Payment by Acceptor*—*by Drawer*—*by a Stranger.*— *When to be made.*— *At what Time of Day.* — *Subsequent Tender.*— *Premature Payment.* — *After Action brought.* — *Payment by Notes or Checks.* —*What amounts to Payment.* — *Legacy.*— *Appropriation of Payments.* — *Part Payment.* — *When Payment will be presumed.* — *Evidence of Payment.* — *Of delivering up the Bill.* — *Of giving a Receipt.* — *Effect of Receipt.* —*Tender of Part Payment.* — *Plea of Payment.* — *Retractation of Payment.*

PAYMENT should be made to the holder and the real proprietor of the bill; for payment to any other party is no discharge to the acceptor, unless, indeed, the money paid finds its way into the holder's hands, and the holder has treated it as received in liquidation of the bill. A drew a bill upon defendant, which defendant accepted. A then endorsed it to the plaintiffs, his bankers, who entered to the credit of plaintiffs' account, and, at maturity, presented it to the defendant for acceptance and it was dishonored. The plaintiffs then debited A with the amount, but did not return him the bill. A few days afterwards, defendant paid the amount to A. A still continued his banking account with the plaintiffs, and at different times paid in more money than was sufficient to cover the amount of the bill, and all the preceding items which stood above it in the account, though there was always a balance against him larger than the amount of the bill. A failed, and the plaintiffs proved for the whole of their balance under his commission. They brought this action on the bill against the defendant, the acceptor. Best, C. J.: "The payment to A would not of itself have discharged the defendant, the plaintiffs having been at that time the holders, and entitled to the amount of the bill; but the ground on which the defendant is discharged is, that the plaintiffs not only entered the bill to the credit of A, but treated it as having been paid."

It is a common practice, in the city of London, to write across the face of a check the name of a banker. The effect of this crossing is to direct the drawees to pay the check only to the banker whose name is written across, and the object of the precaution is to invalidate the payment to a wrongful owner in case of loss. It seems, however, that the holder may erase the name of the banker and substitute that of another banker. It is also not unusual to write the words *and Co.*, only in the first instance, leaving the particular banker's name to be filled up afterwards, so as to insure the presentment by some banker or other. C drew a check on his banker payable to A and B, assignees of C or bearer, and wrote the name of their banker across it. B, who had another private account with the banker, paid the check into that account; it was held that the bankers were justified in applying it to that account, the drawer's writing the name of the bankers of the payee of the check across it not being, according to the custom of trade, information to the bankers that the money was the money of the payees.

There are some cases in which payment to a wrongful holder is protected, and others in which it is not. If a bill or note, payable to bearer, either originally made so, or become so by an endorsement in blank, be lost or stolen, we have seen that a bona fide holder may compel payment. Not only is the payment to a bona fide holder protected, but payment to the thief or finder himself will discharge the maker or acceptor, provided such payment were not made with knowledge or suspicion of the infirmity of the holder's title, or under circumstances which might reasonably awaken the suspicions of a prudent man. "For it is a general rule, that where one of two innocent persons must suffer from the acts of a third, he who has enabled such third person to occasion the loss, must sustain it." And supposing the equity of the loser and payer precisely equal, there is no reason why the law should interpose to shift the injury from one innocent man upon another. But, if such a payment be made under suspicious circumstances, or without reasonable caution, or out of the usual course of business, it will not discharge the payer. If payment be made before the bill or note is due, or long after it is due, or, in case of a check, long after it is drawn, that is a payment out of the usual course of business.

And, therefore, though a check be really drawn by a banker's customer, but torn in pieces before circulation by the drawer, with intention of destroying it, and a stranger, picking up the pieces, pastes them together, and presents the check soiled and so joined together to the banker, and he pays it, the banker cannot charge his customer with this payment, for the instrument was cancelled, and carried with it reasonable notice that it had been cancelled.

If the bill or note be not payable to bearer, but transferable by endorsement only, and be paid to a wrong party, the payer is not discharged.

A bill is not discharged, and finally extinguished, until paid by or on behalf of the acceptor; nor a note until paid by or on behalf of the maker.

It does not appear to be settled, whether part payment by the drawer to the holder will discharge the acceptor *pro tanto*, or whether the holder may, nevertheless, recover the whole amount from the acceptor, and hold an equivalent to the amount received from the drawer, as money received of the acceptor to the drawer's use. It is conceived that the holder can only recover of the acceptor the amount of the bill minus the sum paid by the drawer. The acceptor is the principal, and the drawer is the surety; it should seem, therefore, that a payment by the drawer discharges the acceptor's liability to the holder *pro tanto*, and makes the acceptor liable to the drawer for money paid to his use. Besides, had the drawer paid the whole bill, nominal damages only could have been recovered by the holder of the acceptor. But payment by the drawer of an *accommodation* bill is a complete discharge of the bill.

Payment by a stranger of the amount of the bill to the bankers, at whose house the bill is made payable by the acceptor, the party paying obtaining possession of the bill, is not a payment by the acceptor.

The acceptor of a bill, whether inland or foreign, or the maker of a note, should pay it on a demand made, at any time within the business hours, on the day it falls due. And, if it be not paid on such demand, the holder may instantly treat it as dishonored.

But the acceptor has the whole of that day within which to make payment; and though he should, in the course of that day, refuse payment, which refusal entitles the holder to give notice of dishonor, yet, if he subsequently, on the same day, makes payment, the payment is good, and the notice of dishonor becomes of no avail.

A plea of tender, by the acceptor, after the day of payment, is insufficient.

If a bill or note be paid before it is due, and is afterwards endorsed over, it is a valid security in the hands of a bona fide endorsee. "I agree," says Lord Ellenborough, "that a bill paid at maturity cannot be reissued, and that no action can be afterwards maintained upon it, by a subsequent endorsee. A payment before it becomes due, however, I think, does not extinguish it, any more than if it were merely discounted. A contrary doctrine would add a new clog to the circulation of bills and notes; for it would be impossible to know whether there had not been an anticipated payment of them."

If the holder constitutes any one of the parties liable to him his executor, and die, the appointment is equivalent to payment and a release. A premature release will not, any more than a premature payment, protect the releasee from liability to a subsequent holder, without notice.

But the payment on a note payable on demand will be a defence, even against an endorsee, for value without notice; for the statute, which imperatively prohibits the reissuing of such a note, dispenses with notice.

A payment after an action brought will not prevent the holder from proceeding for his costs.

If the bill be paid, the payer has a right to insist on its being delivered up to him; but, if it be not paid, the holder should keep it. Yet it has been held that an agent is justified, by the usage of trade, in delivering it up on receiving a check, though that check is afterwards dishonored. But the drawers or endorsers, in such a case, would be discharged, for they have a right to insist on the production of the bill, and to have it delivered up on payment by them.

If the holder of a check receive bank notes instead of cash, and the banker fail, the drawer is discharged.

A set-off does not amount to payment, unless it be mutually agreed that one demand shall be set off against the other. But an agreement, even by one of several partners, that a separate debt due from the partner shall be set off against a joint debt due to the firm, binds the firm. Credit given to the holder of a bill by the party ultimately liable is tantamount to payment. Where a banker takes from a customer and his surety a promissory note, intended to secure a running balance, and makes advances on the faith of the note, it is not discharged by subsequent unappropriated repayments made by the customer to the banker, but still continues as a security for the existing balance.

There are many circumstances under which a legacy by a debtor to his creditor, of equal or greater amount than the debt, will be considered a satisfaction of the debt. But a legacy to the holder of a *negotiable* bill or note can never be considered as a satisfaction of the debt on that instrument. For a legacy is a satisfaction when it may be presumed to have been the intention of the testator that it should so operate; but that cannot be presumed, when, from the assignable nature of the debt, the testator could not tell whether or no the legatee was at the time of the bequest his creditor.

Where a man is indebted to another in several items, and makes a partial payment, it often becomes a question, important not only to the parties themselves but to third persons, to which of the items the payment shall be imputed. The rule of the Roman law, and therefore, in general, of continental law is, that a payment shall be appropriated, first, according to the intention of the debtor at the time of making it; but, if that be unknown, then, secondly, at the election of the creditor, signified to the debtor at the time of receiving it. If the intention of neither be known, payment must then be appropriated according to the presumed intention of the debtor, and it will be presumed that he meant to discharge such debts as were most burdensome; as, a debt carrying interest, rather than one which carries none; a debt secured by a penalty, rather than one resting on a simple stipulation; a debt on which he may be made a bankrupt, rather than one which will not subject him to such

OF PAYMENT.

a liability. If all the debts are equal in degree, the payment must then be imputed to them according to their respective priority in the order of time. Such is the rule of the civil law, from which, in some particulars, the common law differs. Wherever the transactions between the two parties form one general account current, or are treated by them as such, payments are to be imputed to debts in the order of time, and the balance is to be struck at the foot of the account. But, if an unappropriated payment be made on account of several distinct insulated debts, which cannot be considered in the light of a running account between the parties, the common law then differs from the civil law, and gives the creditor a right of appropriating it at any time before action, as he pleases, provided a prior appropriation have not been communicated to the debtor.

An appropriation which would have the effect of paying one man's debt with another man's money, will not be allowed. Nor can there be an appropriation which would deprive a debtor of a benefit, such as the taxation of costs.

A payment may be imputed to a demand for which the creditor could not recover at law. But the law will ascribe a payment to a legal debt, rather than to an illegal one. A party receiving money for the use of another from a third person, which is not properly a payment, but a set-off, cannot appropriate the money without the knowledge or consent of him for whom it has been received. It has been held, that a payment may be appropriated to a disputed debt, if it be really a good debt.

Part payment of the debt by the party liable is no discharge of the party liable, but part payment by a stranger may be. And it has been held, that where a promissory note is due and unpaid, so that not only the principal, but interest, (at least to a nominal amount,) is due also, the principal may be taken in satisfaction of the debt and damages.

As the lapse of twenty years is sufficient to raise a presumption that a bond has been paid, so it has been held to be a good defence to an action on a promissory note payable on demand. But if during this period the plaintiff was an alien enemy, and payment to him would consequently have been illegal, such a presumption would not, it seems, arise.

The production of a check drawn by the defendant on his banker, and endorsed by the plaintiff, is evidence of payment; but not if there have been several transactions between the parties without evidence to connect the delivery of the check with the payment in question. The mere production of a bill from the custody of the acceptor is not prima facie evidence of his having paid it, without proof of its having been once in circulation after it had been accepted.

The party paying a bill or note has a right to insist on its being delivered up to him. But where the bill or note is not negotiable, he can not refuse to pay it till it is delivered up.

It was formerly held that a party paying a debt could not in general demand a receipt for the money, and therefore that a tender on condition of having a receipt was insufficient. It is usual to write a receipt on the back of bills, and it has been said that it is the duty of bankers to make some memorandum on bills or notes which have been paid. And a receipt on a distinct piece of unstamped paper, though it cannot be looked at as evidence of the payment, may be shown to a witness who has signed it, to refresh his memory, and enable him to speak to the fact of payment.

A receipt on the back of a bill imports prima facie that it has been paid by the acceptor.

A tender of part of the amount of an entire sum due on a bill or note, seems not to be good even *pro tanto*.

A defendant, where there is a plea of payment, is entitled to reduce the damages by the amount of payment established, though he be unable to prove the plea. But if he plead that a note was given for a part only of the apparent consideration, and allege payment of that part, and on issue joined the plea is found against him, the plaintiff is entitled to a verdict for the full amount of the note.

If the drawee discover, after payment, that the bill or check is a forgery, he may, in general, by giving notice on the same day, recover back the money. And if he have paid the bill with the understanding that he was to receive it back, and do not, he may bring an action to retract the payment.

OF PROTESTING AND NOTING.

Protest necessary on Foreign Bills, and why. — By whom to be made. — Office of a Notary. — When to be made. — Where to be made. — Form of Protest. — For better Security. — Noting, what. — Notice of a Protest. — Copy of Protest. — When Protest excused. — Protest of Inland Bills. — Pleading. — Evidence.

WHEN a foreign bill is refused acceptance or payment, it was and still is necessary, by the custom of merchants, in order to charge the drawer, that the dishonor should be attested by a protest. For, by the law of most foreign nations, a protest is, or was, essential, in case of dishonor of any bill; and, though by the law of England it is unnecessary in the case of an inland bill, yet, for the sake of uniformity in international transactions, a foreign bill must be protested. Besides, a protest affords satisfactory evidence of dishonor to the drawer, who, from his residence abroad, might experience a difficulty in making proper inquiries on the subject, and be compelled to rely on the representation of the holder. It also furnishes an endorsee with the best evidence to charge an antecedent party abroad; for foreign courts give credit to the acts of a public functionary, in the same manner as a protest under the seal of a foreign notary is evidence, in our courts, of the dishonor of a bill payable abroad.

The protest should be made by a notary public; but, if there be no such notary in or near the place where the bill is payable, it may be made by an inhabitant, in the presence of two witnesses.

A notary, *registrarius, actuarius, scriniarius*, was anciently a scribe that only took *notes* or minutes, and made short drafts of writings and other instruments, both public and private. He is at this day, in England, a public officer of the civil and canon law, appointed by the Archbishop of Canterbury, who, in the instrument of appointment, decrees "that full faith be given, as well in as out of judgment, to the instruments by him to be made."

The protest of a foreign bill should be begun, at least, (and such an incipient protest is called noting,) on the day on which acceptance or payment is refused; but it may be drawn up and completed at any time before the commencement of the suit, or even before the trial, and ante-dated accordingly. An inland bill cannot be protested for non-payment till the day after it is due.

A protest is, in form, a solemn declaration, written by the notary, under a fair copy of the bill, stating that the payment or acceptance has been demanded and refused, the reason, if any, assigned, and that the bill is therefore protested. When the protest is made for a qualified acceptance, it must not state a general refusal to accept, otherwise the holder cannot avail himself of the qualified acceptance.

Besides the protest for non-acceptance and for non-payment, the holder may protest the bill for *better security*. Protest for better security is where the acceptor becomes insolvent, or where his credit is publicly impeached before the bill falls due. In this case, the holder may cause a notary to demand better security; and, on its being refused, the bill may be protested, and notice of the protest may be sent to an antecedent party. Yet, it seems, the holder must wait till the bill falls due before he can sue any party. Nor does there appear any advantage from the protest more than from simple notice of the circumstances; except that, after such a protest, there may be a second acceptance for honor. Whereas, without the intervention of a protest, there cannot be two acceptances on the same bill.

Noting is a minute made on the bill by the officer at the time of refusal of acceptance or payment. It consists of his initials, the month, the day, the year, and his charges for minuting; and is considered as the preparatory step to a protest. " Noting," says Mr. J. Buller, " is unknown in the law, as distinguished from the protest; it is merely a preliminary step to the protest, and has grown into practice within these few years." A bill, however, is often noted, where no protest is either meant or contemplated; as in the case of many inland bills. The use of it seems to be, that a notary, being a person conversant in such transactions, is qualified to direct the holder to pursue the proper conduct in presenting a bill, and may, upon a trial, be a convenient witness of the presentment and dishonor. In the mean time, the minute of the notary, accompanying the returned bill, is satisfactory assurance of non-payment or non-acceptance, to the various parties by whom the amount of the bill may be successively paid.

If the drawer reside abroad, a copy, or some memorial of the protest, ought to accompany the notice of dishonor. But notice of the protest certainly is not necessary, if the drawer resides within this country, though, at the time of the non-acceptance, he may happen to be abroad; nor if, at the time of dishonor, he have returned home to this country. " If," says Lord Ellenborough, " the party is abroad, he cannot know of the fact of the bill having been protested, except by having notice of the protest itself; but, if he be at home, it is easy for him, by making inquiry, to ascertain that fact."

And it is now decided that *a copy* of the protest need not in any case be sent.

Proof of a protest of a foreign bill is excused, if the drawer had no effects in the hands of the drawee, and no reasonable expectation that the bill would be honored; or if the drawer has admitted his liability by promising to pay. "By the drawer's promise to pay," observes Lord Ellenborough, "he admits the existence of everything which is necessary to render him liable. When called upon for payment of the bill, he ought to have objected that there was no protest. Instead of that, he promises to pay it. I must, therefore, presume he had due notice, and that a protest was regularly drawn up by a notary."

And it is said, that where the drawer adds a request or direction, that in the event of the bill not being honored by the drawee, it shall be returned without protest, by writing the words "*retour sans protêt*," or "*sans frais*," a protest as against the drawer, and perhaps as against the endorsers, is unnecessary.

It has been held, that a protest is unnecessary on inland bills, except to enable the holder to recover interest; and subsequent and uniform practice, confirmed by a late decision, has settled that it is superfluous even for this purpose.

Foreign bills are very frequently protested, both for non-acceptance and non-payment; but a protest is hardly ever made for non-acceptance of an inland bill, though it is sometimes protested for non-payment. It is conceived that a protest of an inland bill is unknown to the common law, and must, therefore, derive its efficacy from the above enactments; from which it will follow, that it is applicable only to such instruments as are therein described, and that the steps therein required must be taken.

The loss of a bill is no excuse for the absence of protest.

In an action against the drawer of a foreign bill, protest must be averred as well as proved; and it has been held, that, if a protest of an inland bill be set forth in pleading, it must be proved. But this decision proceeded on the ground that an allegation of protest of an inland bill involved a consequential claim for interest and costs; whereas it has been since decided, that such a claim may be made without protest.

In an action on a foreign bill, presented abroad, the dishonor of the bill will be proved by producing the protest, purporting to be attested by a notary public; or, if there is not any notary near the place, purporting to have been made by an inhabitant, in the presence of two witnesses.

A promise to pay is good prima facie evidence of protest, and of notice thereof.

CONTENTS OF BYLES ON BILLS OF EXCHANGE.

                                                                                                  Page

I. HISTORY OF BILLS OF EXCHANGE, ... 60

II. OF PRESENTMENT FOR ACCEPTANCE. — Advisable in all Cases. — Necessary where Bill is drawn at or after sight. — When to be made. — At what Hour. — Excused by putting Bill in Circulation. — Or by other reasonable Cause. — To whom it should be made. — What Time may be given to the Drawee. — Consequence of Negligence in Party presenting. — Proper Course for Holder when Drawee cannot be found, or is Dead. — Pleading, ... 61

III. OF PRESENTMENT FOR PAYMENT. — How made. — In case of Bankruptcy or Insolvency. — Unnecessary to charge a Guarantee. — In case of Drawee's death. — Of Holder's death. — When to be made. — Time, how computed. — Months. — Days. — Bills and Notes at sight. — Usance. — Old and New Style. — Days of Grace. — What in different Countries. — How reckoned. — Sundays and Holidays, how reckoned. — On what Instruments Days of Grace allowed. — When Presentment of Bills payable on Demand is to be made. — Of a common Bill of Exchange payable on Demand. — Of a Check. — Of a common Promissory Note payable on Demand. — Of a Bank Note. — Of other Bankers' Paper. — When no time of Payment is specified. — At what Hour. — Where, when a Bill is made payable at a particular place. — Pleading. — When a Note is made so payable. — Consequence of not duly Presenting. — Presentment not necessary to charge Acceptor. — When Neglect to Present excused. — Of Bill seized under extent. — By circulating. — By the Absconding of the Drawee. — By Absence of Effects in the Drawee's hand. — Not by Declaration of Acceptor that he will not pay. — Advantage from Neglect, how waived. — Pleading. — Evidence of Presentment, ... 67

IV. OF PAYMENT. — To whom it should be made. — Of Crossed Checks. — To a wrongful Holder. — Effect of Payment by Acceptor — by Drawer — by a Stranger. — When to be made — At what Time of Day. — Subsequent Tender. — Premature Payment. — After Action brought. — Payment by Notes or Checks. — What Amounts to Payment. — Legacy. — Appropriation of Payments. —Part Payment. — When Payment will be presumed. — Evidence of Payment. — Of delivering up the Bill. — Of giving a Receipt. — Effect of Receipt. — Tender of Part Payment. — Plea of Payment. — Retractation of Payment, ... 73

V. OF PROTESTING AND NOTING. — Protest necessary on Foreign Bills, and why. — By whom to be made. — Office of a Notary. — When to be made. — Where to be made. — Form of Protest. — For better Security. — Noting, what. — Notice of a Protest. — Copy of Protest. — When Protest excused. — Protest of Inland Bills. — Pleading. - Evidence, ... 79

BILLS OF EXCHANGE.

BY JOHN RAMSEY M'CULLOCH, ESQ.,

AUTHOR OF THE "DICTIONARY OF COMMERCE," &c.

The following observations are taken from Mr. M'Culloch's Essays on Exchange, Interest, Money, &c., published in one volume, octavo, by Crosby & Nichols, Boston; a work which should be in the hands of every banker and money dealer. Price Seventy-five Cents.

I. — LAWS AND CUSTOMS RESPECTING BILLS AND NOTES.

A BILL of exchange may be defined to be an open letter of request or order from one person, the *drawer*, to another person, *drawee*, who is thereby desired to pay a sum of money, therein specified, to a third person, the *payee*. When the *drawee* obeys the request or order, by subscribing the document, he becomes *acceptor*. If the contrary do not appear on the face of the bill, it is presumed that the *drawee* has funds of the *drawer's* in his hands to the amount of the bill, and that the drawer is indebted to the *payee* to that extent. The bill thus operates as a transfer or mercantile assignment to the payee, of the drawee's debt to the drawer. But a bill may also be drawn payable to the *drawer* or his order, in which case, when accepted, the document is not an assignment, but merely the acknowledgment or constitution of a debt. This is also accomplishable by *promissory note*, which is a promise by one person, the *maker*, (Scoticè *granter*,) to pay a sum to another person, the *payee* (Scoticè *grantee*.) The bill and the promissory note have now equally the privilege of being *assignable* or *transferable* from one person to another by endorsement, that is, by the *payee* subscribing his name on the back of the document. In this case the *payee* becomes an *endorser* and the person in whose favor the endorsement is made is called the *endorsee*, who may again endorse to another; and in this manner the bill or note may pass from hand to hand without limitation. Each endorsation may be made *in full* or *in blank;* in full, by filling up the name and description of the party in whose favor it is made, which is attended with several advantages if the document should be lost or stolen; in blank, by merely subscribing the endorser's name, which is equivalent to making it payable to the *bearer*. All the endorsements, or any one of them, may also be *qualified* by the words *without recourse ;* and when this is done, neither the endorsee nor any subsequent *holder* of the bill or note can have recourse on the endorser who thus qualifies his endorsation. If none of the endorsations be so qualified, the *last holder* for value, and *in bona fide,* has all the prior endorsers and other parties to the bill or note bound to him jointly and severally. He may select any one of them, or proceed against them all at the same time; and if all were to become bankrupt, he could claim on the estate of each for the whole debt, and be entitled to receive dividends from all the estates until he obtained *full payment,* but which he must not exceed. An endorser may also qualify his endorsation by the condition that his endorsee shall not have the power of making an endorsement from himself.

From the negotiability thus conferred upon them, bills have been compared to bags of money; but it should be remembered that, in the former case, we transfer only *a right*, in the latter the *property itself.* The comparison is best supported in those transferences which are made without recourse, since, in those instances, the bill passes from hand to hand without any alteration in the rights and duties of those interested in it, and without any one acquiring an additional security. In the simplest case, however, the rights arising on a bill may be preserved or lost by the conduct of the holder; and where there has been even one unqualified endorsation, the duties of the holder are of a delicate and important nature. But these will be more readily understood after we have pointed out the requisites of a bill.

II. — REQUISITES OF A BILL OR NOTE.

The general requisites of a bill are, that it must be payable at all events; that it must be for payment of money only; and that the money must not be payable from any particular fund. Of the more special requisites, the *first* is, that any bill or note drawn or made in Great Britain, (though dated abroad, Chitty, 5th edit. p. 70, 7. T.R. 601, 4 Camp. *Law*, 269,) or in its colonies, is, that it be written on paper *stamped* according to the law of the mother country or colony, as it happens to be drawn in the one or the other. The stamp duty varies according to the sum in the bill, and the extension of the term of payment; but for these particulars, and the mode of complying with the provisions of the law, reference should be made to the statutes in force at the time. The present regulating statute is that of 55 Geo. III. c 184, both as to *inland* bills and notes, and bills of exchange drawn here on foreign countries. As to bills truly drawn in foreign states not colonies of Great Britain, on traders in this country, our law takes no cognizance of them as to whether they are or are not stamped; but *promissory notes* made *out* of Britain are declared *not* to be negotiable or payable unless stamped agreeably to our laws. Bills drawn at home must also be written on the stamp appropriated for bills. If on a stamp of another denomination, though of equal or superior value, they are invalid if not got re-stamped, which they may be for payment of the duty and a penalty of 40s. when carried to the stamp-office before they are due, but when after due, the penalty is £10. If written on a stamp below the proper value, a penalty is incurred of £50, and the bills, besides, are *null* (Bell's *Com. on Bankrupt Law*, vol. ii. p. 249;) but it has been found with us in England, that if a bill be *not* properly stamped, a neglect to present for acceptance or payment will not relieve parties who are *otherwise* liable in the *original debt* in respect of which the bill was granted. The relief in this case is granted by a court of equity, but this relief is not extended to remote endorsers not responsible for the original debt. Relief, however, is given when a party has bound himself to grant a valid note or bill, but gives one by mistake or design on a defective stamp. Negotiable bills under £5 must, by 37 Geo. III. c. 32, be payable within twenty-one days, and bear the name of the *place* where they are made, without which also *checks* on bankers are liable to stamp duty. Penalties are likewise imposed on the post-dating of such *checks*, or of bills, for the purpose of reducing the duty by apparently shortening the term of payment; and there are provisions in those laws respecting bills drawn in sets or otherwise, with which every trader should make himself acquainted. This, however, it is very difficult to do in all its bearings, since the penalties and provisions of the prior statutes are retained in every subsequent one, except as therein specially altered. This is one great evil of our fiscal regulations. Where the law cannot be known, transactions are rendered uncertain, property insecure, and litigation is increased to a mischievous extent. But the worst evil is, that this state of law increases in a prodigious degree the influence of the crown, by the power over traders which is thus placed in the hands of solicitors of stamps, excise, customs, and other crown officers.

The other requisites of a bill are, 2dly, That it should bear the name of the place at which it is made or drawn; and if the street and number of the house be added, it is easier to give and receive the notices tha' may be necessary, in proper time. 3dly, The *date* should be distinctly marked, and, if *written* at length, a higher protection would be afforded against accidental or intentional alterations and vitiations. If a bill have no date, the date of issuing will be held as the date of the bill. 4thly, The time of payment should be clearly expressed, and a *time certain* is necessary to make the document *negotiable ;* that is to say, the payment must not depend on an event that may never happen, such as the *marriage of a person*, though it may on the *death*. 5thly, The *place* at which a bill is made payable should also, for the sake of safe negotiation, be distinctly stated; because at that place *presentment* must be made both for acceptance and payment. If no place be mentioned, the place of doing business, if the acceptor have one, or otherwise his dwelling-house, becomes the place of presentment. 6thly, The sum payable should be clearly written in the body of the bill, and the superscription of the sum in figures will aid an omission in the body. 7thly, It should contain an order or request to pay. 8thly, Of bills drawn in parts or sets, each part or copy should mention the number of copies used, and be made payable on condition that none of the others has been paid. The *forgery* of an endorsement on one of the parts passes no interest even to a *bona fide* holder, and will not prevent the payee from recovering on the other part. 9thly, Every bill should specify distinctly *to whom* the contents are to be paid; but a *bona fide* holder, or his executor, may fill up a blank, if one be left, for the name of the payee, and recover payment. (Chitty, 82.; Bell, vol. ii. p. 251, &c.) 10thly, If it be intended that a bill is to be negotiable, it should contain the operative words of transfer " to order ;" (Chitty, 86.) 11thly, It is advisable in all cases to insert *value received ;* since, without these words, the holder of an *inland* bill for upwards of £20 could not, in England, recover interest and damages against the drawer and endorser in default of acceptance or payment. Bills bearing for value received, and payable *after date*, seem also to possess advantages when lost, under the statutes 9 and 10 W. III. c. 17; but equity would probably extend these to endorsements; and 3 and 4 Anne, c. 9, it is thought, extends the same notes. (Chitty, p. 196.) 12thly, As to foreign bills, the drawee should attend to whether they are to be paid *with* or *without further advice;* since the propriety of his accepting or paying will, in the one case, depend on his having received advice. The more carefully all these requisites are attended to, the greater is the security of all concerned against accidents and litigation. But traders, we fear, have too generally a prejudice in favor of that brevity which approaches to looseness of expression, and against that precision which alone can keep them out of difficulties.

III. — GENERAL EXPLANATORY NOTES AND USAGES.

Business Hours. — Rules of giving Notices. — Effect of Inevitable Accident. — How to act when Bill lost. — Effect of Usury. — Effect of Gaming. — Effect of Forgery. — Effect of Vitiation. — Acceptance by Procuration. — Conditional Acceptance. — Endorsements.

When a bill, check, or note, is payable *on demand*, or when *no time of payment is expressed*, it should be presented within a reasonable time after receipt, and is payable *on presentment*, without the allowance of any days of grace. It is yet *unsettled* (Chitty, 344, *et seq.*) whether bills drawn *at sight* are entitled to days of grace, though the weight of authority is rather in favor of them. If drawn at one or more days after sight, the days of grace must be allowed. The day on which a bill is dated is not reckoned one ; but all bills having days of grace, become due, and must be presented and protested, *on the third day*, and if that day be a Sunday or a holiday, on *the second*. The rule for giving notice of non-acceptance or non-payment is different, since, if the day on which it should have been given be a day of rest, by the religion of the party, such as the Jews' Sabbath, the notices will be good if given on the next day. Calendar months are always understood with respect to bills ; and if dated on the 29th, 30th, or 31st of January, payable *one month* after date, they will fall due on the *last day* of February, from which the days of grace are to be calculated. Presentments of bills should be made within business hours. These are generally considered to be in London from nine morning till six evening, but a protest has been held good against an ordinary trader when made at eight. This would not have been good in the case of bankers, whose hours (from nine to five in London) must be attended to. In Edinburgh, bankers' hours are from ten to three ; traders from ten to three, and from six to eight ; but there are no Scotch decisions holding these as the only business hours. A verbal notice of the dishonor of an *inland* bill is good ; but as such notice is always matter of parole evidence, is better in every case to give notice in writing, and the regular mode of doing so is by post. Such notice, if put into the general post-office, or an authorized receiving house, is good though it miscarry, provided the letter be regularly booked, and reasonable proof be made of its having been put into the post-office. If given only to a bellman in the street, would not in such a case be good. When there is no post, the ordinary mode of conveyance, such as the *first* ship or carrier, is sufficient. As to *foreign bills*, notices of dishonor, with the respective protests, must be despatched by post on the day when the bills become due, or on which acceptance was refused, if any post or ordinary conveyance set out that day, and if not, by the next earliest conveyance. (Chitty, 291.) As to *inland* bills, notice should be made by the first post after the expiry of a day, when the parties reside at a distance ; if in the same town, it is enough if the notice be made so as to be received within business hours of the following day, and this may be done by the twopenny or penny post, if receivable within the time mentioned. When a holder deposits his bill at his banker's, the number of persons entitled to notice is increased by one ; and each party in succession is entitled to *twenty-four hours* for giving notice, (6 East. 3 Bell, 263.) Such notice, as to inland bills, is necessary in England for preserving recourse as to the principal sum only. If protest be made and notice given within fourteen days, the recourse is preserved as *to interest*, damages and expenses. In Scotland a protest is necessary in every case, and there is no distinction made as to the mode of recourse between principal and interest ; but intimation to the drawer within *fourteen* days preserves recourse for the whole (Bell, vol. ii. p. 265 ;) and it has been decided, that notice of an endorser may be good even after the fourteen days, if there has been no unnecessary delay. (*Fac. Col.* 2d June, 1812.) But this applies only to *inland* bills, and a bill drawn from Scotland upon England is in Scotland held to be foreign. (Bell, vol. ii. p. 265.) Every bill should be presented for payment on the day upon which it falls due, unless that be rendered impossible by some unforeseen and *inevitable* accident, such as shipwreck, or sudden illness, or death. To preserve recourse, the accident, and the presentment of the bill as soon as possible afterwards, must be intimated without delay, and, if denied, proved by the party who seeks recourse. The same doctrine will hold as to presentments for non-acceptance and notices of dishonor. But the loss or destruction of a bill is no excuse for not demanding payment and protesting ; the protest in that case being made upon a copy or statement of the bill, if the party who has a right to hold the bill has it in his power to make such a statement. If the destruction of the bill can be proved, action will be sustained in a court of law ; if not, the redress is got upon giving an indemnity in a court of equity ; but as equity will not interfere where law can, it is of importance, in such a case, and indeed in all cases of difficulty, to resort at once to the best professional advice. Inconsiderate attempts to remedy neglects, or cure what is defective, generally make the case worse, and often implicate character. Cases of great hardship and difficulty frequently arose on bills granted partly for *usurious* consideration. A mighty benefit, however, has now been conferred by the statute 58 Geo. III. c. 93, which enacts, " That *no bill* of exchange or promissory note that shall be drawn or made after the passing of this act shall, though it may have been given for a usurious consideration, or upon a usurious contract, *be void* in *the hands of an endorse for valuable consideration,* unless such an endorsee had, at the time of discounting or paying such consideration for the same, *actual notice* that such bill, &c., had been originally given for a usurious consideration, or upon a usurious contract." It is much to be regretted that the same protection was not extended by this statute to the *innocent holder* of a bill granted for a game debt. Such bills are still void in the hands of a *bona fide* endorsee. In Scotland it has been decided otherwise (25th January, 1740, Nielson; Bell, vol. ii. p. 210.) The rage for legislation has not yet extended itself to lawyers, who, as a body, can hardly be expected to display any anxiety to remedy any defects which add to their emoluments and consequence. How much of the learning of this profession is wasted on niceties and difficulties that would readily yield to the spell of an act of parliament! To the law, however, we owe this sound maxim, that, "unless it has been so expressly declared by the legislature, and it formerly was in the case of usury, and still is as to bills for *game* debts, illegality of consideration will be no defence in an action to the suit of a *bona fide* holder, without notice of the illegality, unless he obtained the bill after it became due." (Chitty, 105.) Thus *forgery* does not vitiate a bill. The forged document is good to and against all parties but those whose names are forged. Against one whose name is forged, it is true, it will neither support an action nor ground a claim; "yet if he have given credit to acceptances or endorsations as binding on him, forged by the same hand, he will be liable." (3 Esp. N. P. 50; 2 Bell, 250.) Subsequent approbation also does away an objection on the head of forgery or fraud, and generally all sorts of objections otherwise competent. This doctrine holds as to vitiations when the stamp laws are not concerned; but without the consent of parties, all vitiations or alterations of bills in material parts are fatal. (2 Bell, 252.) A clerk or servant may accept a bill for his master if authorized to so do; and authority will be inferred from a sanctioned practice. The law on this point is dangerous, and would require legislative revision. If the servant or agent do not explain the character in which he acts, but subscribes his own name simply, he will bind himself, not his employer. An acceptor may enlarge the term of payment, or accept for a part, or under any other condition not expressed in the bill; but in that case it is optional in the holder to take the acceptance as thus offered, or to proceed as if no such offer had been made; if rejected, the protest should bear the condition, and the rejection of it; it should also be kept in view, that a *holder* who accepts of a limited or conditional acceptance, liberates the drawer and prior endorser, unless he have their consent. Blank endorsements are held to be of the date of the bill, until the contrary is proved. Endorsements after the term of payment, though for value, do not protect the endorsers like endorsements before maturity; very slight evidence is admitted as proof of knowledge of dishonor, and the holder in that case becomes liable to all exceptions which can be stated against the right of his immediate endorser, or the person who held the bill when it became due. When acceptance is refused, and the bill returned with protest, action may be raised immediately against the drawer, though the regular time of payment is not arrived. His debt, in such a case, is considered as contracted the moment the bill was drawn; if the date of the bill be prior to that of a commission of bankrupt, the debt, in such a case, may be claimed upon. As to current bills and contingent claims, the case is unfortunately different; in these respects England might derive great help from the law of Scotland.

IV. — DUTIES OF DRAWEE.

The *drawee*, who, having funds, refuses to accept, is responsible for the consequences to the *drawer*, and may also be sued for payment by the payee or holder, the presentment and protesting of the bill for non-acceptance operating as an intimated assignment and complete transfer of the debt *to the holder*, who in Scotland is preferred to any subsequent arrester. The *drawee* who has no funds is not bound to accept; but, after protest for non-acceptance, he may accept supra-protest, for the *honor* of the drawer and endorsers, or either of them. A *third party* may thus accept for *honor* supra-protest; and whoever does so, if he give immediate notice and send off the protest, may have immediate recourse on the party or parties for whose honor he has interfered.

V. — PAYEE OR HOLDER. — EFFECT OF BANKRUPTCY. — ACCOMMODATION PAPER. — CROSS PAPER.

It is the duty of a *payee*, when directed by the drawer, and of every one who is merely an agent for the owner, though acting gratuitously, to present a bill for acceptance. The time thought reasonable for this purpose is twenty-four hours, or at least within business hours of the day following that on which the bill was received. It is prudent in all holders of a bill to present for acceptance within this period; and *in all cases* where presentment is made, and acceptance refused, notice should be given to all to whom it is meant to preserve recourse. A draft may be left twenty-four hours with the drawee, if no post go out in the mean time; but if he intimate within that time that he will not accept, or ask *more time* to consider, *notice should be given*. (Chitty, 288, 289.) A verbal acceptance, if it can be proved, or one by a separate writing, binds the drawee; but in Scotland none but a written acceptance on a bill will authorize the usual summary diligence. (Chitty, 217, 270; 2 Bell, 69, 210.) If the drawee had no funds, notice to the drawer is not necessary; but as the not having funds is a matter of fact to be proved, it is safer in this, and indeed in all other cases, to give the usual and regular notice. When a bill is drawn at some certain time *after sight*, presentment is *necessary* to fix the term of payment. Respecting bills of this description, both foreign and inland, the general rule is, that *due diligence must be used*. Foreign bills, so drawn, may be put into the circulation without acceptance, as long as the convenience of the successive holders requires; and it has been found not to be *laches* (in Scotland *mora*, or undue delay) to keep a bill (at three days' sight) out in the circulation for twelve months; but if, instead of circulating, a holder were to lock it up, this would be *laches*. An unacceptable inland bill may also be put in circulation; and any holder, who does not circulate it, has a reasonable time, such as the fourth day respecting a bill drawn within twenty miles of London, for presenting it there for acceptance. Despatch and attention, however, are always advisable. It is said that when a bill has been already protested for non-acceptance, and due notice thereof given, it is not necessary to protest or to give notice on account of non-payment; but it is usual to do so, and the safer practice. The same rules and the same time should be observed, as to non-payment, that are observed as to protest and notice, in the case of non-acceptance. When inland bills are made payable on a day named and fixed in the bills, it is common to delay presenting them for acceptance until they can also be presented for payment, and then, if necessary, to protest for both; but it is better to make a presentment for acceptance as soon as it can be done in the ordinary course of business. It has already been stated, that notice either of non-acceptance when a presentment has been made, or for non-payment, *must* be given *to all the parties* to whom the *holder* intends to resort for payment. Bankruptcy is no excuse for neglecting any step in the negotiation of a bill. If a party be bankrupt, notice of recourse should be given to him and his assignees; if *dead*, to his executor or administrator; if abroad, the notice should be left at his place of residence, if he have one, and a demand of acceptance or payment (when that is necessary) should be made of his wife or servant. Notice should also be made to one who merely guarantees payment; and a person who subscribes a bill not addressed to him is held to be a collateral security. If notice be made to one endorser, he may give notice to prior endorsers, or to the drawer; and, if done timely, it will be available to the holder; but notice by a party not party to the bill, nor agent for a party, will not be available.

Accommodation bills are subject to the same rules as other paper, except among those who agree to lend their names or credit. Among them the rule is, that he for whose use the money is to be raised shall provide for the bill; but as all the others have an action of relief when forced to pay, they are entitled to notice. In Scotland this has been extended to the drawer when he is not the party for whom the credit was intended. With respect to cross paper, it is held that mutual accommodations exchanged are good considerations for each other; that in case of bankruptcy, a dividend from any one estate is to be held as payment of all that can be demanded in respect of that debt; and that there can be no double ranking of the same debt. But questions often arise in such cases, which require the utmost professional skill to comprehend and decide. In a short digest of this nature it is impossible to enter into the niceties of legal questions; and we can only observe, generally, that parties should never act, in cases of difficulty, without taking the best professional assistance.

The *law* respecting bills of exchange is more consonant with reason than almost any other branch of our law, since, where it is silent, recourse is had to the custom of merchants.

The best authorities respecting the law of bills are the treatises of Chitty and of Bayley as to the English law, and Mr. Bell's *Commentaries on Mercantile Jurisprudence* as to Scotch law.

FOREIGN BILLS OF EXCHANGE.

Forms of Bills of Exchange ordinarily used in the French, German, Dutch, Italian, Spanish, Portuguese, Swedish and Danish language.

As many bills drawn in foreign languages pass through the hands of numerous bankers, it may be useful to give a list of some of those words which express the amount and the time, the two main points in a bill of exchange : —

English,	One	Two	Three	Sixty	Ninety.
German,	Ein	Zwei	Drei	Sechzig	Neunzig.
Dutch,	Een	Twee	Drie	Zestig	Negentig.
French,	Un	Deux	Trois	Soixante	{ Quatre-vingt-dix or Nonante.
Italian,	Uno	Due	Tre	Sessanta	Nonanta, or Novanta
Spanish,	Uno	Dos	Tres	Sesenta	Noventa.
Portuguese,	Hum	Dous	Tres	Secenta	Noventa.
Swedish,	En	Twa	Tre	Sexti	Nitti.
Danish,	Een	To	Tre	Tredsindstyve	Halvfemtesindstyve.

English,	Two months after date.	Three days after sight.
German,	Zwei monate nach dato.	Drei tage nach sicht.
Dutch,	Twee maanden na dato.	Drie dagen na zigt.
French,	A deux mois de date.	A trois jours de vue.
Italian,	A due mesi dopo data.	{ A tre giorni vista. A tre giorni dopo vista.
Spanish,	{ A dos meses de la fecha. A dos meses data.	A tres dias vista.
Portuguese,	A dous mezes de data.	A tres dias vista.
Swedish,	Twa manander ifran dato.	Tre dagar efter sigt.
Danish,	To maander efter dato.	Tre dage efter sigt.

In all the above languages, " at sight " is usually expressed by *a vista* except the French, which expresses it by *à vue.* " At usance " is expressed by *a uso* or *ad uso.* The names of the months so nearly resemble the English, that a mistake can but rarely occur.

The following are forms of bills in each of the languages named: —

French.

Lille, le 28 *Septembre,* 1848. *Bon pour* £158 9 *Sterlings.*

Au vingt-cinq Décembre prochain, Il vous plaira payer par ce mandat à l'ordre de nous-mêmes la somme de cent cinquante-huit livres sterlings 9 schellings valeur en nous-mêmes et que passerez suivant l'avis de

A *Messieurs* ———————
    a *Londres.*

German.

Nürnberg, den 28 *October,* 1848. *Pro* £100 *Sterling.*

Zwei monate nach dato zahlen Sie gegen diesen Prima Wechsel an die Ordre des Herrn ——————— Ein Hundert Pfund Sterling den Werth erhalten. Sie bringen solche auf Rechnung laut Bericht von.

Herren ———————
    London.

Dutch.

Grouw, den 1st *November,* 1848. *Voor* £59 17 6

Twee maanden na dato gelieve UEd te betalen voor dezen onzen prima Wisselbrief de secunda niet betaald zynde aan de ordre van de Heeren ——— negen & vyftig Ponden zeventien schelling en zespences sterling, de waarde in rekening UEd stelle het op rekening met of zonder advys van

de *Heer* ———————
    te London.

Italian.

Livorno, le 25 *Settembre,* 1848. *Per* £500 *Sterline.*

A Tre mesi data pagate per questa prima de Cambio (una sol volta) all' ordine ————————————, la somma di Lire cinque cento sterline valuta cambiata, e ponete in conto M. S. secondo l'avviso Addio.

A*i* - ———————
    Londra.

FOREIGN BILLS OF EXCHANGE. 95

SPANISH.

Malaga, á 20 de Setbre de 1848.   Son £300.

A noventa dias fecha se serviran V^s mandar pagar por esta primera de cambio á la orden de los S^{res} _____ Tres cientas libras Esterlinas en oro o plata valor recibido de dhos S^{res} que anotaran valor en cuenta según aviso de

A los S^{res} _____
   Londres.

PORTUGUESE.

£600 Esterlinas.   Lisbon, aos 8 Dezembro de 1848.

A Sessenta dias de vista precizos pagará V _____ por esta nossa unica via de Letra Segura, á nos ou á nossa Ordem a quantia acima de Seis Centas Livras Esterlinas valor de nos recebido em Fazendas, que passera em Comta segundo o aviso de

Ao Senr _____
   Londres.

SWEDISH.

Bjorneberg, den 23 September, 1848.   For £ Sterl. 100

Nittio Dagar efter dato behagade H. H. emot denna prima Wezel (secunao obetald) betala till Herr _____ elle ordres Etthundra Pund Sterling som stalles i rakning enligt avis.

Herrar _____ _____
   London.

DANISH.

Kjobenhavn, 9 December, 1848.   Rbae 4,000.

Tre maaneder efter dato behager de at betale denne Prima Vexel, Secunda ikke, til Herr _____ eller ordre med Fire Tusinde Rigsbank Daler, Valutta modtaget og stilles i Regning ifölge advis.

Herrer _____
   London.

FORMS OF NOTICE OF PROTEST.

The following forms have been prepared after careful investigations of the subject, and with a view to combine all the information required by the latest decisions of the State Courts·

FORM USED BY THE NOTARY OF THE PHENIX BANK, NEW YORK, 1847.

$ —————   *New York,* ————————— 184

Please to take notice that a promissory Note for $—————, *made by* ————————————, *endorsed by you, having been duly presented and payment thereof demanded, which was refused, is therefore protested for non payment, and that the holders look to you for payment thereof.*

————————————— *Notary Public.*

FORM OF NOTICE USED BY THE NOTARY OF THE PHILADELPHIA BANK.

$ —————   *Philadelphia,* ————————— 185

Payment of ————————— *note in favor of* —————, *and by* ————————— *endorsed, for* $—————, *dated* —————, *delivered to me for protest by the* ————— *Bank of* —————, *Philadelphia, being this day due, demanded and refused, it has been by me duly protested accordingly, and you will be looked to for payment, of which you hereby have notice.*

————————————— *Notary Public.*

FORMS OF NOTICE OF PROTEST. 97

Form used by the Notary of the Bank of Virginia.

$_____ Richmond, Va., _____ 185

Take notice that _____ note for $_____, dated the _____ day of _____, 185 , and payable _____ days after date, to the order of _____, at the _____ Bank of Virginia, and endorsed by _____, being due and unpaid, the same was presented by me at said Bank _____, and payment thereof then and there demanded, which was refused. Whereupon the said note was dishonored, and I duly protested the same for non-payment, and the holders look to you for payment, as endorser thereof, for principal, interest, damages and costs.

Done at the request of the Cashier of the Bank of Virginia.

_____ *Notary Public.*

~~~~~~~~~~~~~~~~~~~~

Form adopted by the Cayuga County Bank, New York.

Auburn, _____ 1850.

$_____

Sir,—Take notice that a promissory note made by _____, to order of _____, for _____ dollars, dated _____ at _____ after date, this day due, endorsed by you, was this day presented by me, at the Cayuga County Bank, where the same was made payable, and payment thereof demanded of the _____ of said Bank, and by him refused, and is this day protested for non-payment. The holder looks to you for the payment of the same.

_____ *Notary Public.*

To _____

~~~~~~~~~~~~~~~~~~~~

Form of Notice used in Vermont.

$_____

A promissory note for _____ dollars, dated _____, payable _____ after date, to _____, signed by _____, endorsed by _____, having been duly presented for payment this day, and payment refused, has been protested by me for non-payment. I now hereby give you notice that the holder looks to you for payment, interest, cost, and damages.

_____ *Notary Public.*

NOTICE OF PROTEST.

Form used by the Notary of the Suffolk Bank, Boston.

$_____   Boston, _____, 185_

Sir,—A promissory note for $ _____, dated _____, signed _____, payable to the order of _____, at _____, endorsed by _____, having been protested by me this day for non-payment, I hereby notify you that the holder looks to you for payment, interest, cost and damages, payment having been duly demanded and refused.

Done at the request of the Cashier of the _____ Bank.

_____, Notary Public.

~~~~~~~~~~~~~~~~~~~~

Bill of Exchange.

Boston, _____, 185_

$_____

A bill of exchange drawn by _____, on _____, for _____ dollars, dated _____, 185_, payable _____ after _____, in favor of _____, and endorsed by _____, due this day, is protested for non-payment, by direction of the holder, payment having been duly demanded and refused.

The holder requires of you payment of the same, with interest, cost and damages.

_____, Notary Public.

REMARKS.

Judge Story, in his Treatise on Promissory Notes, says:—The endorsement of a promissory note, in contemplation of law, amounts to a contract on the part of the endorser, with and in favor of the endorsee, and every subsequent holder to whom the note is transferred: *First*, that the instrument itself and the antecedent signatures thereon are genuine. *Second*, that he, the endorser, has a good title to the instrument. *Third*, that he is competent to bind himself by the endorsement as endorser. *Fourth*, that the maker is competent to bind himself to the payment, and will, upon due presentment of the note, pay it at maturity. *Fifth*, That if, when duly presented, it is not paid by the maker he, the endorser, will *upon the due and reasonable notice given to him of the dishonor*, pay the same to the endorsee or holder.

There is no particular form of notice required, but it is indispensable that it should, ei her expressly or by just and natural implication, contain in substance the following requisites: —

1st. A true description of the note, so as to ascertain its identity.

2d. An assertion that it has been duly presented to the maker at its maturity, and dishonored.

3d. That the holder or other person giving the notice, looks to the person to whom the notice is given, for payment and indemnity.

This statement is essential to establish the claim or right of the holder, or the party giving notice, for otherwise he will not be entitled to any payment from the endorser. It will be sufficient, indeed, if the notice sent, necessarily, or even fairly, implies by its *terms* that there has been a due presentment and dishonor at the maturity of the note; but mere notice of the fact that the note has not been paid, affords no proof whatever that the note has been presented in due season, or even that it has been presented at all.

The Supreme Court of the U. S. have decided that "where a notice is sent, after the exercise of due diligence, and inquiry as to the residence of the endorser, a right of action immediately accrues to the holder, and subsequent information of another character as to the true residence of the endorser does not render it necessary for the holder to send him another notice.

The law does not require actual notice. It requires reasonable diligence only, and reasonable efforts, made in good faith, to give it. And if sufficient inquiries have been made, and information received, upon which the holder has a right to rely, a mistake as to the nearest post office does not deprive him of his remedy. He has done all that the law requires; and the notice thus sent, fixes the liability of the endorser as effectually as if he had actually received it.—(*Howard's Reports*, Vol. *ix.*)

Waiver of Notice.—In Maine it has been decided that if the endorser of a promissory note knew that the note would not be paid on presentment, and that the maker had deceased, and his estate insolvent, such knowledge would not relieve the holder from his obligation to make the presentment and give due notice of dishonor.

Decease of Maker.—When the maker of a promissory note dies before it becomes payab e, the holder should make inquiry for his personal representative, if there be one, and present the note at maturity for payment.

By whom held.—It has been held that notice of dishonor need not state on whose behalf payment is applied for, nor where the bill is lying; and a misdescription of the place where the bill is lying is immaterial, unless perhaps a tender were made there.

Kentucky. — The place where a bill of exchange is dated is, prima facie, the residence of the drawer, and, in the absence of proof to the contrary, notice sent to that place will be good.

In *Massachusetts,* (R. S. 303,) all bills of exchange payable at sight, or at a future day certain, and all promissory negotiable notes payable at a future day certain, within that State, in which there is no express stipulation to the contrary, grace is allowed as it is by the custom of merchants on foreign bills of exchange, payable at a certain period after date or sight. These provisions do not extend to any bill of exchange, note, or draft, payable *on demand.*

In *Louisiana,* the 1st of January, the 8th of January, the 22d of February, the 4th of July, the 25th of December, Sundays and Good Friday, are days of public rest. When the 3d or both 3d and 2d days of grace on a bill or note falls upon a day of rest, such bill or note shall become due in the one case on the 2d, and the other on the 1st day of grace. In computing the delay allowed in giving notice of non-payment, or non acceptance of a bill or note, the days of public rest are not counted. (Bullard and Curry's Digest, 40.)

In *Michigan,* days of grace are not allowed upon any bill, note, or draft, payable on demand, but are allowed upon all bills payable at sight, or at a future day certain, within the State, and all negotiable promissory notes and drafts payable at a future day certain within the State, wherein there is no express stipulation to the contrary. (2 R. S. of 1846, 157.)

In *New Hampshire,* days of grace are allowed on all negotiable promissory notes, except those payable on demand, unless the instrument show the intention of the parties to be otherwise. (R. S. 180.)

In *Vermont,* bills and notes executed in any other State, but payable in that State, and all bills and notes executed in that State, and payable in any other State, are entitled to three days' grace; this does not extend to bi..s and notes payable on demand, or in any way but in money. (R. S. 73.)

BANKING AND FINANCIAL MAXIMS.

OPINIONS ON COMMERCE, &c.,

By Addison—Appleton—Edmund Burke—Lord Brougham—Buckle—Lord Campbell—W. H. Crawford—W. E. Channing—P. W. Chandler—A. J. Dallas—Delany—The Edinburgh Review—The London Quarterly Review—Gallatin—A. Hamilton—A. B. Johnson—Dr. Johnson—Jefferson—Lord Jeffrey—Chancellor Kent—J. Stuart Mill—Madison—R. Rush—Smiles—D. Webster.

I. *Capital and Labor.*—Rightfully considered, no principle is more conservative than that which identifies the laborer with the capitalist.—*Edinburgh Review*, 1864.

II. *Co-operation.*—The co-operative principle is that the workers are the capitalists. By this, if it is found practicable, the opposition between Capital and Labor is annihilated.—*Edinburgh Review*, 1864.

III. *The New World.*—America and Australia are the two fields in which the intelligence and inventions of our own age find their widest application. The ordinary growth of centuries is here compressed into two or three generations; and the surface of the earth submitted to changes which have no parallel in the earlier history of nations.—*Edinburgh Review*, 1864.

IV. *Railroads.*—Look further at those admirable constructions, both in Europe and America, by which the railroad is carried across mountain chains, climbing tortuously their steep acclivities, or forced by tunnels through the rock. In the Copiapo Railway of Chili, the locomotive carries its train four thousand and seventy feet above the sea. In the several railroads which cross the Alleghany Mountains, the summit levels are from two to three thousand feet. The new empire of Brazil boasts a work of similar kind, just completed. In the section, now open, of the St. Ander Railroad in Spain, an elevation is reached of two thousand five hundred and twenty-four feet. The Sömmering Pass, between Vienna and Gratz, carries the traveller three thousand feet above the sea. Tunnels from two to three miles in length are familiar to us in England and elsewhere. That which is now in progress under Mount Cenis has for its object and ambition to win a passage into Italy without crossing the Alps . . . The traveller gains a few hours of time upon his journey, and emerges into Italy through a hole in a rock !—*Edinburgh Review*, 1864.

V. *Human Progress.*—It is, in truth, a wonderful picture of human progress—of progress continuous, yet so marvellously quickened during the last fifty years, that the dullest observer of the world around him feels that he is living in a new age; and the most cautious philosopher scarcely ventures to set a limit to what may hereafter be attained. While the instincts and acts of other animals have remained stationary from the earliest recorded time, human intelligence, working with, and in part controlling, the great forces of nature, has covered the globe with monuments of its activity and power. The whole may be received as evidence of the high destiny which God has given to man on earth; a destiny mingled at present with much that is obscure to reason and painful to feeling, but capable of, and intended, as we believe, for some higher and nobler development in the time yet to come.—*Edinburgh Review*, 1864.

VI. *Free Trade.*—We have, in great degree, confined ourselves to proving how unsound is the social philosophy embodied in the Free Trade policy. It would be even an easier task to prove its pernicious moral tendencies. It is in its very essence a mercenary, unsocial, demoralizing system; opposed to all generous actions, all kindly feelings. Based on selfishness—the most pervading as well as most powerful of our vicious propensities—it directs that impulse into the lowest of all channels, the mere sordid pursuit of wealth. It teaches competition and isolation, instead of co-operation and brotherhood; it substitutes a vague and impracticable cosmopolitanism for a lofty and ennobling patriotism; it disregards the claims of humanity towards the poor, if opposed to the pecuniary interests of the rich; it takes no account of all that should exalt man in the scale of being, but elevates to exclusive importance his most degrading tendencies. Wealth is its end and aim, and mammon its divinity. We cannot altogether regret with Burke that " the age of chivalry is past," and though we do with him regret that "an age of sophists, of economists, and of calculators has succeeded," we still trust that " the glory of England is not yet extinguished forever."—*London Quarterly Review.*

VII. *National Resources.*—The wealth of the nation, in the value and products of its soil, in all the acquisitions of personal property, and in all the varieties of industry, remains almost untouched by the hand of Government; for the national faith, and not the national wealth, has hitherto been the principal instrument of finance. It was reasonable, however, to expect that a period must occur, in the course of a protracted war, when confidence in the accumulating public engagements could only be secured by an active demonstration both of the capacity and the disposition to perform them. In the present state of the Treasury, therefore, it is a just consolation to reflect that a prompt and resolute application of the resources of the country will effectually relieve from every pecuniary embarrassment, and vindicate the fiscal honor of the Government.—*A. J. Dallas, Secretary of the Treasury,* 1814.

VIII. *National Debts.*—It is a wise rule, and should be fundamental in a government disposed to cherish its credit, and at the same time to restrain the use of it within the limits of its faculties, never to borrow a dollar without laying a tax in the same instant, for paying the interest annually and the principal within a given term; and to consider that tax as pledged to the creditors on the public faith. On such a pledge as this, sacredly observed, a government may always command, on a reasonable interest, all the lendable money of its citizens; whilst the necessity of an equivalent tax is a salutary warning to them and their constituents against oppression, bankruptcy, and its inevitable consequence, revolution.—*Thomas Jefferson.*

IX. *Origin of Repudiation.*—In proportion precisely as an individual is beyond the reach of compulsory process, should he be inclined to disregard the technicalities of mere law, and base himself upon the broader principles of natural justice. This is still more necessary when an independent sovereignty is concerned; because it is more difficult to procure redress for wrongs committed by a State. The relation between debtor and creditor, in all cases involving the repose of confidence, is pre-eminently a fiduciary relation when the debtor is a sovereign commonwealth. It should be distinguished by that *uberrima fides* which scorns the strict letter of the contract and regards its spirit and intention.—*Peleg W. Chandler.*

X. *Power of Taxation.*—Congress has the power to lay stamp duties on notes, on bank notes, and on any description of bank notes. That power has already been exercised, and the duties may be laid on to such an amount, and in such a manner, as may be necessary to effect the object intended. This object is not merely to provide generally for the general welfare, but to carry into effect, in conformity with the last paragraph of the eighth section of the first article, those several and express provisions of the Constitution, which vest in Congress exclusively the control over the monetary system of the United States, and more particularly those which imply the necessity of a uniform currency.—*A. Gallatin.*

XI. *Taxation.*—The apportionment of taxes on the various descriptions of property is an act which seems to require the most exact impartiality; yet there is, perhaps, no legislative act in which greater opportunity and temptation are given to a predominant party to trample on the rules of justice. Every shilling with which they overburden the inferior number, is a shilling saved to their own pockets.—*Madison (Federalist), November 23,* 1787.

XII. *Public Credit.*—Credit, public and private, is of the greatest consequence to every country; of this, it might be emphatically called the invigorating principle. No well-informed man can cast a retrospective eye over the progress of the United States, from their infancy to the present period, without being convinced that they owe, in a great degree, to the fostering influence of credit, their present mature growth. This credit has been of a mixed nature, mercantile and public, foreign and domestic. Credit abroad was the trunk of our mercantile credit, from which issued ramifications that nourished all the parts of domestic labor and industry. The bills of credit emitted from time to time by the different local governments, which passed current as money, co-operated with that resource.—*Alexander Hamilton.*

XIII. *The Public Debt.*—There can be no more sacred obligation, then, on the public agents of a nation, than to guard with provident foresight and inflexible perseverance against so mischievous a result [the accumulation of public debt]. True patriotism and genuine policy cannot, it is respectfully presumed, be better demonstrated by those of the United States, at the present juncture, than by improving efficaciously the very favorable situation in which they stand for extinguishing, with reasonable celerity, the actual debt of the country, and for laying the foundation of a system which may shield posterity from the consequences of the usual improvidence and selfishness of its ancestors; and which, if possible, may give immortality to public credit.—*Alexander Hamilton, Secretary of the Treasury,* 1795.

XIV. *A Warning.*—By a series of arbitrary acts on the part of government, and by connecting some splendid and illusory schemes with the bank, Law succeeded in putting in circulation about four hundred and twenty millions of dollars in bank notes, or more than twice the amount of the currency then wanted in France. This paper was made a legal tender, to the total exclusion of the precious metals. But the laws and all the power of the French government were unequal to the task of sustaining that excess of currency. The price of every species of merchandise naturally rose 100 per cent. Government, with a view probably to prevent a final catastrophe, reduced, by a decree, the notes to one-half their original value.—*A. Gallatin.*

XV. *Statistics.*—To those who have a steady conception of the regularity of events, and have firmly seized the great truth that the actions of men, being guided by their antecedents, are in reality never inconsistent; but, however capricious they may appear, only form part of one vast scheme of universal order, of which we, in the present state of knowledge, can barely see the outline—to those who understand this, which is at once the key and the basis of history, the facts just adduced, so far from being strange, will be precisely what would have been expected, and ought long since to have been known. . . . Statistics have already thrown more light on the study of human nature than all the sciences put together.—*Buckle.*

XVI. *Mineral Wealth.*—Great Britain is indebted to its mines for its colonization in the mists of time—for much of its present importance—and, according to Bochart and others, even for its name. Its whole history, indeed, is associated with these subterranean treasures. The most ancient nations of the East resorted to it for tin and copper. Julius Cæsar, like the Spanish conquerors of the West, was attracted to its shores chiefly by rumors of its mineral wealth; and Pliny, and even the severer Tacitus, invested Britain with the splendors of an El Dorado. These golden visions, to be sure, were not realized. But the Romans worked extensively its mines of lead, and extracted silver from the produce. It was reserved for much later times to discover that the stratification of Britain was of almost unequalled variety, and that it contained, to an extent never dreamed of, the most abundant supplies of coal and iron. The manufacturing industry of the north originated in and was long satisfied with, the power derived from the uncertain streams issuing from its mountains. But the steam-engine at last opened out visions of national wealth more gorgeous than the mines of Peru. It not only enabled the deeper metallic and other mines to be worked, and thus added new realms of happy conquest to the nation, but it formed in itself a matchless power for all the industrial arts of life. All that this many-handed and munificent giant demanded for its unceasing labors, was a sufficient supply of its peculiar food; and, fortunately for Britain, this food was found within her shores in a profusion and of an excellence unparalleled in Europe.—*Edinburgh Review.*

XVII. *The Standard.*—There is not, however, in nature, any perfect or altogether permanent standard of value. There is not a single commodity, the relative value of which, as compared to that of all other commodities, is not subject to great and permanent changes, as well as to temporary fluctuations. But it will be found that the nature of the demand for precious metals, the comparative regularity of the supply, and especially their much greater durability and intrinsic value than those of any other substance otherwise fitted for a circulating medium, restrain the fluctuations to which the relative value is liable, within far narrower limits, than is the case with any other commodity, which might have been selected for a currency.— *A. Gallatin.*

XVIII. *Railroads and Steam.*—Among the innumerable benefits derived from advancing knowledge, there are few more important than those improved facilities of communication which, by increasing the frequency with which nations and individuals are brought into contact, have, to an extraordinary extent, corrected their prejudices, raised the opinion which each forms of the other, diminished their mutual hostility, and thus diffusing a more favorable view of our common nature, have stimulated us to develop those boundless resources of the human understanding, the very existence of which it was once considered almost a heresy to assert.—*Buckle.*

XIX. *Steam.*—It has increased indefinitely the mass of human comforts and enjoyments; and rendered cheap and accessible, all over the world, the materials of wealth and prosperity. It has armed the feeble hand of man, in short, with a power to which no limits can be assigned; completed the dominion of mind over the most refractory qualities of matter; and laid a sure foundation for all those future miracles of mechanic power which are to aid and reward the labors of after generations. It is to the genius of one man, too, that all this is mainly owing. And certainly no man ever bestowed such a gift on his kind. The blessing is not only universal, but unbounded; and the fabled inventors of the plough and the loom, who were deified by the erring gratitude of their rude contemporaries, conferred less important benefits on mankind than the inventor of our present steam-engine.—*Francis Jeffrey,* 1819.

XX. *Mechanical Progress.*—Machinery is made to perform what has formerly been the toil of human hands, to an extent that astonishes the most sanguine; with a degree of power to which no number of human arms is equal, and with such precision and exactness as almost to suggest the notion of reason and intelligence in the machines themselves. Every natural agent is put unrelentingly to the wheel. The winds work, the waters work, the elasticity of the metals works; gravity is solicited into a thousand new forms of action; levers are multiplied upon levers; wheels revolve upon the peripheries of other wheels. The saw and the plane are tortured into an accommodation to new uses; and, last of all, with inimitable power, and "*with whirlwind sound,*" comes the potent agency of steam.—*Daniel Webster,* 1828.

XXI. *Facts.*—Facts are to the mind the same thing as food to the body. On the due digestion of facts depends the strength and wisdom of the one, just as vigor and health depend on the other. The wisest in council, the ablest in debate, the most agreeable companion in the commerce of human life, is that man who has assimilated to his understanding the greatest number of facts.—*Burke.*

XXII. *Commerce.*—An unrestrained intercourse between the States themselves will advance the trade of each, by an interchange of their respective productions, not only for the supply of reciprocal wants at home, but for the exportation to foreign markets. The veins of commerce in every part will be replenished, and will acquire additional motion and vigor, from a free circulation of the commodities of every part. Commercial enterprise will have much greater scope from the diversity in the productions of different States. When the staple of one fails, from a bad harvest or unproductive crop, it can call to its aid the staple of another. The variety, not less than the value of products for exportation, contributes to the activity of foreign commerce.—*Hamilton, Federalist.*

XXIII. *Board of Directors.*—Regard to reputation has a less active influence, when the infamy of a bad action is to be divided among a number, than when it is to fall singly upon one. A spirit of faction, which is apt to mingle its poison in the deliberations of all bodies of men, will often hurry the persons of whom they are composed into improprieties and excesses, for which they would blush in a private capacity.—*Hamilton, Federalist, December, 1787.*

XXIV. *Opportunities.*—They who have turned their attention to the affairs of men, must have perceived that there are tides in them; tides very regular in their duration, strength, and direction, and seldom found to run twice exactly in the same manner or measure. To discern and to profit by these tides in national affairs, is the business of those who preside over them; and they who have had much experience on this head inform us, that there frequently are occasions when days, nay, even when hours, are precious.—*Hamilton, Federalist, March 7, 1788.*

XXV. The revenue of the State is THE STATE; in effect, all depends upon it, whether for support or for reformation.—*Burke.*

XXVI. *Protection.*—The merchant, like the manufacturer, requires, at proper junctures, the helping hand of Congress, and may suffer without it. Hence it has been the object, as it was the duty, of the Department, to invoke legislative favor for both these great interests, under the belief that they flourish most when they flourish together; that, in proportion as both flourish, in conjunction with agriculture (the invariable feeder of both), is the public treasury most likely to be kept full; and that all plans of finance that do not take the co-operating prosperity of these three primary interests of the State as their foundation, must prove fallacious or short lived.—*Richard Rush, Secretary of the Treasury, 1828.*

XXVII. *Public Faith.* –Every breach of the public engagements, whether from choice or necessity, is, in different degrees, hurtful to public credit. When such a necessity does truly exist, the evils of it are only to be palliated by scrupulous attention, on the part of the Government, to carry the violation no further than the necessity absolutely requires; and to manifest, if the nature of the case admit of it, a sincere disposition to make reparation whenever circumstances shall permit. But, with every possible mitigation, credit must suffer, and numerous mischiefs ensue. It is, therefore, highly important, when an appearance of necessity seems to press upon the public councils, that they should examine well its reality, and be perfectly assured that there is no method of escaping from it, before they yield to its suggestions.—*Alexander Hamilton, Secretary of the Treasury,* 1790.

XXVIII. *The Future of the United States.*—There will be no more oppression, either of conscience or any other species; no oppression of one class by another, or of all classes of society by a permanent army. North America will only have an army for appearance sake; consisting, at most, of twelve thousand men, disseminated in little bands over the entire extent of her territory. Then, there will be no unpleasant traces of the past; no law of primogeniture; no exclusive academies; no embroidery of distinctive rank; no crosses and decorations; no cringing courtiers; no sinecure offices; no charity under the name of reward. Men will be estimated at their real value; nothing will be respected save work and money—the incarnation of labor—but it will have to be earned by the sweat of one's brow, for the *dolce far niente* will be looked upon, in America, as a robbery committed upon society in general.—*Address to King Cotton.*

XXIX. *The American Gold Region.*—The great auriferous region of the United States, in the western portion of the continent, stretches from the 49th degree of north latitude and Puget Sound, to the 30° 30' parallel, and from the 102d degree of longitude west of Greenwich, to the Pacific Ocean; embracing portions of Dacotah, Nebraska, Colorado, all of New Mexico, with Arizona, Utah, Nevada, California, Oregon, and Washington Territories. It may be designated as comprising seventeen degrees of latitude, or a breadth of eleven hundred miles, from north to south, and of nearly equal longitudinal extension; making an area of more than a million of square miles.—*Annual Report of the Commissioner of the Land Office.*

XXX. *Public Debt.*—Persuaded, as the Secretary is, that the proper funding of the present debt will render it a national blessing, yet he is so far from acceding to the position, in the latitude in which it is sometimes laid down, that "public debts are public benefits"—a position inviting to prodigality, and liable to dangerous abuse—that he ardently wishes to see it incorporated as a fundamental maxim, in the system of public credit of the United States, that the creation of debt should always be accompanied with the means of extinguishment. This he regards as the true secret for rendering public credit immortal. And he presumes that it is difficult to conceive a situation in which there may not be an adherence to the maxim.—*Alexander Hamilton, Secretary Treasury,* 1790.

XXXI. No expectation of forbearance or indulgence should be encouraged. Favor and benevolence are not the attributes of good banking. Strict justice and the rigid performance of contracts are its proper foundation.—*Appleton.*

XXXII. *Specie and Paper.*—The essential difference between banking and other commercial business is, that merchants rely, for the fulfilment of their engagements, on their resources, and not on the forbearance of their creditors; while the banks always rely, not only on their resources, but also on the probability that their creditors will not require payment of their demands. We have already seen that this probability is always increased or lessened in proportion as the issues of the banks are moderate or excessive. One of the most efficient modes to reduce the amount of bank notes, as compared to the total amount of the currency of the country, consists in the increase of the metallic currency which circulates amongst the people, independent of that which is kept in reserve in the vaults of the banks.—*Albert Gallatin.*

XXXIII. *Requisites of Bankers.*—A banker should possess a sufficiency of legal knowledge to make him suspect what may be defects in proffered securities, so as to submit his doubts to authorized counsellors. He must, in all things, be eminently practical. Every man can tell an obviously sufficient security and an obviously abundant security, but neither of these constitute any large portion of the loans that are offered to a banker. Security practically sufficient for the occasion is all that a banker can obtain for the greater number of loans he must make. If he must err in his judgment of securities, he had better reject fifty good loans than make one bad debt; but he must endeavor not to err on the extreme of caution or the extreme of temerity; and his tact in these particulars will, more than any other, constitute the criterion of his merits as a banker.—*A. B. Johnson.*

XXXIV. *Directors.*—Directors are, *virtute officii*, something more than irresponsible dummies. They are not, it is true, strictly trustees, in every sense of the word; they are not, for all purposes, like persons in whom property is vested upon specific trusts; but they fill what the law calls a fiduciary character. They are at all times, in the nature of trustees, partaking of their liabilities and participating in their immunities; and they are, as to the application of funds belonging to the company which come into their hands, or which are dealt with by their orders, in general, strictly trustees.

XXXV. *Specie Payments.*—It is, then, believed that the evils which are felt in those sections of the Union where the distress is most general, will not be extensively relieved by the establishment of a national currency. The sufferings which have been produced by the efforts that have been made to resume and to continue specie payments have been great. They are not terminated, and must continue until the value of property and the price of labor shall assume that relation to the precious metals which our wealth and industry, compared with those of other States, shall enable us to retain. Until this shall be effected, an abortive attempt, by the substitution of a paper currency, to arrest the evils we are suffering, will produce the most distressing consequences.—*Wm. H. Crawford, Secretary of the Treasury, Feb.*, 1820.

XXXVI. *Bank Loans.*—If banks were established only in the principal commercial cities of each State; if they were restrained from the issue of notes of small denominations; if they should retain an absolute control over one-half of their capital and the whole of the credit which they employ, by discounting to that amount nothing but transaction paper, payable at short dates, the credit and stability of the banks would at least be unquestionable. Their notes could always be redeemed in specie on demand. The remaining part of their capital might be advanced upon long credits to manufacturers, and even to agriculturists, without the danger of being under the necessity of calling upon such debtors to contribute to their relief, if emergencies should occur.—*Wm. H. Crawford, Secretary Treasury,* 1820.

XXXVII. *Money Saving.*—The saving of money, for the mere sake of it, is but a mean thing, even though earned by honest work; but where earned by dice-throwing, or speculation, and without labor, it is still worse. To provide for others, and for our own comfort and independence in old age, is honorable and greatly to be commended; but to hoard for mere wealth's sake, is the characteristic of the narrow-souled and the miserly. It is against the growth of this habit of inordinate saving, that the wise man needs most carefully to guard himself; else what in youth was simple economy, may, in old age, grow into avarice; and what was a duty in the one, may become a vice in the other.—"*Self-Help,*" *by Smiles.*

XXXVIII. *Money.*—The power of money is, on the whole, overestimated. The greatest things which have been done for the world have not been accomplished by rich men, or by subscription lists;

but by men generally of small means. Christianity was propagated over half the world by men of the poorest class; and the greatest thinkers, discoverers, inventors, and artists, have been men of moderate wealth—many of them little raised above the condition of manual laborers—in point of worldly circumstances. And it will always be so. Riches are oftener an impediment than a stimulus to action; and, in many cases, they are quite as much a misfortune as a blessing.—"*Self-Help*," *by Smiles*.

XXXIX. *Money.*—Money is, with propriety, considered as the vital principle of the body politic; as that which sustains its life and motion, and enables it to perform its most essential functions. A complete power, therefore, to procure a regular and adequate supply of it, as far as the resources of the community will permit, may be regarded as an indispensable ingredient in every Constitution. From a deficiency in this particular, one of two evils must ensue; either the people must be subjected to continual plunder, as a substitute for a more eligible mode of supplying the public wants, or the Government must sink into a fatal atrophy, and, in a short course of time, perish.— *Hamilton, Federalist, December* 28, 1787.

XL. *Social Advancement.*—The multitude is rising from the dust. Once we heard of the few, now of the many; once, of the prerogatives of a part, now of the rights of all. We are looking, as never before, through the disguises, envelopments, of ranks and classes, to the common nature which is below them; and are beginning to learn that every being who partakes of it, has noble powers to cultivate, solemn duties to perform, inalienable rights to assert, a vast destiny to accomplish. The grand idea of humanity, of the importance of man as man, is spreading silently, but surely.—*W. E. Channing.*

XLI. *Statistics.*—Whoever is at all acquainted with what has been done during the last two centuries, must be aware that every generation demonstrates some events to be regular and predictable which the preceding generation had declared to be irregular and unpredictable; so that the marked tendency of advancing civilization is to strengthen our belief in the universality of order, of method, and of law. . . . It becomes, therefore, in the highest degree, important to ascertain whether or not there exists a regularity in the entire moral conduct of a given society; and this is precisely one of those questions for the decision of which statistics supply us with materials of immense value.—*Buckle, History of Civilization.*

XLII. *Paper Money.*—The loss which America has sustained since the peace, from the pestilent effects of paper money on the necessary confidence between man and man, on the necessary confidence in the public councils, on the industry and morals of the people, and on the character of republican Government, constitutes an enormous debt against the States chargeable with this unadvised measure, which must long remain unsatisfied; or rather an accumulation of guilt, which can be expiated no otherwise than by a voluntary sacrifice on the altar of justice of the power which has been the instrument of it.—*Madison, Federalist, January* 25, 1788.

XLIII. *Powers and Duties of Agents.*—An agent who is entrusted with general powers must exercise a sound discretion, and he has all the implied powers which are within the scope of the employment. A power to settle an account, implies the right to allow payments already made. If his powers are special and limited, he must strictly follow them; but whether the authority be special or general, each case includes the usual and appropriate means to accomplish the end. An agent cannot be both buyer and seller, for this would expose his fiduciary trust to abuse and fraud.—*Kent's Commentaries.*

XLIV. *Literary Pursuits of Merchants.*—Biography abounds, in truth, with examples of the union of the pursuits of literature and science with those of every department of active life. The most elegant of the writers of ancient Rome was also the most renowned of her warriors. It was amid the hurry and toils of his campaigns that Julius Cæsar is said to have written those Commentaries, or memoirs of his military exploits, which have immortalized his name more than all his victories, and thus amply justified the anxiety he is recorded to have shown to preserve the work when, being obliged to throw himself from his ship, in the bay of Alexandria, and swim for his life, he made his way to the shore, with his arms in one hand, holding his Commentaries with his teeth.—*Lord Brougham.*

XLV. *Merchants.*—I am wonderfully delighted to see a body of men thriving in their own fortunes, and at the same time promoting the public stock; or, in other words, raising estates for their own families, by bringing into their country whatever is wanting, and carrying out of it whatever is superfluous. Nature seems to have taken a particular care to disseminate her blessings among the different regions of the world with an eye to their mutual intercourse and traffic among mankind, that the nations of the several parts of the globe might have a kind of dependence upon one another, and be united together by their common interest.—*Addison.*

XLVI. *Merchants.*—There are not more useful members in a Commonwealth than merchants. They knit mankind together in a mutual intercourse of good offices; distribute the gifts of nature; find work for the poor, and wealth for the rich; and magnificence for the great. . . . Trade, without enlarging the British territories, has given us a kind of additional empire; it has multiplied the number of the rich; made our landed estates infinitely more valuable than they were formerly; and added to them an accession of other estates as valuable as the estates themselves.—*Addison.*

XLVII. *Frugality.*—It appears evident that frugality is necessary even to complete the pleasure of expense; for it may be generally remarked of those who squander what they know their fortune not sufficient to allow, that, in their most jovial expense, there always breaks out some proof of impatience and discontent; they either scatter with a kind of wild desperation and affected lavishness, as criminals brave the gallows when they cannot escape it, or pay their money with a peevish anxiety, and endeavor at once to spend idly, and to save meanly; having neither firmness to deny their passions nor courage to gratify them, they murmur at their own enjoyments, and poison the bowl of pleasure by reflection on the cost.—*Johnson.*

XLVIII. *Circumspection.*—Men with a multiplicity of transactions pressing on them, and moving in a narrow circle, and meeting each other daily, desire to write little, and leave unwritten *what they take for granted* in every contract. In spite of the lamentations of judges they will continue to do so; and, in a vast majority of cases, of which courts of law hear nothing, they do so without loss or inconvenience; and, upon the whole, they find this mode of dealing advantageous, even at the risk of occasional litigation.—*Lord Campbell.*

XLIX. *Payment of Debts.*—Paying of debt is, next to the grace of God, the best means in the world to deliver you from a thousand temptations to sin and vanity. Pay your debts, and you will not have wherewithal to buy a costly toy or a pernicious pleasure. Pay your debts, and you will not have what to lose to a gamester. In short, pay your debts, and you will, of necessity, abstain from many indulgences that war against the spirit, and bring you into captivity to sin, and cannot fail to end in your utter destruction, both of soul and body.—*Delany.*

L. *Wealth.*—In the wealth of mankind, nothing is included which does not of itself answer some purpose of utility or pleasure. To an individual anything is wealth which, though useless in itself, enables him to claim from others a part of their stock of things, useful or pleasant. Take, for instance, a mortgage of a thousand pounds on a landed estate; this is wealth to the person to whom it brings in a revenue, and who could, perhaps, sell it in the market for the full amount of the debt. But it is not wealth to the country; if the engagement were annulled, the country would be neither richer nor poorer; the mortgagor would have lost a thousand pounds, and the owner of the land would have gained it.—*J. Stuart Mill.*

A CHAPTER ON YOUNG MEN.

Alexander, of Macedon, extended his power over Greece, conquered Egypt, rebuilt Alexandria and overrun all Asia, and died at 33 years of age.

Hannibal was but 26, when, after the fall of his father, Hamilcar, in Spain, and Asdrubal, his successor, he was chosen commander-in-chief by the Carthagenian army. At 27, he captured Saguntum from the Romans; before he was 34 he carried his arms from Africa into Italy, conquered Publius Scipio on the banks of the Ticinus; routed Sempronius near the Trebia; defeated Flaminius on his approaches to the Apennines; laid waste the whole country; defeated Fabius Maximus and Varro, marched into Capua, and at the age of 36 was thundering at the gates of Rome.

Scipio Africanus was scarcely 16 when he took an active part in the battle of Cannæ, and saved the life of his father. The wreck of the Roman cavalry chose him then for their leader, and he conducted them back to the capital. Soon after he was 20, he was appointed pro-consul of Spain, where he took New Carthage by storm. He soon after, successfully, defeated Asdrubal, Hannibal's brother, Mago and Hann; crossed into Africa, negotiated with Syphax, the Massasylian king, returned to Spain, quelled insurrections, drove the Carthagenians wholly from the peninsula, returned to Rome, devised the diversion against the Carthagenians by carrying the war into Africa; was appointed pro-consul of Africa, crossed thither, destroyed the army of Syphax, compelled the return of Hannibal and defeated Asdrubal a second time. All this was done before he was 31.

Charlemagne was crowned king of the Franks before he was 26. At 28 he had conquered Aquitania, and at 29 he had made himself master of the whole German and French empires.

Charles XII., of Sweden, was declared of age by the states and succeeded his father at 15. At 18 he headed the expedition against the Danes, whom he checked, and with a fourth of their numbers, he cut the Russian army to pieces commanded by the czar, Peter, at Narva—crossed the Dwina, gained a victory over the Saxons, and carried his arms into Poland. At 21 he had conquered Poland and dictated to her a new sovereign. At 24 he had subdued Saxony;

and at 27 he was conducting his victorious troops into the heart of Russia, when a severe wound prevented his taking command in person, and resulted in his overthrow and subsequent treacherous captivity in Turkey.

Lafayette was a major-general in the American army at 19 ; was but 20 when he was wounded at Brandywine ; but 22 when he raised supplies for his army, on his own credit at Baltimore ; was but 23 when he stormed the redoubt at Yorktown ; and was but 32 when the French revolution raised him to the office of commander-in-chief of the national guards.

Napoleon Bonaparte commenced his military career as an officer of artillery at 17. He successfully commanded the artillery at the siege of Toulon at 24. His splendid and victorious campaign in Italy was performed at the age of 27. The following year, when he was but 28, he gained battle after battle over the Austrians in Italy, conquered Mantua, carried the war into Austria, ravaged the Tyrol, concluded an advantageous peace, took possession of Milan and the Venitian republic, revolutionized Genoa, and formed the Cisalpine republic. At 29 he received the command of the army against Egypt; scattered the clouds of Mameluke cavalry ; mastered Alexandria, Aboukir and Cairo, and wrested the land of the Pharoahs and Ptolemies from the proud descendants of the prophet. At 30 he fell among the Parisians like a thunderbolt, overthrew the directoral government ; dispersed the council of five hundred, and was proclaimed first consul. At 31 he crossed the Alps with an army and destroyed the Austrians by a blow at Marengo. At 32 he established the Code Napoleon ; in the same year he was elected consul for life by the people ; and at the age of 34 he was crowned emperor of the French nation.

Papinian, who was the greatest lawyer Rome ever produced, was put to death by Carracella at the age of 36. He had even at that early age composed more than fifty books on legal subjects. So profoundly learned were his views considered, that Valentinian III. ordered that whenever the judges were divided in opinion, that Papinian's should be followed. In fact he was the great oracle of the Roman law before he arrived at the age of 34.

William Pitt, the first earl of Chatham, was but 27, when, as a member of parliament, he waged the war of a giant against the corruptions of Sir Robert Walpole.

The younger *Pitt* was scarcely turned of 20 when, with masterly power he grappled with the veterans of parliament, in favor of America. At 22 he was called to the high and responsible trust of chancellor of the exchequer. At 24 he was appointed first lord of the treasury and chancellor of the exchequer. It was at that age when he came forth in his might on the affairs of the East Indies. At the age of 29, during the first insanity of George III., he rallied around the Prince of Wales.

Edmund Burke, at the age of 19, planned a refutation of the metaphysical theories of Berkley and Hume. At 20 he was in the temple, the admiration of its inmates, for the brilliancy of his genius and the variety of his acquisitions. At 26 he published his celebrated satire, entitled " A Vindication of Natural Society." The same year he published his essay on the sublime and beautiful—so much admired for its spirit of philosophical investigation, and the elegance of its language. At 25 he was first lord of the treasury.

George Washington was only 27 when he covered the retreat of the British troops at Braddock's defeat ; and the same year was appointed commander-in-chief of all the Virginia forces.

General *Joseph Warren* was only 29 when, in defiance of the British soldiery stationed at the door of the church, he pronounced the celebrated oration which aroused the spirit of liberty and patriotism that terminated in the achievement of independence. At 34 he gloriously fell gallantly fighting in the cause of freedom, on Bunker's Hill.

Alexander Hamilton was a lieutenant-colonel in the army of the American revolution, and aid-de-camp to Washington at the age of 20. At 25 he was a member of congress from New York ; at 30 he was one of the ablest members of the convention that formed the constitution of the United States. At 31 he was a member of the New York convention, and joint author of the great work entitled "The Federalist." At 32 he was secretary of the treasury of the United States, and arranged the financial branch of the government upon so perfect a plan, that no great improvement has ever been made upon it by his successors.

Thomas Heyward, of South Carolina, was but 30 years of age, when he signed the glorious record of the nation's birth—the Declaration of Independence ;—*Elbridge Gerry*, of Massachusetts, *Benjamin Rush* and *James Wilson*, of Pennsylvania, but 31 ; *Matthew Thornton*, of New Hampshire, 32 ; *Thomas Jefferson*, of Virginia, *Arthur Middleton*, of North Carolina, and *Thomas Stone*, of Maryland, 33 ; and *William Hooper*, of North Carolina, but 34.

Thomas Jefferson, at 26, was a leading member of the colonial legislature in Virginia. At 30 he was a member of the Virginia convention ; at 32 a member of congress ; and at 33 years of age he drafted the Declaration of Independence.

John Jay, at 29, was a member of the old revolutionary congress, and being associated with *Lee* and *Livingston* on the committee for drafting an address to the people of Great Britain, drew up that paper himself, which was considered one of the most eloquent productions of the time. At 32 he penned the old constitution of New York, and in the same year was appointed chief justice of that state. At 34 he was appointed minister to Spain.

Fisher Ames was highly esteemed as a public man in his own state at the age of 30 ; at which age he was chosen as member of congress from the Suffolk district, Massachusetts ; and before he was 34, held the assembled statesmen of the nation breathless by his eloquence.

Milton, at 26, had written his finest miscellaneous poems, including his L'Allegro, Penseroso, and Comus.

Lord *Byron* at the age of 20 published his celebrated satire upon the English bards and Scotch reviewers; at 24 the two first cantos of Childe Harold's Pilgrimage. Indeed, all the vast poetic treasures of his genius were poured forth in their richest profusion before he was 34 years old : and he died at 37.

Mozart, the great German musician, completed all his noble compositions before he was 34, and died at 35.

Raphael, the illustrious painter, by his incomparable works, had acquired the appellation of the "divine Raphael" long before he arrived at the age of 30.

Pope wrote many of his published poems by the time he was 16 ; at 20 his Essay on Criticism; at 24 the Rape of the Lock, and at 25 his great work, the translation of the Iliad.

Sir *Isaac Newton* had mastered the highest elements of the mathematics, and the analytical method of Descartes before he was 20 ; had discovered the new method of infinite series of fluctions, and his new theory of light and colors. At 25 he had discovered the principles of the reflecting telescope, the laws of gravitation, and the planetary system. At 30 he occupied the mathematical chair at Cambridge.

Dr. *Dwight's* Conquest of Canaan was commenced at 19, and finished at 22. At the latter age he composed his celebrated dissertation on the history, eloquence and poetry of the Bible, which was immediately published and republished in Europe.

Henry Clay was a member of the Senate, and speaker of the House of Representatives, before he was 33.

Oliver Hazard Perry was but 27 when he achieved the victory of Lake Erie.

A MAGIC SQUARE OF SQUARES.

From the "*Young Folks*," published by Ticknor & Fields, Boston.

1	27	14	57	80	67	20	52	42
75	71	58	47	43	33	19	18	5
38	34	51	10	9	23	66	62	76
25	15	2	81	68	55	53	40	30
72	59	73	44	31	48	16	6	20
35	49	39	7	24	11	63	77	64
13	3	26	69	56	79	41	28	54
60	74	70	32	46	45	4	21	17
50	37	36	22	12	8	78	65	61

The above square contains the numbers from 1 to 81 inclusive, and has the following properties:

1. The sum of any row of nine numbers, vertical, horizontal, or diagonal, is 369.

2. The sum of any nine numbers forming a square, wherever taken, is 369.

3. If the four corner numbers (1, 42, 50, 61), the middle numbers of the four outside rows (80, 72, 20, 12), and the central number (31) be added together, their sum will be 369.

4. The sum of the nine numbers similarly situated in any square formed by twenty-five or forty-nine numbers is 369. [For instance, 71, 74, 13, 21, 43, 46, 59, 6, and 31.]

One or more vertical rows may be transferred from the left to the right, or from the right to the left, or one or more horizontal rows from the top to the bottom, or from the bottom to the top, and the properties of the square be unchanged.

Curiosities of Numbers.—When the number 9 is multiplied by any other number, the digits of the product when added together will always be 9 or a multiple of 9. Thus 9 multiplied by 2 equals 18; and 1 and 8 make 9. Nine by 11 equals 99. Nine by 14 equals 126; and 1, 2, and 6 make 9.

Another singular fact is, that if any number be taken, its digits reversed in order, and the new number subtracted from the other, the remainder will be 9 or a multiple of 9, and the sum of its digits will be 9 or a multiple of 9. Thus 63 minus 36 equals 27; which is thrice 9, and 2 plus 7 equals 9.

The same property is found in the squares, cubes, etc., of any numbers thus transferred. Thus the square of 63 is 3,969, and that of 36 is 1,296. Subtracting the latter, the remainder is 2,673, a multiple of 9, and the sum of its digits is twice 9.

DECISIONS OF THE SUPREME JUDICIAL COURT OF MASSACHUSETTS.

I. Cashier, &c. — II. Promissory Notes and Bills of Exchange. — III Bank Notes. — IV. Notaries Public. — V. Stockholders, &c. — VI. Banks Banking, &c.

I. CASHIER, ETC.

General Authority. — The authority of officers of banks is restricted to such modes of binding the company as result from the nature of their duty and the powers vested in them by their offices. The property of stockholders is not bound by their irregular transactions, or by the declarations or confessions of their officers, beyond the legal sphere of their action. *Wyman* v. *Hallowell, &c., Bank,* 14 Mass. 62. 17 Mass. 29.

Bond. — Where a statute prohibited any bank from issuing bills payable at any place except at the bank, and a cashier, on receiving bills not proved to have been issued after the statute was passed, (which had been taken up and paid by another bank, at which they were made payable,) put them again into circulation for his own use; it was *held* to be a breach of his bond given for the faithful performance of his duty, for which his sureties were liable. *Dedham Bank* v. *Chickering,* 4 Pick.

Aliter, where he embezzled new bills, made by consent of the directors, and intended to be privately kept and surreptitiously issued by him, after the statute was passed, and in direct violation of it, such bills not being intended to make part of the ostensible funds of the bank, and not being entered on its books, nor noticed in the half-yearly returns to the governor and council. *Ib.* 314.

Nor are a cashier's sureties liable on his bond for his not accounting to the bank for their money collected by him as an attorney at law. *Ib.*

Nor for his surreptitiously conveying his shares in the bank to a third person by means of blank certificates signed by the president and deposited in the cashier's hands, though he had previously pledged the shares to the bank as security for the payment of his notes. *Ib.*

But, in such case, the bank may apply, towards payment of the cashier's notes, a balance standing on its books in his favor, instead of applying it for the sureties' benefit, in reducing damages for breach of the bond. *Ib.*

Bond. — Where a board of directors, by a vote, approved of two persons as sureties in a bond to be given by the cashier, and a bond, duly executed by them and the cashier, was afterwards found in the possession of the president, it was *held,* that there was a sufficient acceptance thereof by the corporation. *Dedham Bank* v. *Chickering,* 3 Pick 335 S. P 1 Har. & Gill, *ubi sup.*

Bond. — Where a cashier, before his re-appointment to office, had misapplied the funds of the bank, and, after his re-appointment, borrowed money, as cashier, and placed it in the bank, to conceal his delinquency, and afterwards returned the money so borrowed, and was dismissed as a defaulter, it was *held* that the sureties on his last bond were answerable; as the money that he so placed in the bank became the property of the bank, and his subsequent conduct was a breach of the condition of that bond. *Ingraham* v. *Maine Bank*, 13 Mass. 208.

Endorsement. — Where a note endorsed by the payee to a bank of which P. H. F. was the cashier, was again endorsed as follows: "P. H. F., cashier," it was *held*, that such second endorsement was sufficient. And *it seems*, that in an action upon such note, by the second endorsee against the payee, if the second endorsement is not sufficiently certain, the plaintiffs may, at the trial, prefix the name of the bank to such endorsement. *Folger* v. *Chase*, Pickering's Mass. Reports, 63.

An endorsement written on a slip of paper, which was attached to the back of a note by a wafer, for the purpose of writing receipts of partial payments thereon, there not being room on the back of the note, was *held* to be sufficient; the endorsement having been made after several of such receipts had been written on such attached paper. *Ib.*

Appointment. — Where, by the charter of a bank, the directors were to be chosen annually, and they, "for the time being, have power to appoint a cashier, and such other officers under them, as may be necessary for executing the business of said corporation," a cashier so appointed is an officer of the corporation, the duration of whose office, in the absence of an express limitation, is limited only by the duration of the charter; but he is liable to be removed by the directors as occasion may require, and is not necessarily an annual officer. *Union Bank of Maryland* v. *Ridgely*, 1 Har. & Gill, 324. S. P. *Dedham Bank* v. *Chickering*, 3 Pick. 341.

Act of President. — The president of a bank may transfer, by his endorsement, a note made, &c., to the corporation, if he has a general authority for that purpose from the directors; and the seal of the corporation need not be affixed to the transfer, nor a particular vote therefor be passed on the subject. *Spear* v. *Ladd*, 11 Mass. 94. *Northampton Bank* v. *Pepoon*, 11 Mass. 288.

Transfer of Securities. — The cashier of a bank cannot assign notes belonging to it, unless authorized by the bank, or by the directors, pursuant to powers vested in them. *Hartford Bank* v. *Barry*, 17 Mass. 94.

But his endorsement of such notes would authorize the holders to deliver them to the makers or endorsers who should pay them; and payment to the holders would be a discharge. *Ib*

I. PROMISSORY NOTES AND BILLS OF EXCHANGE.

Memorandum Check. — A bona fide holder of a memorandum check, (a check not addressed to any particular bank or person,) payable to bearer, may maintain an action on it against the drawer, in his own name, though it came into his hands five years after its date. *Ellis v. Wheeler*, 3 Pick. 18.

But the burden of proof, in case of a check of this kind, is on the holder; and he cannot recover on it without proof that he obtained it fairly and for a valuable consideration. *Ball v. Allen*, 15 Mass. 433.

Joint Note. — Where a joint and several promissory note was executed and left in the hands of M., one of the promisors, to be delivered to the payee, when it should be demanded by him, in exchange for a note for the same amount, but of a previous date, and signed by M. alone, and no demand was made therefor by the payee before the death of M., it was *held*, that the new note did not operate *de facto* as a payment of the old note, that the property in such new note had not vested in the payee, and that he could not recover the possession of it from the administrator of M., it being presumed that the interest which had accrued upon the old note was to be paid upon making the exchange. *Canfield v. Ives.* Pickering's Mass. Reports, 253.

Note on Demand. — In the case of a note endorsed after it has become due, the endorser is not liable unless payment be demanded of the maker and notice of the non-payment given to the endorser; and as such a note has become payable on demand, the demand on the maker must be made within a reasonable time, and immediate notice of non-payment given to the endorser. *Colt v. Barnard*, ib. 260.

Void Notes. — A promissory note given for compounding a public prosecution for a misdemeanor, is founded upon an illegal consideration. *Jones v. Rice*, ib. 440.

Drawer of Bill. — The drawer of a bill of exchange having no effects in the hands of the acceptor from the time when the bill was drawn to the time when it became due, was held liable without proof of demand and notice of non-payment. *Kinsley v. Robinson*, Pickering's Reports, 327.

In an action by the endorsee against the drawer of a bill of exchange, the acceptor is a competent witness to prove that he has not had in his hands any funds of the drawer. *Ib.*

Foreign Law. — In an action against the endorser of a promissory note of hand, made in Illinois, the plaintiff must prove that judgment has been recovered against the original promisor, and remains unsatisfied.

" We think the law of Illinois is to govern in this case. This provision, respecting the liability of endorsers goes not to the remedy merely, but to the substance of the contract and is a part of it; and it makes no difference that the note in the present case is payable generally to order. There being no evidence that the plaintiff has complied with the law of Illinois, the default which was entered, must be set aside, and the cause stand for trial."

Mutilation. — Where a promissory note has been mutilated of its signature, if the facts shown explain the mutilation, it is not necessary, in Massachusetts, that the party suing on it should first apply to a court of equity for a complete instrument. *Spencer* v. *Bemis,* Mass. Court of Common Pleas.

Delivery. — A negotiable note, payable to order, is transferable by delivery merely, so that the party receiving it may be authorized to demand payment of it and deliver it up to the maker, though it is unendorsed. *Ib.*

Title. — Possession of a negotiable note is *prima facie* evidence of title and ownership in the holder. Therefore, where the makers of a note, payable to order, took it up in good faith from a party presenting it for payment, the note bearing on it an endorsement alleged to be forged, it was *held,* on the question of rightful payment by the makers, that the party presenting it was to be presumed to have authority to receive payment for it and deliver it up; and that proof of forgery of the endorsement would not be conclusive against his right to bind the payee by his acts.

Lost Notes. — If a negotiable promissory note be stolen or lost, and paid by the makers in good faith on a forged endorsement, *it seems* that a delay of eighteen months and upwards by the payee to notify the makers of his loss, (it not being shown when he first discovered it,) is not such absolute evidence of negligence on his part, as to prevent his recovering the value of the note from the makers. *Ib.*

Foreign Law. — When the drawee of a bill of exchange, who resides in New York, writes a letter there to the drawer, who resides in this state, accepting the bill, which was drawn in this state, the contract of acceptance is made in New York, and is governed by the law of that state; and the bill must be presented there to the acceptor for payment. *Worcester Bank* v. *Wells,* 8 Metcalf's Massachusetts Reports, p. 107.

By the law of New York, an acceptance of a bill of exchange, " written on a paper other than the bill, shall not bind the acceptor, except in favor of a person to whom such acceptance shall have been shown, and who, on the faith thereof, shall have received the bill for a valuable consideration." A. drew a bill on B., in New York, and procured it to be discounted at a bank: B. afterwards wrote a letter to A., accepting the bill, and A. exhibited the letter to the officers of the bank. *Held,* that the bank could not maintain an action against B. on his acceptance. *Ib.*

A promise to accept a bill of exchange is a chose in action, on which no one beside the immediate promisee can maintain a suit in his own name. *Ib.*

Genuineness. — To prove forgery of a party's hand-writing, other specimens of it, though not belonging to the case, or admitted to be genuine, may be introduced in evidence on collateral proof of their genuineness. *Ishi Spencer* v. *Seth Bemis et al,* Mass. Reports Common Pleas, 1815.

Damages. — An acceptor of a bill of exchange is not liable to the payee or endorsee for damages caused by non-payment, but only for the amount of the bill, with interest and costs of protest. *Bowen* v. *Stoddard,* 10 Metcalf, 375.

Foreign Law. — The statute of Maine, which enacts that, in an action on a bill of exchange drawn or endorsed in that state, payable in this state, and protested for non-payment, the holder shall recover three per cent. damages, in addition to the contents of the bill and interest, does not entitle the holder to recover those damages in a suit brought against the acceptor in the courts of this state. *Fiske* v. *Foster,* ib. 597.

Usury. — The Bank of Orleans, at Albion, in the State of New York, discounted a bill of exchange, deducting a little less than legal interest for the time it had to run, and gave the holder, at his request and for his accommodation, a draft payable in its own bills, on a bank at Albany, where by law it was required to redeem them at a discount not exceeding one half of one per cent.; and the holder received those bills at par. The bank at Albany was the agent of the Bank of Orleans for the redemption of its bills, and paid the holder of the discounted bill in the paper of the latter bank, which then passed current at par: and that bank paid to the bank at Albany the amount of said draft in full. *Held,* that these facts did not prove that the bill was discounted on an usurious consideration or agreement. "To constitute usury, within the prohibitions of the law, there must be an intention knowingly to contract for or take usurious interest; for if neither party intend it, but act *bona fide* and innocently, the law will not infer a corrupt agreement." *Bank of Orleans* v. *John Curtis and others,* 11 Metcalf, 359.

Usury. — A. gave a note to B., on demand, and B., at the expiration of a year, computed the interest thereon at nine per cent., and took from A. a new note for the principal sum and for the interest so computed. Nineteen months afterwards, B. computed the interest on the second note, at ten per cent. per annum, and added compound interest, and A. gave him a new note for a sum which included the principal of the second note, and the interest thereon, so computed, and also, another sum which was justly due from him to B. *Held,* in a suit on this last note, that by the Revised Statutes, c. 35, the plaintiff, on proof of the usurious contract, was entitled to recover the amount of the note, with interest thereon, deducting therefrom three-fold the amount of the interest, compound as well as simple, computed on the first two notes, and of the interest which had accrued on the note in suit. *Upham* v. *Brimhall*, ib. 526.

Interest. — A promissory note, for the payment, "ten years after date," of "seven hundred and fifty dollars, with interest semi-annually, fifty dollars of the principal to be paid annually until the whole is paid," is a contract that the interest shall be paid semi-annually, that fifty dollars of the principal shall be paid annually, and that the whole amount of the note, principal and interest, shall be paid in ten years after date. *Emer* v. *Myrick*, 1 Cushing, 16.

The promisee, by an agreement under seal, executed on the same day with the note, covenanted with the promisor, that "if said note should not be paid at the expiration of the said ten years," he would "give up said note" to the promisor, provided the latter should execute to him a quit-claim deed of certain land mentioned in the agreement. It was held, that this agreement (assuming that the note and agreement constituted an entire transaction, which the court did not decide) did not preclude the promisee from enforcing payment of the interest, and such instalments as should become due, before the expiration of the ten years. *Ib.*

Dissolution. — B. H., after the dissolution of a partnership between himself and S. W., made a negotiable promissory note, in the name of the late firm of W. & H., payable to S. W. and S. F. as partners under the firm of W. and F.; and, after a dissolution of the last-named firm, and the death of S. W., S. F., in the name of W. and F., indorsed the note to himself: — it was *held*, that S. F., could not maintain an action on the note, as indorsee; but that as surviving promisee he was entitled to recover, on the money counts, against B. H., either as surviving promisor, if the note had been subsequently ratified by S. W., or as sole promisor, if it had not been so ratified. *Fowle* v. *Harrington, Ib.* 146.

Consideration. — A promise to forbear, for six months, to sue a third person, on a just cause of action, is a valid and sufficient consideration for a promissory note. *Jennison* v. *Stafford, ib.* 168.

Forbearance. — In a suit, by the payee against the maker, on a promissory note, given in consideration of a promise to forbear to sue a third person for six months, the burden of proof is not on the payee, to show that he has forborne according to his promise, but on the maker, to show that he has not. *Ib.*

Title. — Where the payee of a negotiable promissory note, for the purpose of indemnifying one who had become his surety for the payment of the fees and expenses attending the institution of proceedings in insolvency, negotiated and transferred the note to the surety, before the commencement of such proceedings, it was *held*, that, in the absence of fraud, the maker of the note could not set up in defence the title of payee's assignee, and that it was immaterial whether the note was endorsed by the payee before or after his insolvency. *Fogg* v. *Willcutt, ib.* 300.

Letter of Credit. — Mills & Co., of Boston, wrote letters to B., in New Orleans, as follows: " 1. You may have opportunities to make advances on cotton shipped to this port, and we should be willing to accept against shipments to us, the necessary papers accompanying the bills, for such sums as in your judgment may be safely advanced. 2. We do not want cotton under limits. Your advances ought not to exceed three quarters the value. Under these restrictions, you may go on, and your bills shall be duly honored, accompanied by bills of lading and orders for insurance." B. showed these letters to C., and sold to him bills drawn on M. & Co., in favor of C.'s principals, and paid, with the money received from C., for cotton, which he shipped to M. & Co., in his own name. No bills of lading nor orders for insurance accompanied these bills, and M. & Co. refused to accept or pay them. *Held*, in suits by the payees against M. & Co., as acceptors of the bills under their promise to accept and pay them, *that they were not liable ;* that B.'s authority was limited and special, and that he had exceeded it by drawing the bills without accompanying them with bills of lading and orders for insurance ; and that C., the payee's agent, knowing the contents of M. & Co.'s letters to B., took the bills on his personal confidence in B., and not on the obligation of M. & Co. to honor them. When merchants in Boston authorize an agent to make advances on cotton at New Orleans, to be shipped to them for sale at Boston, and promise to accept bills drawn on them to an amount not exceeding three fourths of the value of the cotton, the value at New Orleans is intended ; and therefore, in a question as to the amount for which the agent is authorized to draw, evidence of the value of cotton at Boston is not admissible. *Murdoch & Coolidge* v. *Mills*, Metcalf, Sup. Jud. Court Reports, vol. xi

III. — BANK NOTES.

Redemption in Coin. — Under the act establishing the Chenango Bank, which imposes a penalty of 14 per cent. until tender, for refusing payment of its notes, it was held that payment must be made within a reasonable time after demand, according to circumstances ; that a sum of ordinary magnitude should be paid at least during the day of demand ; that the officers must employ themselves diligently. in paying, in the order of time that demands are made ; that the bank cannot, at its option, pay in small pieces when it has large in its vault, thus causing delay; that it should keep money counted out, or servants sufficient to count it out in a reasonable time, and that unreasonable delay was refusal to pay, and subjected the bank to said penalty. *Hubbard v. Chenango Bank*, 8 Cow. 88. See 3 Mason, 1.

Void Notes. — Before the passing of the Massachusetts statute of 1816, chapter 91, there was nothing in the charters of the banks of that state which prohibited them from issuing drafts on a bank in another state, where they had funds deposited, for small sums, with the intention of their being circulated as bank bills. *King v. Dedham Bank*, 15 Mass. 447. See *Post*, 63.

Re-charter. — Where a new bank was incorporated with the same name as the old one, whose charter was expiring, the new bank was held not to be responsible for the notes of the old, though a major part of the stockholders were the same in each. *Bellows v. Hollowell, &c. Bank*, 2 Mason, 31. See also 14 Mass. 58.

Illegal Issues. — The statute of 1816, c. 91, sect. 2, so far as it enacted that every bank, which *had issued* any bill, &c., payable at any other place than where the bank was established by law and kept, should be liable to pay the same on demand at said bank, without a previous demand at the place where it might, on its face, be made payable, was inoperative, and not binding on the parties to such bills, &c., nor on the courts. *King v. Dedham Bank*, 15 Mass. 447. See *Ante*, 38.

Hence, if a banking company, incorporated by the same name of a former one, appoint the same president and cashier, and the officers receive and issue the notes of the former company, and declare that there is no difference between the notes thus issued and those of the new company, the new company, never having authorized these proceedings, are not liable to pay such notes. 14 Mass. 62. See also *Bellows v. Hallowell, &c., Bank*, 2 Mason, 31.

Forged Signatures. — Where a bank paid notes on which the president's name was forged, and did not return them till fifteen days afterwards, it was *held* that it had lost its remedy against the person from whom the notes were received. *Gloucester Bank v. Salem Bank*, 17 Mass. 33.

Stolen Notes. — Where the bills of a bank, after being prepared by the cashier for the president's signature, were stolen, and a forged signature of the president added, the bank was held not to be liable to pay a *bona fide* holder, on the ground that the cashier had declared them to be genuine, nor by reason of the negligence of the directors in so keeping the paper prepared for signature. *Salem Bank v. Gloucester Bank, ib.*

Payment in Coin. — The holder of bank bills is entitled to be paid in specie upon demand made on the bank, within the usual banking hours; and he is not obliged to take foreign gold and silver at the bank count but the payment must be by weight. *Suffolk Bank* v. *Lincoln Bank*, 3 Mason, 1.

Where one bank holds the bills of another, and demands payment, it is not obliged to receive its own bills in payment, at the other's banking-house. *Ib.*

IV. — NOTARIES PUBLIC.

Presentment for Payment. — If a note is made payable at a bank, there is no default of payment on the part of the maker until the close of the usual banking-hours, on the last day of grace, at such bank. If no particular bank is named, the hour will be determined by the usual banking hours of the bank, or several banks, in the place where the note is payable. *Chase* v. *Clark*, 21 Pickering, 310.

Notice to Administrator. — Where the administrator of an endorser of a promissory note had been appointed to that office before the maturity of the note, and had given due notice of the appointment, it was *held*, that he was entitled to the same notice of the non-payment of the note, as is required by law to be given to an endorser. *Oriental Bank* v. *Blake*, 22 Pickering, 24.

Demand. — Where a note is payable on demand at a specified bank, no demand need be made at any other place, and in an action against an endorser, it will be presumed, in the absence of evidence to the contrary, that the note was at the bank, and that some officer of the bank was in attendance to receive payment. *Folger* v. *Chase*, 18 Pickering's Reports, 63.

It is a sufficient demand and refusal to constitute a dishonor of a note, if the maker, on the day it is due, calls on the holder at his place of business, where the note is, and declares that he is unable to pay it, and shall not pay it, and desires the holder to give notice to the endorser 3 Metcalf, 495.

Notice. — A notice given to the endorser of a note, in the forenoon of the day on which it becomes due, merely stating that the person giving notice holds the note, and that it is due and unpaid, and demanding payment, is not sufficient to charge the endorser. *Ib.*

Notice Insufficient. — A notice to the endorser of a note, which merely states that the note remains unpaid, and that the holders look to him for payment, is not sufficient to charge the endorser, although such notice is given by a notary public. 9 Metcalf, 174.

V. — STOCKHOLDERS, RIGHTS OF, ETC.

Liability for Issues. — An act incorporating a banking company provided that if the corporation should refuse or neglect to pay their bills on demand, "the original stockholders, their successors, assigns, and the members of the corporation," should, in their private capacities, be liable to the holder. *Held,* that such only of the original stockholders, their successors, &c., as were members of the corporation at the time payment was refused, were liable. *Bond* v. *Appleton,* 8 Mass. 472.

Subscription to Stock. — A stockholder in a bank that is authorized to commence business with one amount of stock, and to increase the amount afterwards, is entitled to subscribe for and hold the additional stock, in proportion to his original shares; and the bank is liable to him, if its officers, or the corporation, refuse to allow him thus to subscribe therefor; and the measure of damages will be the excess of the market value above the par value of the number of shares to which he was entitled, with interest on such excess. *Gray* v. *Portland Bank,* 3 Mass. 364.

Sale of Pledged Stock. — A stockholder of a bank transfers his shares to the corporation by a writing absolute in form, and surrenders his certificate of stock, and at the same time leaves with the cashier an agreement, in which, after reciting that he had transferred the shares as collateral security for the payment of a certain note to the bank, he covenants that if the note shall not be duly paid, the bank may sell the shares and apply the proceeds to the payment of the note, and hold the surplus to his use; he pays interest from time to time upon the note after it had fallen due, and continues to receive the dividends upon the shares. *Held,* that he is still a member of the corporation. *Merchants Bank* v. *Cook,* 4 Pick. 405.

Collateral Shares. — A subscriber for 90 bank shares, of $100 each, paid $2,750 towards an instalment of 80 per cent., and drew a draft in favor of the bank for the balance, and transferred to the bank all his right, &c., in his shares, (excepting and reserving the sum he had paid in money,) as collateral security for payment of the draft. The draft was not paid, nor did the bank pass to the subscriber's credit any stock, nor give him any certificate for shares. *Held,* that the subscriber was once an owner of the shares, and that the effect of the reservation in his conveyance to the bank was, that an amount equal to 34 shares, of the par value of $80 a share, remained his property, and was liable to be sold on an execution against him. *Hussey* v. *M. and M. Bank.* 10 Pick. 415.

The application, by the bank, of the $2,750 to an account of the subscriber, which was independent of the shares, was held to be unauthorized, and not to affect his title to the shares. *Ib.*

Liability for Deficiency. — If stockholders, while their charter is in force and their bills in free circulation, should divide and withdraw their capital, so that their debts could not be paid, they would be liable to the person thereby injured. Per Jackson, J. 15 Mass. 519. Bu where the capital stock of a bank was divided, after its charter had expired, so that funds were not left to pay its debts, it was *held* that an action would not lie against an individual stockholder, who had received his proportion of the dividends. *Vose* v. *Grant*, 15 Mass. 505. *Spear* v *Grant*, 16 Mass. 9.

Action for Fraud. — A stockholder may sustain a bill in equity against the corporation, the directors, and other stockholders, on allegation of fraudulent practices, depreciating the value of the stock, suspending banking operations, refusing cash payments, and withholding dividends; and in such bill, he may join individual stockholders with the corporation, may pray for an account of stock and funds, and for restoration of whatever has been fraudulently withdrawn from the common stock. *Taylor* v. *Miami Exporting Co*, 5 Ham. 165. See 15 Mass. 522.

Liability for Circulation. — Where a bank divided among its stockholders three fourths of its capital stock, before its charter expired, and did not provide funds adequate to meet its outstanding notes, it was *held* that a bill in equity might be maintained by *some* of the holders of the notes against *some* of the stockholders, the impossibility of bringing *all* before the court being sufficient to dispense with the ordinary rule of making all parties in interest parties to the suit. *Wood* v. *Dummer*, 3 Mason, 308.

The decree, in such case, against the stockholders before the court, should be only for their contributory share of the debt, in the proportion which their stock bore to the whole. *Ib.*

Where the charter of a bank makes a stockholder personally liable, an action of debt lies against him by the holder of a dishonored bank note. *Bullard* v. *Bell*, 1 Mason, 243.

VI. — BANKS, BANKING, FAILURE, LIQUIDATION, ETC.

Assignment of Securities. — The Massachusetts statute of 1812, c. 57, which prohibited banks, after the expiration of their charters, from issuing or putting into circulation any securities for money, did not extend to the assignment of a note for the purpose of paying a debt owed by the bank before the charter expired; no new obligation being contracted by the bank. *Hallowell, &c. Bank* v. *Hamlin*, 14 Mass. 178.

Penalty for Suspension. — The statute of 1809, c. 38, imposing (prospectively) a penalty of two per cent. a month on the amount of bank notes, which the bank issuing them should refuse or neglect to pay on demand, was held to be constitutional and valid. *Brown* v. *Penobscot Bank*, 8 Mass. 415.

Capital. — A bank incorporated with the privilege of creating a stock not less than one sum, nor greater than another, may commence business with the smaller capital and afterwards increase it to the larger Grey v. *Portland Bank*, 3 Mass. 364.

Special Deposits. — Where gold coins, deposited in a bank for safekeeping, are fraudulently taken away by the cashier, the bank is not answerable to the owner, unless gross negligence is proved. *Foster v. Essex Bank*, 17 Mass. 459.

Where the officers of a bank have been in the practice of receiving money and other things to be deposited in its vault for safe-keeping, the corporation, and not the officers, will be considered as the depositary. *Ib.*

Uncurrent Notes. — A bank that is prohibited, by its charter, from vesting, using, or improving any of its moneys, goods, &c., in trade or commerce, may nevertheless lawfully take notes payable in bills of other banks, and receive such bills at a discount in payment for their notes. *Portland Bank v. Storer*, 7 Mass. 433.

And may make loans in their own bills, on a contract that if any of the bills shall be returned during the continuance of the loan, the borrower shall redeem them with specie, and that he shall also receive of the bank a certain amount of the bills of other banks, for which he should pay specie. *Northampton Bank v. Allen*, 10 Mass. 284.

Void Loans. — The Massachusetts statute of 1809, c. 38, (which made penal the receiving as a deposit, or in other way negotiating, loaning, or passing payment, *by* any banking corporation, of the bank bills or notes of any banking company not incorporated by the Legislature of Massachusetts, except the bills of the United States Bank,) rendered void any note made payable to a bank in such prohibited bills ; and the subsequent repeal of the statute did not purge the illegality of the contract. *Springfield Bank v. Merrick*, 11 Mass. 322.

Power of Directors. — The directors have authority to control all the property of the bank ; and they may authorize one of their number to assign any securities belonging to the corporation. A blank endorsement, in pursuance of such authority, by the person so authorized, is sufficient to transfer a note ; and the endorsement may be properly filled at the bar. 11 Mass. 288.

Custom. — Where a bank has established usages and by-laws respecting demands on makers of promissory notes and notices to endorsers thereof, the dealings and contracts of persons doing business with such company are to be understood and enforced according to such usages and by-laws. *Lincoln and Kennebec Bank v. Page*, 6 Mass. 125. *Same v. Hammatt.* ib. 159. *Smith v. Whiting*, 12 Mass. 8.

The usages of a bank, at which parties are accustomed to transact business, concerning demand and notice on notes, &c., are given in evidence, not as rules of judicial decision, but as evidence of the contract of the parties, and their assent to usages, and of their waiving their strictly legal claims. *Ib. Blanchard* v. *Hilliard*, 11 Mass. 88. *Jones* v. *Fales*, 4 Mass. 252. *Widgery* v. *Monroe*, 6 Mass. 450. *Renner* v. *Bank of Columbia*, 9 Wheat. 585. *Yeaton* v. *Bank of Alexandria*, 5 Cranch, 52. *Bank of Columbia* v. *Fitzhugh*, 1 Har. & Gill, 239. *Hartford Bank* v. *Stedman*, 3 Conn. 489.

In *Mills* v. *Bank of U. S.*, 11 Wheat. 431, the parties were not acquainted with the usage of the bank; but as the note was made payable at the bank, it was held that the parties were bound to know its usages, and had impliedly agreed that those usages should become a part of their contract.

And this doctrine was afterwards held to be applicable to the parties to a bill of exchange drawn on a person at Washington, on the ground that the bill would probably be put into bank there for collection. *Bank of Washington* v. *Triplett*, 1 Pet. 25. See, also, *Whitwell* v. *Johnson*, 17 Mass. 452.

Bank Notice. — So an established custom that notice, &c., to directors of a bank shall be left on the cashier's desk, is binding on the directors whose notes come into the bank. *Weld* v. *Gorham*, 10 Mass. 366.

So of a custom to make demand of the maker of a note lodged in a bank, without presenting the note to him. *Whitwell* v. *Johnson*, 17 Mass. 452. *City Bank* v. *Cutter*, 3 Pick. 414. S. P. *Pearson* v. *Bank of Metropolis*, 1 Pet. 93. *Raborg* v. *Bank of Columbia*, 1 Har. & Gill, 231.

In all these cases, a knowledge, express or implied, of the usage, must be brought home to the party who is to be affected by it. *Pierce* v. *Butler*, 14 Mass. 303. 11 Wheat. 431.

Damages. — A bank is liable to an action for wrongfully refusing to transfer shares; and the measure of damages is the value of the shares at the time of the refusal, with interest to the time of the rendition of judgment. *Hussey* v. *M. & M. Bank*, 10 Pick. 415. See, also, 10 Johns. 485. 3 Mass. 364.

Attachment of Shares. — Where the owner of shares assigned them to two persons, and gave a power of attorney to one of them to transfer them on the books of the bank, the power was held to be valid, whether the power authorized the transfer to be made to both assignees, or to the attorney alone; and the bank was held not to be liable for refusing to transfer the shares to a subsequent attaching creditor, who sold them on execution. *Plymouth Bank* v. *Bank of Norfolk*, 10 Pick. 451.

Exhibition of Books. — A bank is bound to exhibit its books to a depositor, on proper occasions, and the officers having charge of them are, *quoad hoc*, the agents of both parties. *Union Bank* v. *Knapp*, 3 Pick. 96

Payment in Suspended Bills. — A bank is, in New York, legally bound to take its own bills in payment of debts due to it. Per *Woodworth*, J

Niagara Bank v. *Roosevelt,* 9 Cow. 409. *Aliter,* in Massachusetts. 13 Mass. 206. See, also, *Tillou* v. *Britton,* 4 Halst 120

In Ohio, if a bank has *bona fide* parted with all interest in a debt due to it, the debtor cannot pay the assignee in the paper of the bank. *Pancoast* v. *Ruffin,* 1 Ham. 381. S. P. *Hallowell, &c.. Bank* v. *Howard,* 13 Mass. 235.

Tax on Stock. — The Legislature of a State may constitutionally impose a tax on the capital stock, &c., of a bank previously incorporated by it, unless the right has been expressly relinquished. *Portland Bank* v. *Apthorp,* 12 Mass. 252. *Providence Bank* v. *Billings,* 4 Pet. 514. *Judson* v. *State,* Minor, 150.

Rights of Third Parties — Collection Paper. — When there have been, for several years, mutual and extensive dealings between two banks, and an account current kept between them, in which they mutually credited each other with the proceeds of all paper remitted for collection, when received, and charged all costs of protests, postage, &c.; accounts regularly transmitted from the one to the other, and settled upon these principles; and upon the face of the paper transmitted, it always appeared to be the property of the respective banks, and to be remitted by each of them upon its own account; there is a lien for a general balance of account upon the paper thus transmitted, no matter who may be its real owner. *New England Bank* v. *Bank Metropolis,* Supreme Court U. S. 1 Howard, 234.

A bank that receives from another bank, for collection, a note endorsed by the cashier of that bank, is bound to present the note to the maker for payment, at maturity; and, if it is not paid, to give notice of non-payment to the bank from which the note was received; is not bound, unless by special agreement, to give such notice to the other parties to the note. *Phipps* v. *Millbury Bank,* 8 Metcalf's Massachusetts Reports, p. 79.

A bank receiving paper for collection at Philadelphia, or elsewhere, is liable to its depositors for the neglect or mistakes of its correspondents in protesting paper, or in placing notes, &c., in the hands of notaries for protest. *Ballister* v. *Farmers' & Mech. Bank,* Phil. (Before the Court of Common Pleas, Boston, Feb. 1846, for collection paper remitted by State Bank, Boston. For full report of this case, see Bankers' Magazine, vol. 1, pp. 13, 14.)

Injunction. — A party who brings an action against a bank, that is afterwards restrained, by injunction, from further proceeding in its business, and whose property and effects are put into the hands of receivers, does not, by proving his claim before the receivers, but without receiving a certificate thereof, or taking a dividend, bar his right to proceed in the action. *Watson* v. *Phenix Bank,* 8 Metcalf's Mass. Reports.

In a suit on a demand due from a bank, the plaintiff is entitled to recover interest thereon from the time of action brought, although the bank is afterwards restrained, by injunction, from proceeding in its business, and its property is put into the hands of receivers. *Ib.*

Attachment. — The Bank of Michigan placed funds in the hands of W. & Co., in New York, for the special purpose of paying its drafts made in favor of various individuals, and not then due and payable; and afterwards drew an order on W. & Co., in favor of D., of Springfield, for the amount of said funds, and desired D. to make arrangement with W. & Co., to provide for the payment of said drafts, so far as the funds should be sufficient therefor; and W. & Co. placed said funds on their books to the credit of D., who instructed them to pay the drafts as they should be presented at maturity; the holders of the drafts had notice that said funds were placed at D.'s control for payment of their claims, and assented thereto, and D. had notice of this assent; a creditor of the bank, residing in this state, afterwards sued the bank here, and attached said funds in D.'s hands, by the trustee process. *Held*, that the process could not be maintained against D. *Edmund Dwight* v. *Bank of Michigan*, vol. 10, Metcalf's Massachusetts Supreme Court Reports, p. 605.

Liquidation by Receivers. — In adjusting the concerns of a bank, by receivers of its assets appointed pursuant to the provisions of Statutes, the bank tax imposed by Revised Statutes, c. 9 and 36, and due from the bank, may be set off against money due from the Commonwealth to the bank on loan: so, of money deposited in the bank by the agent of Charles River Bridge, in his capacity as agent, — *aliter*, of money deposited in the bank by the warden of the State Prison, in his capacity of warden. 11 Metcalf.

Insolvent Banks. — An incorporated bank is not a person within the meaning of the act of Congress, (1797,) which requires priority of payment to be made to the United States, when any person indebted to them shall become insolvent, not having sufficient property to pay all his debts, or shall make a voluntary assignment of his property; or when his property shall be attached by process against an absconding, concealed, or absent debtor, or when a legal act of bankruptcy shall be committed by him.

When the assets of a bank are put into the hands of receivers, pursuant to statute of 1838, to have its concerns adjusted according to the provisions of Revised Statutes, c. 44, the United States, if creditors of the bank, are not entitled to priority of payment, under the act of Congress of 1797, there not being, in that case, such an insolvency of their debtor as is contemplated by that act. *Commonwealth* v. *Phœnix Bank* ibid. p. 129.

Agency.— *Collection of Paper.*— An agent has no right to delegate his authority to a sub-agent, without the assent of his principal; but where, from the nature of the agency, a sub-agent must necessarily be employed, the assent of the principal must be obtained; as, where a draft, payable at a distant place, is left with a bank for collection, it must be presumed that it is intended to be transmitted to a sub-agent, at the place where it is payable, and not that the bank is to employ its own officers to proceed there, for the purpose of obtaining payment. *Dorchester and Milton Bank* v. *New England Bank*, 1 Cushing, 177.

A bank, by which notes and bills, payable at a distant place, are received for collection, without specific instructions, is bound to transmit or to cause the same to be transmitted, by suitable sub-agents, to some suitable bank, or other agent, at the place of payment, for that purpose; and where suitable sub-agents are thus employed, in good faith, the collecting bank is not liable for their neglect or default. *Ib.*

The D. and M. Bank, at M., having discounted a number of drafts, payable in W., transferred the same, by a general endorsement, and without any specific instructions, to the N. E. Bank, in Boston, their general agents for collection : the latter, having no correspondent in W., transferred the drafts, by a like general endorsement, to the C. Bank, in Boston, then and afterwards in good credit, for collection; the C. Bank transmitted the drafts to their correspondent, the Bank of the M., in W., for the same purpose : the C. Bank having subsequently failed, the N. E. Bank demanded the drafts of the B. of the M. before they became due : the latter refused to deliver the drafts, but collected them, and applied the proceeds to the payment of a balance due them from the C. Bank; whereupon the N. E. Bank commenced an action against the Bank of the M. to recover the amount : — it was *held*, 1st, that the N. E. Bank, having acted in good faith, and the C. Bank being a suitable agent, had authority to employ the latter to make the collection; 2d, that no proof of general usage was necessary to give the N. E. Bank such authority; and, 3d, that, as the drafts were transferred to the N. E. Bank by a general endorsement, that bank might transfer them in the same manner to the C. Bank, and were not bound to make a restricted endorsement. *Ib.*

Loans — Collateral, &c. — The agent of the H. M. Co., at Ware, being authorized for the purpose by a vote of the corporation, made drafts on D. B. & Co., of New York, payable to the order of G. S., treasurer of the company, and one of the firm of G. S. & Co., the agents of the company in Boston, which drafts were there accepted by D., one of the drawees, who was also a member of the firm of G. S. & Co., and were then endorsed by G. S., treasurer, and by G. S. & Co., and negotiated and disposed of by them for their own benefit, under an agreement with the H. M. Co. that they would pay them at maturity : G. S. & Co., having failed before the drafts became due, and being unable to take them up at maturity, the drafts, when due, were proved and allowed as claims against the H. M. Co., who had also failed in the mean time, and dividends were paid thereon by the assignees of the latter : — it was *held*, that the assignees of the H. M. Co. were entitled to charge the amount of said drafts against G. S. & Co. in account : notwithstanding that, on some of them, the endorsement of G. S., treasurer, was made by attorney ; — that some of them were paid by one of the endorsers, subsequent to G. S. & Co., without previous demand of the acceptor, and notice to such endorser ; — and that some of them had been negotiated and received in payment of, or as collateral security for, illegal loans. *Shaw* v. *Stone*, 228.

Endorsement. — A draft, by the agent of a corporation, payable to " G S., treasurer" thereof, is payable to him personally, though described as treasurer, and not merely as treasurer for the time being, and may be endorsed by him, as treasurer, either in person, or by attorney. *Ib.*

Bond. — A bond well and truly to execute the duties of cashier or teller, includes not only honesty, but reasonable skill and diligence. If, therefore, he perform those duties negligently and unskilfully, or if he violate them from want of capacity and care, the condition of his bond is broken, and his sureties are liable for his misdoings. *Minor* v. *Mechanics' Bank*, 1 Pet. 46. *State Bank* v. *Chetwood*, 3 Halst. 25. *Barrington* v. *Bank of Washington*, 14 S. & R. 405. *American Bank* v. *Adams*, 12 Pickering, 303.

Collateral Stock. — A bank cannot legally be taxed for railroad stock pledged to it as collateral security for a debt. *Waltham Bank* v. *Inhabitants of Waltham*, Metcalf's Reports, vol. x., 331.

Individual Liability. — Under the Rev. Sts. c. 36, § 31, which provide that "the holders of stock in any bank, at the time when its charter shall expire, shall be liable, in their individual capacities, for the payment and redemption of all bills which may have been issued by said bank, and which shall remain unpaid, in proportion to the stock they may respectively hold at the dissolution of the charter," it was *held*, that the bill-holders cannot severally maintain a bill in equity against the stockholders, to compel payment and redemption of the unpaid bills held by them respectively, but that all of them must join in one bill, or one or more of them must file a bill for the benefit of all, against all the stockholders. *Crease* v. *Babcock*, ibid. 525. [Case of the Chelsea Bank.] *Crew* v. *Breed*, ibid. 575.

Unpaid Bills. — *Held, also,* that a holder of bank bills, purchased by him as trustee, is entitled to maintain a bill in equity in his own name, without joining the cestui que trust, against the stockholders, for himself, and for all other holders of unpaid bills. *Grew* v. *Breed*, ibid. 569 [Case of the Nahant Bank.]

Held, also, that one who buys bank bills of a broker, at a discount, under an agreement to keep them from circulation for a certain time, is entitled to the statute remedy against the stockholders, for the full amount of the bills, unless he has notice, when he buys them, that they are improperly issued by the officers of the bank; but that such a sale to him by a broker is not evidence of such notice. *Ibid.*

Held, also, that when the bills of the bank are sold by its officers, on a usurious contract, a subsequent bona fide purchaser of them is entitled to recover of the stockholders the full nominal value thereof, without any deduction on account of the usury in the sale by the officers of the bank. *Ibid.*

Held, also, that an agreement by a bank, with a holder of its bills, to convey property to him in payment thereof, which agreement is not executed, by reason of an injunction on the bank and the placing of its assets in the hands of receivers, does not impair the bill-holder's remedy against the stockholders. *Ibid.*

Held, also, that when part of the stock is owned by the bank itself, the individual stockholders are not, for that reason, liable to any further extent than they would have been if none of the stock had been so owned. *Crease* v. *Babcock,* ibid. 525.

Held, also, that holders of stock are not jointly responsible for each other; that each is severally liable in such a sum, not exceeding the par value of his shares, as the amount of unpaid bills may require; and that the liability of solvent holders cannot be extended by reason of the insolvency of other holders. *Ibid.*

Held, also, that those who hold stock as collateral security, and those who hold it in trust, whether the trust does or does not appear on the books of the bank, are liable for the payment and redemption of unpaid bills; and that administrators of deceased stockholders are so liable, in their representative capacity, as for other debts of their intestates. *Crease* v. *Babcock,* ibid. 525. *Grew* v. *Breed,* 569.

Held, also, that the remedy against the individual stockholders is not confined to those who held the bills of the bank at the time when the charter expired, but extends to those who, after the charter expired, took the bills in the ordinary course of business, or otherwise acquired a good title to them. *Ibid.*

Held, also, that the terms "bills which shall remain unpaid" mean bills that shall be ultimately unpaid, after the application of the assets of the bank towards payment thereof, and that the holders of unpaid bills are not entitled to a decree for payment, against the individual stockholders, until after the assets of the bank have been so applied. *Crease* v. *Babcock,* ibid. 525.

Held, also, that stockholders are not liable to pay post-notes issued by the bank. *Crease* v. *Babcock,* ibid. 525.

Held, also, that when the assets of the bank are placed in the hands of receivers, the holders of its bills, who do not present their claims to the receiver, cannot recover of stockholders the full amount thereof, but only the balance which they would have been entitled to recover, if they had proved their claims before the receivers had obtained part payment. *Grew* v. *Breed,* ibid. 569.

Held, also, that holders of stock are not liable to pay any interest on unpaid bank bills, either from the time when payment was demanded of the bank, or the time of filing a bill in equity to compel payment. *Crease* v. *Babcock,* ibid. 525. *Grew* v. *Breed.*

Held, also, that an attachment of the property of the bank, made on a bill in equity (inserted in a writ) by the holders of unpaid bills against the individual stockholders, is wholly unavailing. *Crease* v. *Babcock,* ibid. 525.

Bill of Exchange.—An acceptor of a bill of exchange is not liable to the payee or endorsee for damages caused by non-payment, but only for the amount of the bill, with interest and costs of protest. *Bowen* v. *Stoddard,* ibid. 375.

The statute of Maine, which enacts that, in an action on a bill of exchange drawn or endorsed in that State, payable in this State, and protested for non-payment, the holder shall recover three per cent. damages, in addition to the contents of the bill and interest, does not entitle the holder to recover those damages in a suit brought against the acceptor in the courts of this State. *Fiske* v. *Foster,* ibid. 597.

ON THE

DUTIES, OMISSIONS, AND MISDOINGS
OF
BANK DIRECTORS.

BY A. B. JOHNSON.

TO THE HON. JOHN GREIG, OF CANANDAIGUA, VICE CHANCELLOR OF THE
STATE UNIVERSITY, AND PRESIDENT OF THE ONTARIO BANK.

My DEAR SIR:—The following reflections, you, of all men, need the least, still I inscribe them to you, for you have been in my thoughts whenever I have spoken of conduct commendable in a bank director. Indeed, your entire Board are models of what bank directors should be, no member of your direction, and no officer of your bank, having been, for many years, its debtor, in any shape; while you, and all the directors have performed faithfully your duties, with no pecuniary consideration, except what proceeds from the bank dividends, which are shared in common by all the stockholders. Though I have been an officer of your corporation for nearly the third of a century, I never saw your Board but once—the fall of 1843—and then I saw the same men, to a great extent, who, thirty years previously, in the same chamber, and around the same table, commenced banking. The Board had met to discharge a pleasant duty, in dividing among the stockholders, out of surplus profits that had been earned at the Canandaigua office, 20 per cent. on the invested capital of half a million of dollars. To say that no director, and no officer of the bank had purchased up stock in anticipation of this great and unexpected dividend, is only what is known to everybody; and what has passed unnoted by everybody, for the reason that no different conduct could be expected from the actors. Indeed, in alluding to it now, I hesitate, as a man falters in naming a disreputable woman in the hearing of chaste matrons but I can not avoid knowing that the conduct of your Board, in this particular, contrasts gratefully with the spasmodic rise in price which occasionally occurs in the quoted stocks of some prosperous corporations; and which rise reveals, to a practical observer, that the directors are competing with each other for the stock, in anticipation of a secret forthcoming surplus dividend.

Eight more years are passed since the event referred to, and you are still President of the same Board, with the same Midas in charge of the executive department of the bank, and he is again amassing surplus profits, which, on the first day of January, 1856, when the bank is to die a natural death, will be again faithfully given to the stockholders. That the same Board may survive, with strength and health, to that ultimate consummation of all banking things to you, and them, and me, devoutly prays

Your friend during more than eight lusters,

A. B. JOHNSON.

UTICA, *April 1st*, 1851.

Who are Bank Directors?—In the year 1829, the State of New York, to protect the public against bank insolvencies, originated the Safety Fund System of banking, by which every bank subject thereto, was compelled to pay annually into the State Treasury the half of 1 per cent. on its capital, till the payments should amount to 3 per cent. thereon; payments were then to be intermitted, till the fund should become exhausted by losses, when a further 3 per cent. was to be collected by processes similar to the first. Soon after the year 1836, several Safety Fund banks became insolvent, absorbing, by means of various frauds, not only the existing collections of the Safety Fund, but all the annual payments that would be made by solvent banks during the limit of their corporate existence.

Influenced by this sad aspect of an experiment which had lived down its original many enemies, the State, in the year 1838, discontinued the further creation of Safety Fund bank charters, and originated what are called Free Banks; voluntary associations, whose bank-notes are secured by pledges to the State of certain governmental stocks (State and National), or by such stocks, and by mortgages on unincumbered real estate, in equal parts each. Our purpose includes not the comparative merits of the systems, or the positive merit of either. So far as the banks of both systems are managed by directors, they will be within the purview of our remarks; but the Safety Fund Banks are subjected by their charters to a board of twelve or thirteen directors, while the Free Banks may adopt any number, or any other mode of government which the proprietors shall prefer, hence the proprietors, in some cases, constitute a pecuniary democracy, governing personally, and to such the following treatise will be inapplicable:—

THE DUTIES OF BANK DIRECTORS.

A Director should possess a good Theory of Conduct.—Bank directors usually commence their duties with honest intentions toward their stockholders and the public. The misconduct which may supervene, will proceed from temptations incident to their office, and perhaps from the absence of well-digested notions of the conduct that is proper. To remedy this defect, the present miniature treatise is offered, and its good intention is avowed as a palliative for its presumption. Some years ago, a person was asked whether he would accept the office of director then vacant in a bank of this city. After deliberating, he replied, that as the office might result in some benefit to him, he would accept. When the answer was reported to the Board who were to fill the vacancy, they refused to appoint him, lest he should sit at the Board mousing to catch something beneficial to himself, while they wanted a director who would accept office to benefit the bank. A man ought to watch his own interest, when conducting his own affairs, but when he is acting officially, he should lose himself in his public duties. We expect a soldier to sacrifice his life, if necessary, to the discharge of his duty, and we should condemn him for professing a less self-denying creed, how much soever our knowledge of human fallibility might induce us to pardon his short-comings, when death should obstruct his path. Fortunately the performance of bank duties will peril only some forbearance from pecuniary acquisitions, and our creed ought to be self-denying enough to renounce these, instead of avowing them to be the motive of our services; nor is the principle new. The law will not permit a trustee to derive any indirect benefit from his trust, or any judge or juror to decide in his own controversies; and the State of New York has, in its Constitution, consecrated the principle, by prohibiting our legislators from regulating their own compensation, or even the number of days which shall be occupied in legislative duties. In some cities, also, no civic officer can become legally interested in any municipal contract; and who censures not some recent high officers of our National Government, for participating in a private claim, which they officially aided in adjusting and paying. Thus thinking, the President of a large railroad corporation of our State refused to supply iron for his road, though his associate directors, with the complaisance which is as vicious as it is common, offered him the contract. In this case, no contractor could have been more eligible, but the rejector established a precedent that is more profitable for his corporation than the money it would have saved in purchasing the iron of him.

Direct Compensation to Directors is purer than Indirect.—The remuneration of bank directors, consists, with us, in an indefinite claim for bank loans, and which claim led formerly to so great an absorption of the country banks, whose capitals are small, that a law was enacted interdicting bank directors* from engrossing, directly or indirectly, more than a third part of the capital of their respective banks; a quota which is, in some banks, divided equally among the directors, irrespective of any business merits of the borrower. This mode of compensation, when founded on ample security for the borrowed money, and when the amount taken, directly or indirectly, is limited to the legal quota, may, in small banks, constitute a less objectionable mode of remunerating directors than any other indirect mode, or than most other direct modes. The Legislature, however, seems to have contemplated that the motives for accepting a directorship shall consist in being a stockholder, and thereby a participant in the general profits of the bank. We infer this from the requirements of law, that the director of every bank shall own at least five hundred dollars of its capital; divesting himself of which causes a forfeiture of his office. No mode of compensation is so pure as what proceeds thus from a ratable interest in the common loss and gains of a bank; and should a negation of other compensation deter small stockholders from accepting a bank direc-

* This law, like most other legal regulations of bank directors, was made before the existence of banking associations; hence the directors of such associations are not included therein.

torship, large stockholders could be substituted, and banks would thereby become assimilated to private institutions that are managed by their owners—the most efficient and honest of all management. A man may, however, properly refuse the office of bank director, unless he can obtain for his services a satisfactory pecuniary compensation; and banks must comply with such a requirement, if suitable men are not otherwise obtainable; but such a contingency promises to be remote, under the avidity for accidental distinctions by our citizens, consequent, probably, on their legal equality. But when such a contingency shall occur, a direct compensation will generally be purer than any indirect, and a definite compensation cheaper than an indefinite; and usually money is the most economical mode of paying for services that are not to be deemed honorary.

No Director should assume Antagonistic Duties.—The law usually regards bank directors as an entirety under the title of a Board. The duties and powers which are conferred on the Board by the charters of Safety Fund Banks, may be classed as legislative, supervisory, and appointing. The legislative power consists in creating such offices as the business of the bank shall render necessary, regulating their duties and salaries; directing the modes in which the bank shall be conducted, and generally all that pertains to the management of the stock, property, and effects of the corporation. The appointing power consists in selecting proper incumbents for the created offices; while the supervisory power is indicated by all the foregoing, and by the ability to dismiss the appointees at pleasure. But a man can not properly supervise himself in the performance of public services, nor limit and regulate their scope and extent, nor fix his compensation therefor; hence the powers of the Board can be exercised efficiently only on persons who are not members of the Board. Nor is the inexpediency of uniting in the same person the duties of grantor and grantee, master and servant, agent and principal, a contrivance of man; it proceeds from his organization. No person can sit at a Board of Directors without observing that agents who are not directors, are supervised more freely than agents who are directors. A practical admission of this is evinced by some discount Boards, who, in deciding on paper offered by directors, vote by a species of ballot, while in other Boards, the offered notes are passed under the table, from seat to seat; and a note is deemed rejected, if, in its transit, some director has secretly folded down one of its corners. Had the United States Bank been supervised by a Board disconnected from executive duties, it would not have permitted its chief officer to persevere in the measures which ultimately ruined the corporation, though its capital was thirty-five millions of dollars. Even the separation o a Legislature into two chambers, checks the *esprit du corps*, and pride of opinion which would urge one chamber into extremes, with no means of extrication from a false position. A separation operates like the break of continuity in an electric telegraph, arresting a common sympathy, passion, or prejudice, which, in a single chamber, rushes irresistibly to its object. Still, in many banks (the Bank of England included), the President (entitled Governor in the Bank of England) is the chief executive officer, as well as head of the legislative department. The Bank of England is, however, controlled by twenty-four directors, the largeness of which number naturally mitigates the influence of the members individually, and hence diminishes ratably the objection against its executive organization. Such an organization may operate well, where the Board consists of a small number of members, yet the good is not a consequence of the organization, but in despite thereof; for whatever weakens the power of supervision, must diminish its benefits. The joint stock banks of England are all controlled by officers called Managers, and who are not members of the Board, though they sit thereat *ex officio*, for mutual explanation and instruction.

The Executive should be Single, not Multiform.—That the Board should legislate, supervise, and appoint, but not execute, occasioned probably the exclusion from the directorship that early prevailed, and widely continues, of the person who occupies the office of cashier, and who, with us, was once almost universally the chief executive bank officer. But the executive power, located, should center in only one person; a divided responsibility creating necessarily a divided vigilance. Thirteen men acting as an executive, will not produce the vigilance of one man multiplied by thirteen; but rather the vigilance of one man divided by thirteen. The inspection of a picture by ten thousand promiscuous men will not detect as many imperfections in it as the scrutiny of one person, intent on discovering to the extent of his utmost vigilance; hence large assemblies refer every investigation to a small committee, the chairman of which is expected to assume the responsibility of the examination, while the other members are more supervisors than actors. Here again, as in most other modes which business assumes by chance apparently, our organization dictates the mode. When, therefore, we want an army of the highest efficiency, we possess no alternative but to intrust it to a single commander-in-chief; and if we want a bank of the highest efficiency, as respects safety and productiveness, we must intrust it to a single executive, under any title we please; but to one man, who will make the bank the focus of his aspirations, and know that on his prudence and success will depend the character he most affects, and the duration of his office, with all its valued associations and consequences.

Appointment of the Executive.—If the proposed organization is the best that can be devised for a bank, the magnitude of power to be delegated is no proper argument against its delegation, but only a motive for prudence in selecting the delegate. A man of known skill and established fidelity is not always procurable for the proposed duties, especially by small banks that can not render available a breach of the tenth commandment. But providentially the world is not so dependent on a few eminent men, as their self-love, and our idolatry may believe. Every well organized person possesses an aptitude to grow to the stature of the station in which circumstances may place him; and some of the most successful bankers of our State acquired their skill after they became bankers. The like principle is discoverable in all occupations, the highest not excepted. Few of our judges, generals, diplomatists, legislators, or civil executives, were accomplished in their vocation before they became invested therewith. Skill is consequent to station and its excitement, though a vulgar error expects (what is impossible) that official dexterity and competence should be possessed in advance.

The Power to be Granted to the Executive.—On the chief executive should be devolved the responsibility of providing funds to meet the exigences of the bank; hence he is entitled to dictate whether loans shall be granted or withheld, and the length of credit that shall be accorded to the borrowers respectively. With him rests also a knowledge of the banking value of each customer; he should therefore be permitted to select from applicants the persons to whom alone loans shall be granted. The responsibility should also be cast on him of making the bank pecuniarily profitable to the stockholders; hence he will be stimulated to obtain good accounts, and to extend business to the utmost capacity that his judgment will justify. On his untiring vigilance should be reposed the safety of the capital; hence no loans should be granted with whose security he is dissatisfied, nor any except those with which he is satisfied—even the improper negation of a loan being usually a small evil to the bank, how important soever it may be to the proposer. The Bank of England, with a capital of about (including surplus) $90,000,000, intrusts the loaning thereof to the governor alone. He has under him a sub-governor, selected from the directors, while an executive committee, designated by the Board, may be consulted by him; but the committee employs itself in digesting matters for the action of the court of directors, rather than in clogging the proceedings and diminishing the discretion of the governor. All the joint-stock banks of England are organized with a like self-depending executive, under the name of general manager; and a bank organized thus to grant loans at all times, during its business hours, will present a great inducement to customers over a bank whose discounts are accorded at only stated days, and after a protracted deliberation by directors—loans being often useful only when obtained promptly. Even the due protesting of dishonored paper, and notifying of endorsers—the enforcement of payment, or the obtainment of security on debts which prove to be unsafe, will all wholesomely fall under the control of the chief executive, by reason that the vigilance of one person can control them better than a divided vigilance; and that the debts having come into the bank by his agency, his self-love is interested in their collectability. He must feel a like responsibility against losses by forgery, overdrawn accounts, the depredation of burglars, and the peculation of subalterns. To secure in the highest degree his vigilance in these particulars, he should be intrusted with the selection of all subordinate agents, even of the notary and attorneys. At least none should be appointed or retained with whom he is not satisfied. His self-respect can not be too much fostered by the Board, and no measure should be enforced, and no loans granted, which can wound his sensibility, or diminish his influence with his subordinates, or the customers of the bank. The more he can thus be brought to identify himself with the bank, the more the bank will be exempt from the disadvantages which make corporations contrast unfavorably with private establishments; and which a proverb alludes to in saying that what is every man's business is nobody's. So great is their assimilation to their bank which some managers attain, that a poignancy of solicitude in relation to the debts of the bank, the preservation of its credit, and the productiveness of its capital, becomes the greatest evil of their position; especially when they are predisposed to morbid nervousness, which, with disease of the heart, their position induces and fosters. Such a man will obtain from his Board all the information it can yield him in relation to the pecuniary responsibility of his dealers; and the directors should give him their opinion—not mandatory, to relieve his responsibility, but to inform his judgment, though he will soon discover that his only safe guide will consist of his feelings founded on personal observations too subtle often to be described, much less enumerated.

His Salary.—His salary should be liberal, for nature will not otherwise produce the activity of mind and body that are essential to his duties. Besides, he must engage in no private business, and will possess neither leisure nor taste to attend minutely to his domestic expenses. No salary can equal in value the devotion of such an officer; still extravagance is unwise as an example, and unnecessary as a stimulant. The more capable the officer, the more he will appreciate money; and instances are frequent where bank services of the most valuable kind are accorded on salaries that would be deemed unsatisfactorily small by officers whose habits are less suited for the station.

The Supervision of the Board over the Manager.—The duties of a Board will rather commence than end with the appointment of its executive. Their proper duties are supervisory. Nature aids the discharge of such duties when the supervisor is distinct from the supervised; indeed, one of the most difficult tasks of a supervisor consists in restraining the undue captiousness that is natural to the position. The president of the bank, as head of the corporation, can not perform too efficiently supervisory duties, and he may well be entitled to a pecuniary compensation therefor. He should deem them under his special charge; but not to supersede therein the modified duties of the other directors. Supervision over the manager's official proceedings will be as salutary to him as proper to the Board. Darkness is proverbially unfavorable to purity, but only by reason of the concealment it creates: every other means of concealment is equally productive of impurity. A man can easily reconcile to his judgment and conscience what can not be reconciled to disinterested supervisors; hence, if an officer knows so little of human nature as to deem supervision offensive, he is unfit to be trusted. That the supervision may be full, it must be systematic. Every director will usually attend meetings of the Board in a degree inverse their frequency, but twice a week, or certainly once, where the bank is not very small, will be as short as is compatible with a due inspection, singly, of the loans, in some regular order, that may have been granted by the manager, since the last session of the Board. The directors will thus learn individually whether the power to make loans has been prudently exercised; and he will learn the opinion which any of the Board may express in relation to the borrowers or their sureties, especially in cities where borrowers are generally known to the Board; and a manager may advantageously defer to it the consummation of many loans in relation to which his own information is questionable, or about which he desires time to deliberate. Such a deferring will often constitute a less offensive mode of avoiding an objectionable discount, than a direct and personal refusal; though truly the kindest act a banker can perform, next to granting a loan, is to promptly inform an applicant that he can not succeed, when the banker knows the loan will not be granted.

Supervision in Relation to Business Principles.—The supervision of the Board must be as comprehensive as the powers of the manager. The revisions of loans will enable the board to ascertain, not merely the solvency of the bank's assets, but whether its business is conducted without partiality, or unwholesome bias of any kind. Nearly every undue partiality possesses concomitants that may lead to its detection;—for instance, an unusual laxity of security, or length of credit; with unusual frequency of renewals in a direct form, or an indirect, so as to screen the operations. A manager, properly sensitive of his reputation, and properly diffident of his natural infirmities, will be reluctant to grant loans to his relatives, or special friends; and never to himself, or any person with whose business operations he is connected. To enable directors to judge of these particulars, a regular attendance at the stated meetings is necessary; but memory alone must not be relied on, except to suggest queries, which should always be capable of solution by proper books and indexes, that must be within reach of the directors; who should habitually inspect the books, that the practice may, in no case, seem an invidious peculiarity. In all scrutinies, however, the directors should remember that in mere judgment and expediency they may differ from the manager, and he may still be right, for banking constitutes his business, while to them it is an incidental occupation. Lenity is proper even to his undoubted errors, when they are of a nature which experience may correct; but time will only inveterate bad intentions, and their first unequivocal appearance should produce an unrelenting forfeiture of his office.

Supervision over Liabilities and Resources.—The Board must understand the liabilities of the bank to its depositors, bank-note holders, and other creditors; also the funds of the bank, and its available resources; so as to judge how far the honor of the bank is safe in the care of its manager. The character of depositors and borrowers are also proper subjects of general scrutiny by the Board, by reason that the reputation of a bank is inferable from the reputation of its dealers;—not that disreputable people should be rejected as depositors, but a bank is not an exception to the proverb which speaks " of birds of a feather ;" and when the customers of a bank are generally respectable in their character and business, we may be sure that the management of the bank is at least ostensibly moral and mercantile.

Supervision founded on Results.—The ticklers of a bank are books which show in detail the debts due, prospectively to a bank, and the days of payment. The aggregate footing of the ticklers will accordingly exhibit the amount of loans not yet matured, and inductively the amount that is past due. The information which relates to the amount past due is often given reluctantly, but a knowledge of it is vastly important in the proper supervision of a bank; and when tested by the ticklers, the information can not well be deceptious, or evaded. In knowing the amount of past due loans, the Board can pretty accurately conjecture the character of the bank's customers. Such loans should be satisfactorily explained by the manager, and the means he is taking in their collection. The like may be said of over-drafts,* which are rarely permitted by American bankers, though in England they seem to constitute one of the regular modes of advancing money to customers. Whether they shall be permitted is within the proper discretion of the Board, and should they occur, inadvertently, the occurrence ought to be manifested to the Board. An exemption from losses is impracticable in long continued operations; yet all grades of intellect are procurable, hence the retention of an officer is unwise when his results are unsatisfactory. Every man can adduce excuses which no person may be able to controvert; but when miscarriages are frequent, or import-

---

* A list of all the credits due to individual depositors, will, by its aggregate amount, show, inductively, the amount of over-drafts.

ant, the Board should assume that something wrong exists and eludes detection, rather than that nature deviates from her accustomed processes, making vigilance unsafe, and skill unprofitable. The recent "Rochester Knockings," which some people endeavor to unravel, by reason that they deem the noises supernatural, if they can not be otherwise explained; saner intellects pass without scrutiny, being confident that the inexplicability of the knockings can prove only that the shrewdness of observers is baffled by the artifice of the exhibiters.

Supervision against Frauds.—The examination of vaults, and counting of money, rarely reveal defalcations, till the defaulter no longer endeavors to conceal his delinquencies. The counting is not pernicious, if the Board choose to amuse their vigilance therewith; but we have not attempted to designate modes in which frauds are detectable; the ingenuity of concealment being naturally as great as the ingenuity of detection. Besides, the detection of intestine frauds requires a greater familiarity with banking accounts, and a more laborious inspection of bank-books, than can ordinarily be expected of bank directors. For the detection of frauds, therefore, the best practical reliance is a supervision, in the way we have indicated, of the bank's business, and a familiar observation of the general conduct, habits, and expenses of the manager, as well as of all the subordinate officers;—the latter, however, are more especially within the duties of the manager. The ruin of a bank, by fraud, commences usually in the personal embarrassment of the delinquent, contracted by improper self-indulgences, or the assumption of secret hazards. Men rarely plunder till their conduct is otherwise disorganized, external symptoms of which observant directors may discover. A bank officer, therefore (and the higher his official position the more urgent the rule), who will not keep disengaged from all suretyship, and business that may render him pecuniarily necessitous, is as unfit to be intrusted with a bank, as a nurse who frequents small-pox hospitals, is unfit to be trusted with unvaccinated children. In menageries, animals are kept peaceful by preventing the cravings of hunger; bank executives require a similar assuasive; not by being glutted with great salaries, but by preserving themselves from expenditures unsuited to their income, and from pecuniary liabilities. A bank manager of undoubted wealth presents therein the best attainable guaranty against misconduct, and is entitled to greater freedom of action in his personal transactions than officers of ordinary circumstances; still we will terminate this part first of our undertaking, by venturing the advice, that when a man wants to be more than a bank manager, especially when he wants to employ much more than his own funds, he had better cease from occupying a station which he is too ambitious, or too avaricious to fill under restraints, which experience shows are alone safe.

PRIZE ESSAY ON BANKING.

SUGGESTIONS TO YOUNG CASHIERS ON THE DUTIES OF THEIR PROFESSION.

BY LORENZO SABINE,
OF FRAMINGHAM, MASS.

[The following Essay was published in the " Bankers' Magazine" in January, 1852, and was well received, not only by bank officers, but by the press. The demand for it has continued, and, unable to supply further orders, we reprint it.

Mr. Sabine, at our request to present such new thoughts as should seem to him advisable, has made very considerable additions.]

The "Bankers' Magazine" is an instrument of good. The observation of every-day life clearly shows that, in consequence of disastrous losses by bank failures, of sorrow and ruin to friends by the misconduct of bank officers, and of wounded feelings by reason of morose and irritable cashiers, many persons entertain strong dislike to banks, and to those who are connected with them. Such persons, forgetting that incapable, unfaithful, and disagreeable agents have been found in *all* corporations, and that bankruptcies and defalcations have occurred in every walk and pursuit, affect the sentiment of a celebrated English essayist, and say, that "nothing truly good can be expected from men who are ever poring over cash-books and balancing accounts;" while others, relying upon the strange remark of our own great moralist and philosopher, Franklin, aver that the wealth acquired by commerce is "generally" acquired by "cheating," and that "agriculture" is the "only honest" employment.*

It must be admitted that defalcations sometimes occur of a nature to warrant almost universal distrust. In 1803, the Bank of England lost, by the frauds of Astlett, one of its clerks, and a nephew of the cashier, the enormous sum of one and a half million of dollars; the frauds and forgeries of the banker Fauntleroy, in 1824, amounted to over a quarter of a million more; and the defalcation of the banker Stephenson, in 1828, was upward of a million and a quarter. These are the memorable delinquents in the history of English banking. The first suffered imprisonment in Newgate many years; the second was executed; the last fled to the United States. The largest indi-

The Magazine, then, by imparting correct information relative to the management of moneyed institutions, and by teaching bank officers that prudence, skill, and method are as essential to success as integrity, is performing a most valuable service to bankers, and to the whole community. It deserves, and should receive, the pecuniary support of every bank in the United States. So, too, I venture to say, that not only executive officers, but presidents and directors, are bound to increase its usefulness by contributing to its pages the results of their experience.

Banking has become a part of the very framework of our system of business. Even Mr. Calhoun said as long ago as 1816, when the whole banking capital in the United States was only eighty millions of dollars, that "the question whether banks are favorable to public liberty and prosperity, was one purely speculative. The fact of the existence of banks, and their incorporation with the commercial concerns and industry of the nation, prove that inquiry to come too late. The only question was, on this hand, under what modifications were banks most useful," etc. Banks now exist, in some form or other, everywhere: and will continue, probably, as long as property shall be bought and sold on credit. In all coming time, therefore, we are to have a class of men to deal in money, in promissory notes, and foreign and domestic exchange. The avocation has ever been honorable, to the last degree responsible, and exposed to many and to peculiar temptations.

Wrecked and ruined bank officers are around us on every hand. The world, seemingly more inexorable with our profession than with others, deals out its direct maledictions upon those of us who err, and will hardly forgive the managers of a broken bank, or the officer whose "cash is short," even when there is no other guilt than credulity, too easy good-nature, or incapacity. To stand upon our defense against *unjust* accusations, and to do what we can to diminish the causes of corporate and of individual delinquency, are duties which we owe to ourselves and to those who are to succeed us. Dispersed, as we are, over a vast extent of country, we can only correct public sentiment, and afford counsel and admonition to one another, as well as render our knowledge of banking available as common stock, by means of the work established for, and devoted to, our benefit.

Banks, with us, both public and private, differ—as none need to be told

vidual defaulters on this side of the Atlantic, as the facts now stand, have been among the officers of railroads.

As regards bank failures, it may well be doubted whether mismanagement, as a cause, has been as extensive in this country as in Ireland. There, according to Sir Henry Parnell, who is good authority, the issuing of paper money has been carried to such an injurious excess as to be without a parallel, perhaps, in the commercial world. The twenty-five years ending with the year 1825, was a period of nearly general bankruptcy. Eleven failures followed in quick succession; and of fifty banks in operation in 1834, eight alone maintained their standing. During this quarter of a century, Ireland, says Sir Henry, was, "from time to time, involved in immense distress."

—in many things from those of England and of Continental Europe. It is known, also, that our system is far from being uniform, and that essential improvements can be made in it. Hence, whatever the value of essays upon foreign banking, papers devoted to our own are far more useful to us, regarded as a class; and hence, too, the necessity for a free interchange of thought by bankers in different parts of the Union.

Entertaining these views, I can not but hope that the Magazine will be enriched, from time to time, not only with "Suggestions to Young Cashiers on the Duties of their Profession," but with articles on the subject of American banks and banking generally.

I pass now to topics immediately connected with the duties of a Cashier. The limits indicated do not admit of elaborate reasoning, but demand, indeed, that mere suggestions shall be made with the brevity of proverbs. I may be permitted, then, to address myself to the young officer, directly, and, as it were, personally.

You are to lead a life so confined, sedentary, and in some respects so mechanical, that, unless you observe great care, you will become, in the lapse of years, a sort of machine for computing discounts, counting money, writing letters, and keeping books.* You are to transact business, and to have a constant intercourse, with men of every shade of character, of every variety of disposition, and of every degree of intelligence. Your temper is to be tried by interruptions at the most unseasonable moments, to attend to the calls of the impatient, or to answer the inquiries of the ignorant or inquisitive. You are to be tempted to embark in speculations in stocks; to be solicited to allow overdrawings and other irregularities by the companions of your social hours, and, it may be, by one or more of your own directors; and you are to have the same domestic cares and afflictions, the same personal aches and pains, as other men; and yet you are expected to be ever at your post, to be ever courteous, to stand fast in your integrity, and to seem cheerful, and even happy. In a word, and as Girard said at the decease of his old and faithful cashier, "*the bank must go on,*" whatever your private griefs, or individual disabilities. Your position is thus one of much difficulty, responsibility, and peril; and you need a knowledge of the laws of your physical being, the counsel of wise friends, strict and daily self-

---

* Every person of observation will attest to the need of the caution in the text. Long and close application to one branch of business, and the habit of being at one place for a course of years, produce wonderful transformations in the character. The case of Mr. Rippon, late chief Cashier of the Bank of England, furnishes an illustration well worth citing. He was connected with that institution for more than half a century, and asked for but a single leave of absence from his post during the entire period, and in this instance, even, he applied at the suggestion of his physician, on the ground of ill health. Permission was granted; and our bank officer departed from London, to be absent two weeks. But the country was without charms; idleness preyed upon his spirits, and the habit of years was so strong, that, at the end of three days, he returned to the bank, solely to become happy again.

examination, and deep religious principle, to enable you to sustain it in health and honor. But be of good cheer; be a true man, and you will overcome every obstacle in the way of a long and of a useful life.

Your duties may be considered under various heads. And first, those which are general. Your bank has secrets; and, that they be kept inviolable, adopt a rule to speak of its affairs only to persons connected with you in its management. An incident to which I was a party, may serve as a story, and, perhaps, to show the necessity of the rule here enjoined upon you. Some years ago, I was in the direction of a bank (in a town on the eastern frontier of the United States) which earned a considerable part of its dividends by receiving the notes of the banks of one of the British colonies, at a small discount, and sending them home for redemption. The general suspension of specie payments occurred; and we were left with an inconvenient amount of these notes on our hands, which the banks, one and all, refused to redeem. The situation of our customers was such, in the mistrust that prevailed, that after much deliberation, we resolved to continue our regular business. The result was that we became indebted to the Boston bank which kept our accounts, in a sum quite equal to one half of our capital stock. This state of things produced much anxiety. My own disquietude caused many sleepless nights. We were in almost constant session to devise some plan of relief. *But we kept our secret.* Though solvent and with a surplus, we felt sure that, excited as the public mind then was, a whisper of our condition out of doors would be disastrous. Meanwhile, colonial bank-notes accumulated every day. We bartered off some for Mexican dollars at a high premium; we bought a thousand Spanish doubloons with others, and lost nearly one thousand dollars by the operation. These, and similar efforts to reduce our debt in Boston, were too expensive, and we determined, at last, to wait the course of events. Months elapsed: *but we still kept our secret.* In time, intelligence reached us that one of the debtor banks had ordered from New York twenty-five thousand dollars in American gold, and that the precious coin was actually on the way in a vessel called the *Teazer.* We met without delay. A vote was passed by a majority of one to send the sheriff of the county to sea to intercept the *Teazer* on her passage to the colonial port to which she was bound, and, finding her within the jurisdiction of the United States, and within the waters of the sheriff's own county, to attach the gold on our account. The proceeding, under the circumstances, was thought hazardous; three of our number refused assent; the sheriff demanded a bond of indemnity. We designed to conduct the enterprise quietly; but, by means which we never ascertained, the colonial bank got wind of our intention, and dispatched several pilot-boats, with their directors on board, to defeat us. The sheriff was a shrewd man; and, accompanied by a sagacious old shipmaster, was successful. The cashier of the debtor bank soon presented himself at our counter, and demanded the gold as his private property. A person in whom he reposed confidence intimated to us that an officer, with a writ of replevin, would take the well-canvased box from our possession. Thereupon, three of our number hurried to our vault as fast as feet could move, divided our prize, and strode rapidly homeward. My share, in the excitement of the moment, or in my excess of zeal, was ample. Afraid to use desk or drawer as a place of deposit, I concluded to thrust my part of the "spoils of victory" into a cat-hole in the cellar floor, over a drain. The end was not yet. The master of the *Teazer*, on his arrival at the port of destination, was sued for the gold, and cast into prison; and before terms of settlement were arranged, many other vexatious measures disturbed us. The affair gave rise to a great deal of talk; and some incidents which I have omitted, as not pertinent to my purpose, afforded infinite amusement to the lovers of fun. *The secret of our great indebtedness to our Boston bank was, however, treasured for years.*

You should embrace every opportunity to acquire information as to the standing of your customers; and whatever is imparted to you on the subject, whether in confidence or otherwise, should be communicated to your directors, and to them alone.

You should become acquainted with the laws relative to banking, and especially with those of your own State; and should be familiar with some work which treats of notes and bills, of the liabilities of sureties, drawers, and indorsers. I recommend as the easiest way to obtain, and to retain, knowledge in these particulars, that you make a manual, or brief digest, with marginal references to the authorities which you consult. The best books are the latest American editions of Bayley on Bills and Notes generally, and Story's Commentaries on the Law of Promissory Notes. To master these works, or even to obtain common knowledge of the immense learning which they contain, will require time—much time. But the leading principles applicable to promissors and other parties to commercial paper, are easily fixed in the memory, and no time should be lost in consulting the latter treatise, at the very least. So, too, chapter eleven of Story, which relates to checks, should also be well studied, since this kind of currency has, as that distinguished jurist observes, "grown into daily and general use," and will be presented at your counter almost as often as money itself. I recommend to the young cashier to devote a part of his leisure to professional reading of a more general nature. The history of the system of credit is not only curious, but interesting and instructive. Strangely enough, as he will find, banking owes its origin to the Crusades, for the earliest institution of which there is any account was a mere bank of *deposit*, established at Venice, late in the twelfth century, for the purpose of aiding those who fought to win the Holy Land from its unholy possessors. Such was the first element; and the degree of security and facility of commercial transactions of the period may be seen in the fact that, in England, contracts between individuals were discharged by payments in cattle, horses, dogs, and even hawks; and that rents, fines, and taxes due the crown were paid in the same kinds of property, in products of the soil, and in merchandise generally. In a word, the idea of paper money based on the precious metals, or on personal estate and credit, or on lands, had not been conceived, we may fairly conclude, anywhere. Next, if the notes of my own reading be accurate, and equally strange, we hear of some sort of *paper credit*, early in the thirteenth century, not in any trading country of Europe, but in far-off, and, as we commonly say, in barbarous China. So, again, toward the close of the last-mentioned century, we are told that the hated and hunted Jews and Lombards invented the *bill of exchange*, which afforded means for the silent and secret transfer of funds from country to country, to the infinite discomfiture of robber kings and of robber outlaws. Next, probably, in chronological order, was the *promissory note*, which strange device, grave and learned judges, in solemn wig and ermine, dared at length to pronounce to worn and weary litigants, might, if traffickers so willed, pass current from one person to another, and be lawfully collected by the final owner.* Still again, about the middle of the fourteenth century, we meet with the origin of *public scrip* in the governmental certificates of Florence, which, I suppose, were the first ever issued in Europe. Thus we have five elements in modern banking. Two others, namely, those of *discount* and *circulation*, were yet wanting. Neither power was conferred upon the Bank of Amsterdam, which, founded near the opening of the seventeenth century, was designed merely, as it would seem, to check the evils of a clipped and worn metallic currency. Nor was the Bank of Hamburg, which was established immediately after, hardly more than an institution for deposit and transfer. In the progress, however, of civilization, of commercial dealing and necessity, we come at last, and toward the close of the seventeenth century, to the Bank of England, which was invested with authority to receive deposits, to buy and sell exchange, to aid in the management of public securities, to discount promissory notes, and to issue a paper currency. And so it appears from this rapid view, that more than five hundred years elapsed before *all* the elements of modern banking were combined, arranged, and reduced to a system in which statesmen and merchants reposed confidence.

The young cashier having, by his researches, convicted me of inaccuracy, or having established the truth of the foregoing outlines of bank history, may, as opportunity occurs, pursue the subject still further. The first charter of the Bank of England is accessible, and he may study it with profit, and to ascertain the immense progress which has been made in the principles of banking, whether as relates to rights of stockholders, or to public con-

* As late down as the reign of WILLIAM AND MARY, the courts of England refused to consider an inland bill of exchange a legal instrument; nor was it until the time of ANNE, that a promissory note, in the hands of an indorsee, could be collected by law of the maker.

venience and safety. He will find valuable lessons in the legislation of his own country; in the issue of paper money prior to the Revolution, which at times flooded the colonies, and which, in spite of the clamors of our fathers, was suppressed by Parliament; in the marvelous tales and traditions which have come down to us of the never-to-be-forgotten "continental money," without which the bonds of colonial vassalage would not have been broken when, and as, they were; in the earlier charters of the different State governments; and in the two charters of Congress of the great national institution which has now ceased to exist.

This general inquiry concluded, he will have improved his own mind, and be ready to meet and to reason with those who, because the system has not been perfected in a century and a half (dating from the establishment of the Bank of England), demand its entire abolition, or at least such changes as would render it powerless for good, alike to individuals and to communities. He can say and prove that CREDIT, wide, liberal, beneficent credit, belongs to the era of liberty, and that it was unknown even in free England until after the expulsion of the Stuarts, and until the Revolution there had secured personal freedom. He may stand upon the emphatic declaration of a great statesman,[*] that the system of credit, as it now prevails, is the vital air of commerce, and that "it has done more, a thousand times, to enrich nations than all the mines in all the world." He should, indeed, admit that its fluctuations, its ebbs and flows, sometimes cause desolation and ruin; yet he should not fail to insist that good and wise men steadily strive to improve it—that, as sweeping conflagrations allow of the straightening and widening of streets; and as disasters in traveling by steam suggest more careful management and better machinery, so do bank failures and the delinquencies of bank officers, however appalling the circumstances at the moment, serve to discover and to apply new checks and new remedies.

If your bank is old enough to have been through "a crisis," and if you have not served in it as an inferior officer, you have much to learn of its past business. Such an institution, for example, has a "suspended debt" account, or at best overdue paper secured by mortgage or other collateral; and assets of this description *always have a history*, and sometimes a very intricate, a very perplexing one. But you must become master of that history. Directors change every year; and in a little time, all who were at the "Board" when this class of paper was taken will have vacated their seats; while, then, some are still in the direction, make written memoranda of the principal facts.

Let it be manifest to your associates and stockholders, that you feel an interest in every thing which relates to their welfare. To work the whole of your capital and of your deposits, to keep both actively employed at all times, and yet to be always able to meet your bills at the point of redemption, require great wisdom; and the most skillful and experienced financiers

[*] Mr. Webster.

sometimes find themselves at fault for the moment. Still your duty demands continual experiments to effect this great object; the recollection and correction of your own mistakes of judgment, as well as a careful eye upon *some* of your customers, who obtain discounts under promises to give your money "a good circulation."

Need I suggest the benefits of a fixed system, and of method, even in matters seemingly of little consequence. Every body finds—as seamen have it—that "a stern chase is a long chase." The business of to-day should never be deferred till to-morrow. Answer letters, and file papers, at the instant. Remember every thing, if possible; but trusting to memory in nothing: let your books contain a record of all transactions. Allow no outstanding bills against the bank; and have a voucher for the smallest item charged to "Expense Account."

You can be, and you ought to be, ready for an "examination" by the "Commissioners," or other functionaries of the government, and of your own "Board," without previous notice, and without the slightest special preparation. In fine, close your vault daily with the reflection that no act has been neglected, and that, if sickness or death should occur "the bank can go on" with no loss to your family, sureties, or stockholders. Do not smile, if I add, that your banking-rooms should be swept, and your desks and counters be dusted daily; that *one* "slut-hole" is ample for all the twine and waste-paper; and that the accumulation of official papers and memorandums in your *private* drawer will cause both you and your associates serious delays and much inconvenience.

Panics and pressures are as certain in banking as storms in winter. When either exist, firmness and courage, if not really possessed, must be assumed. You are presumed to know the nature and extent of your resources under *all* circumstances, and at periods of general distrust especially; and if the amount of those *immediately* available are insufficient for every possible call upon you, thus advise your directors without delay. Should there be "a run for specie," pay your bill-holders the kinds of coin they ask for so cheerfully, and with so careless an air, that they shall observe no reluctance to part with it, but, on the other hand, an apparent joy to be rid of it.

A knowledge of human character is indispensable. Study it. The "actions, looks, words, and steps" of your customers "form an alphabet:" and your "eyes are spectacles to read others' hearts with." Careful, close, and continued observations will enable you to detect a counterfeit man as readily as you now do a counterfeit bank-note. My own experience is, that those who change countenance, or the weight of the body from one foot to the other, when meeting a full, searching, and fixed gaze, are not truthful; that those who ask for additional accommodations, prefacing the request with a story divided into acts like a drama, are already bankrupt; and that those who petition in whispers, in an unnatural tone of voice, in a cant, or a whine, are hypocrites. Some years hence, I shall be glad to ascertain how nearly *your* experience accords with mine.

You should be courteous and respectful to all. Self-command is a great virtue; indulgence of passion is a great fault. Impertinence and stupid ignorance might sometimes be rebuked, were it not for the danger of contracting a morose and irritable habit of speaking. There is no loss of dignity, or of self-respect, in perfect silence under the greatest provocation, and that, accordingly, is your safest course. The cashier's popularity or unpopularity gives character to a bank. The directors are seldom visible, and sometimes unknown, to occasional customers; but their executive officer is an ever-present and a known man, and should bear in mind the Latin proverb, namely, to "be cautious *what* he says, *when*, and to *whom*."*

Should you acquire a reputation, you may be solicited to change your place; or, becoming discontented, may seek to do so on your own motion. In the former case you are to consider your directors as your friends, and, stating *all* the facts fairly, obtain *their* views before taking a single step to meet the overture made to you. This is an imperative duty; and performing it in honor, and acting under the advice of wise counselors, you can hardly come to a wrong conclusion. I assume here that your bank is sound, and that it is under the direction of competent and safe men. If unfortunately otherwise, if your reputation be at stake, and your directors, or a governing part of them, are ignorant or regardless of the principles of banking, or are "speculators," who seek their own accommodation, you should retire at once. But upon this point I will not dwell, since it is to be hoped that such institutions and such men have nearly passed away.

It is related that the eminence of the five brothers Rothschild, as bankers, is to be attributed in a great measure to their strict observance of their father's dying injunction, to "remain united." Well may it be so. Unanimity in the direction of a bank is always an element of success; and the result of my observation in this regard is, that more losses occur from divisions, than from any other single cause. Accommodation notes, large and standing loans to particular parties, and similar departures from legitimate banking, are only to be tolerated in cases which receive the assent of the entire direction. Yet, I have known one and all of these departures to be consummated, time and again, by directors who owned the smallest possible amount of stock, in opposition to the remonstrances of older and abler associates who were large stockholders; and years afterward, when legal remedies had been exhausted, and levies and set-offs had failed to restore more than costs of suit, have personally made wearisome journeys and devoted weeks to the service of closing up, as I best could, these unfortunate

---

* "A bill-broker," says Mr. Windham Beaves, "should avoid babbling, and be prudent in his office, which consists in one sole point, that is, *to hear all and say nothing.*"

illustrations of the rule that "a majority should govern" in the directors' room, as in politics. In short, such, in my view, are the evils of the majority principle in this connection, that I would counsel a cashier, whether young or old, to insist upon a reasonable change, and a change refused, to seek an institution more wisely, more safely conducted.

You may be discontented without cause. I remember to have read a story, in which one of the characters was in possession of every thing that heart could ask, but was miserable from this very circumstance, or because he *wanted—a want.* Such persons exist in real life. Be not of that unhappy class. Accommodate yourself to your condition. Do not seek for happiness in change of place, but in change of disposition. "The lazy ox wishes for the trappings of the horse, and the steed sighs for the yoke," is an old saw that has not yet lost its meaning. Nor should the topic be dismissed without recalling the pithy epitaph composed for the hypochondriac, who quacked himself into his grave: "I was *well;* but by endeavoring *to be better*—am here." Let the young cashier heed the moral contained in these several apt sayings, and remember that care and perplexity exist everywhere. To smooth and fashion the rough stone of life is a religious duty. The change of one's home involves a change of society, of privileges of worship, of schools, of facilities in traveling, of household expenses, of access to books, and various other essentials; and should be carefully considered in every aspect before it is actually undertaken. And I bestow the more attention upon the point, because the propensity to remove from one place to another is so common, and because, within the circle of my acquaintance, many have been ruined, and but few have improved their condition or increased their happiness, by seeking a new abode. In middle age, the experiment is doubly hazardous. Take up a full grown tree, and will it live unless some of the old earth go with it? Sunder the ties of sympathy and affection; exchange old faces and associates for new ones, and what is the condition of a man?

To resume my personal address to the young cashier. You should not possess an overweening desire of praise, nor invite commendation. Nor should you be intoxicated with your own merits.

You should never speak of your official acts, except in explanation and in self-defense. In all pleasantry, I will add, that, in old age, you may tell the son who succeeds you what you were in your youth; but, now, be content with the quiet appreciation of others. Delicate attentions and marks of respect are the surest and best manifestations of regard, and if you have these, do not pine in discontent or discouragement.

In your *official* intercourse with the president and directors, observe great deference; and at the "Board" it may be proper to address the former by his title.

Never speak of the real or supposed faults of character of a director in the social circle, nor bear tales or remarks from one director to another.

Whatever your preferences, likes, and dislikes—and you will probably have both—your *conduct* should be uniformly respectful to all. Whenever your opinion is asked, or given, without solicitation, state your views modestly, and in a conversational tone of voice. Should the "Board" differ from you in judgment, and decide contrary to your convictions, betray no feeling, but promptly and cheerfully execute their vote.

Frequent communications with the directors, relative to the general concerns of the bank and to your own particular duties, will be of essential service: since *they* will thus obtain a knowledge of details, and *you* will have the benefit of their reflections and suggestions. "Conference," says the wise Lord Bacon, "maketh a ready man."

Your style of living is a matter of momentous consequence; and, possibly, the hinge on which your final destiny will turn. Not only live within your income, but so regulate your expenses that, unavoidable misfortunes or sickness excepted, you shall be sure to save at least a quarter part of your salary, as a fund for old age; unless, indeed, your patrimonial estate be ample for such a purpose.* But, whatever be your receipts or expectations from other sources, do not allow your expenditures to exceed your personal earnings. Be this the great economic maxim of your life.

Economy is the parent of honesty, of freedom, and of mental ease and quiet. Poverty can never enter your abode, if content with satisfying your

---

* I designed to say a word in the text on the subject of salaries. As a general rule, the compensation to bank officers is too small. According to a return to Parliament, in 1832, the number of persons employed in the Bank of England and its branches, was nine hundred and forty, who (to average the salaries) received only £225, or about eleven hundred dollars each, per annum. Since several who filled the higher posts were paid very much larger sums, it is evident that a considerable part of this numerous corps could not have received more than a moiety of the above average. Yet, as at the same time there were one hundred and ninety-three on the pension list who enjoyed annually (on the average) £161, or about eight hundred dollars each, the faithful officers of that institution who were then in actual service, could hope for relief in their declining years. In the United States, the system of pensions is not, perhaps, practicable or desirable. But since marriage, a flock of little ones, *the owning of a house unincumbered with mortgage*, and a choice collection of books, are all Virtue's sentinels, directors ought always to have reference to the support of a family in fixing the compensation of their executive officers. Indeed, such officers, like capable and faithful men in other pursuits, should be allowed to provide something for old age. It is fair, I suppose, to assume that the expense of the executive department, as a common thing, is not far from one per cent. on the capital stock, or, in the proportion of one thousand dollars salary to one hundred thousand dollars capital. If this be so, it is manifest, at a glance, that a large part of the bank officers in the United States (as gentlemen are now *compelled* to live both in city and country) are required to consult the maxims of " Poor Richard" every day, in order to secure a moderate competence. The interests of stockholders are not promoted, in the long run, by low salaries; for low salaries, not infrequently, as experience shows, induce speculations in stocks, and other irregularities, which terminate in defalcation. As a class, bank officers are not so well paid as officers of railroads and manufacturing establishments, while their duties are quite as responsible.

real wants; while you will never enjoy independence, if you live in accordance with the world's caprice.* If you possess an inordinate craving for great wealth, or a desire to indulge in luxuries and amusements such as men of fortune alone can afford, you have mistaken your profession, and should abandon it. For your life, if you remain in it, will be a perpetual struggle against your natural inclinations; and the danger is, that, finally yielding to them, you will involve yourself in irretrievable woe.

The road to disgrace is short. Persons who have traced the footsteps of more than one unhappy bank officer that has trodden it, have found that EXTRAVAGANCE and DEFALCATION were but a few strides apart.† A sensual man is disqualified, by his very physical organization, for *any* office in the executive department of a bank, and ought no more to be there than in a pulpit. I make the remark considerately—for good reasons—and not to round out a period. And should this Essay meet the eye of the father of a son ready, by age and education, to enter upon some employment, I venture to counsel that, if banking be thought of, the moral qualities and the strength of the appetites, as developed in early life, are the first things to be considered. The youth who, in childhood, stole slyly to the closet for his mother's sweetmeats, who was never content at table with the share of niceties allotted to him, who shirked his known tasks, and imposed their performance upon a younger and more dutiful brother, and who, as years wore on, evinced a disposition to rely upon others, and to earn nothing for himself, but yet who showed a determined purpose to feed on the best, and to dress in the finest—such a youth, though as quick at figures as Colburn himself, should never be placed in a bank.

"Speculation in stocks" is another fruitful source of ruin, and I can not forbear a word of admonition. The careful investment of your earnings or

* The great English banker, Thellusson, who, at one time, was partner with Mr. Necker, the celebrated French financier, left three sons, and a fortune of three and a half millions of dollars, which estate, he said, he acquired by "industry and honesty." In his will he remarks: "*It is my earnest wish and desire that my sons avoid ostentation, vanity, and pompous show,*" etc. The three, it may be added, became members of the House of Commons, and the eldest, a peer of the realm.

† "The London banker of the old school," says Lawson, "had little resemblance to the modern gentleman who is known by the same title. He was a man of serious manners, plain apparel, the steadiest conduct, and a rigid observer of formalities. As you looked in his face, you could read in intelligible characters that the ruling maxim of life, the one to which he turned all his thoughts and by which he shaped all his actions, was: '*That he who would be trusted with the money of other men should look as if he deserved the trust, and be an ostensible pattern to society of probity, exactness, frugality, and decorum.*'" And further, says the same writer: "The fashionable society at the West End of the town, and the amusements of high life, he never dreamed of enjoying, and would have deemed it nothing short of insanity to imagine that such an act was within the compass of human daring, as that of a banker lounging for an evening in Fop's Alley at the opera, or turning out for the Derby with four grays to his chariot, and a goodly hamper swung behind, well stuffed with perigord pies, spring chickens, and iced champagne."

patrimony, and a similar service for friends and customers, define, in my judgment, the general limits of your operations in the stock market. To say nothing of the hopes and fears consequent upon the adventures of a dealer, and nothing of their influence upon your mind and temper—already sufficiently tasked—I may ask, in all seriousness, What assurance have you, what assurance can you have, that your virtue will resist the temptations sure to beset you? Once embarked and afloat on the stock-exchange, either alone or with partners, you can not move without means: and who shall answer for the money intrusted to your care? Who shall answer that you will not "borrow" from your vault—as others have done—feeling sure that you can "return" the sum you need "in a few days, with interest?" At the outset you will not "risk much;" you desire only "to gain something to add to a moderate salary." But encouraged, at length, by your own success in small operations, or excited by the real or reported good fortune of those around you, the resolution *may* be formed to win a competence at a single cast of the die: YOU LOSE, AND ARE RUINED! Be warned, I entreat, in time. No bank officer—in charity, we may believe—ever meant to be a defaulter; no one, at the beginning of an irregular course, thought defalcation and disgrace possible. Yet, alas for the many victims of self-deception! alas for the self-confident, and for those who neglected the great duty of self-examination! Most affectionately and earnestly do I charge you, as you value your peace, as you would save your integrity, as you would not be driven forth, a broken and shunned man, to resist every seduction of avarice from within, and every solicitation of companions from without. No matter what pretense or excuse a stifled conscience may allow you to frame, *the cash in your vault is not your cash, and you touch it for your private benefit or relief even as a robber, and at the peril of your soul!* Think, ere you yield, of the long roll of sad-faced men who once were honored and trusted, but who, when tempted, fell! Think of those who, wrecked in character, in fortune, and in hope, have become bloated, ragged wanderers! Think of those of whom fathers and mothers, and even wives and children, dare not speak save in whispers, and at the family fireside! Think of those who have been hurried to the prisons and to the tribunals! Think of the graves of the suicides!

A single warning more, and I pass to less painful topics of discourse. Allow no customer to overdraw his account upon your own responsibility, or without the express sanction and authority of directors.* The habit is a bad one, every way, under *any* circumstances; and I wish it could come to an end at once, everywhere and forever. But if it be permitted in particular cases in your bank, have neither part nor lot in the matter, save to execute a positive order. Discourage the practice in every possible manner, and if fortunate enough to put an end to it, you will deserve the

* I believe that no customer of the Bank of England, whatever his rank, is allowed to overdraw.

praise of every correct banker in the country. At your post, and in bank hours, you are to have no friends to indulge with favors, no enemies to punish with refusals. Then and there all men should be alike to you. The motto of the "Bankers' Magazine" should be yours, without reservation or condition.* In fine, perform no act that you would omit in the presence of the full "Board," or in that of the sureties on your official bond. This rule will carry you safely through every difficulty and every temptation.

Pardon me if I now suggest the importance of maintaining a reputation for strict, exact veracity. An aged judge is said to have remarked, ironically, that "half the cases he had tried on the bench arose from '*good understanding*' between the parties;" and by this he meant, that half-made bargains and agreements lead to disagreement and litigation. Avoid misunderstandings from this source. Many, indeed most, of your transactions will be upon verbal contracts. But you may use words so terse, so precise, that misconception will be hardly possible.

The honor of a cashier and the honor of a woman are alike. Suspicion of either in the public mind is as fatal to reputation as convicted guilt. Stand by, stand for *your* honor, then against all comers, and to the last. Preserve your own respect, though you be fed by the hand of public or of private charity. Napoleon, at the hour of his downfall, deposited the remains† of his fortune with Laffitte, and refused an offered and customary certificate, saying: "I KNOW YOU—I HOLD YOU TO BE AN HONEST MAN." The Paris banker, in the course of events, became a cabinet minister; but such a testimonial to his probity from a man whose estimate of human virtue was too low to be just, and who, at the moment he uttered it, was, as he imagined, the victim of faithlessness and treachery, will be remembered when the records of his political honors are torn and scattered. But yet, any man, in his own circle, may, if he will, have it said of him: "I KNOW YOU—I HOLD YOU TO BE AN HONEST MAN." My young friend—now starting upon a banker's career—burn these words deep into your memory!

As in some things there are marked distinctions between banks in different sections of the country, and between country and city banks in the same State, and corresponding differences in the duties of a cashier, it is obvious that no series of "suggestions" can be alike applicable to all. But I may still hope that the *young and inexperienced* officer will not fail to find *some* useful hints in the preceding remarks, whatever his particular position or special charge.

And while this may be so, the country cashier may yet need cautions and recommendations adapted to his peculiar official and social relations.

---

* "No expectation of forbearance or indulgence should be encouraged. Favor and benevolence are not the attributes of good banking. Strict justice and the rigid performance of contracts are its proper foundation."

† Five millions of francs.

Such, then, as I deem the most important, I shall briefly and respectfully offer. First, as it sometimes happens that the person selected for the executive department has had little or no experience in banking, and is to be connected with directors whose knowledge is as limited as his own, the duty of consulting well-informed officers of city banks is manifest. The country cashier is often alone. Without paying or receiving tellers, book-keeper, or discount or collection clerks, but invested with the functions of all, skill, system, and an economical use of time, are indispensable to success. I have known gentlemen who, though possessing quick and clear perceptions, and almost every other natural endowment, were still, at the time of their election, incapable of opening or of properly keeping a single bank-book. Some of these, remarkably cautious in their habits of business, and profiting by mishaps, escaped serious losses, and, in the end, became accomplished officers; while others, more sanguine in temperament, and more self-confident, and unwilling to *seem* novices, involved themselves in difficulties which caused them much mental disquietude and pecuniary embarrassment. Now, it is apparent at a glance, that both classes, had they started right, might have avoided a great deal of painful experience.

I commend to you, therefore, if not bred to banking, the sources of information which are open to you, and to all who desire to increase their knowledge. Accuracy in the count of money is the first, accuracy in the keeping of accounts is the second, qualification in a country cashier; and, while you may acquire the first by practice, you may go wrong with your records all your life.

A small bank should be conducted on a plan as systematic and as regular as a large on. Experience has shown, I think, that bank accounts should be kept in "double entry," and that each department of bank business requires a separate book. Thus, in an institution with a capital of only fifty thousand dollars, I consider that a general and a deposit leger, that books for cash, deposits, discounts, credits, collections, and trial-balances, are as essential as in one of a million of dollars. And the same remark is true of stockholders' and directors' records, of a book to show the state of the bank, and of another to exhibit the paper to mature in any given week.

The general and the deposit leger may be one; the former occupying some seventy-five or one hundred pages, and embracing accounts with *things*, the latter with *persons*. The cash should be settled daily at the close of business, when, also, a trial balance should be taken of the general leger postings. On the last business day of the month, the depositors' accounts should be adjusted, and the balance of each be transferred to the trial-balance book to ascertain whether the deposit leger has been correctly posted. The daily settlement of the cash—neglected in *some* country banks, unless the reform has been very recent—need occupy but a few minutes, since a vault-book, accurately kept, leaves for actual count the cash in drawer only. "Memorandum checks," and similar vouchers—to say nothing of the grave consequences which sometimes result from their use—are great pests in a cashier's drawer, and should not be allowed there, except in the most urgent cases. Some cashiers keep "ragged bills," never intended to be reissued, in vault for months, and even years; but the practice is attended with obvious risk and inconvenience, and should not exist.

As already intimated in another connection, your directors, however worthy and respectable as citizens and gentlemen, may be poorly versed in the science of banking, and may not, at first, appreciate the force and the reason of the rules which you deem necessary to adopt, in transactions with them and with others. But evince no impatience. I assume that a majority of any and of every "Board" are men of honor, and mean to do right; and that, in explanations and conversations with yours, you have but to calmly point out the evils likely to arise from a course opposite to that which you insist upon, to obtain their approbation. Yet you yourself should be well assured that these rules are consonant to law, or are such as are imposed in well-regulated banks, or such as, in your peculiar position and relations, are imperatively demanded.

It is possible that your predecessor allowed improper indulgences to a particular director, or had favorites among your customers, and that you will feel constrained to put an end to these and to similar irregularities. To accomplish this, in harmony, will require all the wisdom and good-nature that you can command. It is possible, too, that overtures may be made to you to grant favors inconsistent with your duty; but, as such cases will arise from thoughtlessness or ignorance, as often as from unworthy motives, you should be silent, except when corrupt intentions are too apparent to be mistaken, or the importunities of the same person become so frequent as to be troublesome.

The customers of a country bank, unlike the merchants of large and busy cities, expect of the cashier some inquiries about their families, and remarks upon the news of the day, upon the crops, the weather, and other matters of personal or local interest. To a reasonable extent this expectation should be gratified. But discussions across your counter on topics of sectarian theology and party politics are to be avoided—entirely avoided. Nor, if you hear, should you reply to, or take part in, tales of scandal and neighborhood gossip. Polite to all, sociable to a degree not to interfere with your duties, inviting and giving friendly greetings, your deportment is yet to be dignified, and such as becomes a well-bred gentleman.

You will transact business with persons who can not even write a note of hand in proper form; with those who can not be made to acknowledge the necessity of a notice to an indorser; and with those who will pertinaciously insist upon having their own way, whatever your reasoning or objections to the contrary. Teach the ignorant, without giving them pain; be firm with the self-willed, without evincing impatience or anger; for the smart of a sharp word, or of a proud toss of the head, is sometimes felt for years. "Contempt," says an Eastern proverb, "will penetrate the shell of a tortoise;" be sure to remember, that it will pierce deeper into the epidermis of a fellow-man.

To require, and to insist upon, regular bank hours will occasion *some* difficulty in *some* places. People whose business at banks is rare, seem to forget that a cashier, like other men, has a love of fresh air, or that he needs exercise and relaxation; and thus can not or will not understand why he is not ready to accommodate them early in the morning, and late in the evening. These persons seek him in his moments of rest and recreation, ask him to receive money at his house, or in the village stores, and complain if he refuses so *reasonable* requests. You will be unjust to yourself if you submit to these, or to similar demands. The intervals between bank hours are yours by positive contract, and by the very necessities of your physical and mental being. Do not permit inroads upon them, save in extraordinary exigences; in these, leave your bed even, to serve a customer. Still, as loose and unsafe habits may have been encouraged by your predecessors, or countenanced by directors, measures of reform will be odious, unless gradual. Under kind and considerate treatment your laggards may become punctual, and untimely requests to open your vault entirely cease.

A single "suggestion" more. The private and social relations of a country cashier are of consequence, and ought not to be overlooked. And, first, a salary officer, under ordinary circumstances, needs not to be in debt for his personal or family expenses; and, as cash payments are sure to show whether he is "living beyond his means," may I not commend the safe rule of "paying as you go?"

Again, may I not be allowed to suggest the duty of constant attendance at church, even though you can not worship with persons of your own faith; and also of manifesting an interest in schools, public lectures, lyceums, and other means employed to promote the welfare of society? The community in which you live have a claim upon you, not only for an exemplary life, but for contributions of money in proportion to your ability, to aid in the maintenance of the religious, literary, and benevolent associations established among them.

To conclude. Should it be thought that I might have omitted the discussion of some topics, and have treated others with greater brevity, I submit, with deference, that I have endeavored to be a careful observer. More than twenty-five years have elapsed since the commencement of my connection with banks and banking; and, as I now look back and recall the facts elicited by judicial inquiry, and the facts embraced in other well-authenticated accounts which relate to bank officers who have fallen, never again to rise, or whose lives have been saddened and embarrassed by want of firmness in resisting the allurements of pleasure, or the solicitations of the companions of their social hours—by an overweening self-confidence—by too great faith in others; as, too, I remember the complaints against another class, who, though without a moral stain, have still injured themselves and the institutions with which they are concerned by churlishness and irritability; I find no cautions and admonitions to omit, no recommendations that may not, I think, assist in forming the character of the officer for whom these suggestions are intended.

A single word more. Many of the cashiers whose private virtues and professional ability adorn the annals of banking in the United States, receive salaries nearly equal to the emoluments of cabinet ministers, or military officers of the highest rank, and are intrusted with powers so ample, that they seem to be private bankers, wielding their own capital. These gentlemen have attained the crowning honors of their profession. Let the "young cashier" aim to reach the same eminence among men and among bankers. Let him remember that, whatever the influence of friends at the outset of his career, his position in the maturity of his years must, in the very nature of things, depend upon himself, upon his capacity, his courage, and his probity.

I have here spoken to him as to my only son, and take my leave, in the earnest hope that, in the labors of some one of his seniors, communicated to the "Magazine" upon the invitation which, perhaps, I have unwisely accepted, he will be sure to find a path marked out for him which will lead him to the rewards of a well-spent life.

THE

NUMISMATIC DICTIONARY

OR,

COLLECTION OF THE NAMES OF ALL THE COINS KNOWN, FROM THE EARLIEST PERIOD UP TO THE PRESENT DAY, WITH THEIR COUNTRIES, VALUES, MULTIPLES, DIVISIONS, ETC., ETC.

A

ABACUS, The Roman calculation Table.
ABASSI, Persian, Silver, value 6d. Qu. Shahee.
ABBEY PIECES, various countries, Brass, possibly current for small sums, but chiefly used in computation as Jetons.
ABRA, Polish, Silver, value 1s.
ABUQUELP Egyptian, Silver, value 30 medini, 1s. 6d. See Griscio.
ACHESON, Scots Billon, value 8d., named from Atkinson, mint master.
ACHTZEHNER, Swedish, Silver.
ACKEY, colonial, Silver, coined in 1818.
ACKIE, Ashantee, Gold, value 5s. 4d. from Ackee, seed of Guinea, Af.
AES, Roman, term for money in general, Brass.
AEFORTIATI, Roman, Senatorian coins of the 12th and 13th centuries.
AHMULAHS, Abyssinian salt money, various sizes, new, 20 to a Dollar.
AIGNEL, Anglo-Gallic, Gold. Bearing the Agnus Dei.
ALBERT, Flemish, Gold. Also Dollars and Groschen.
ALBUS, German, Copper, value 12 Hellers, at Cassel, Cologne, etc.
ALFAZZAT, Persian, Silver.
ALLEVURE, Swedish, Copper, the smallest value.
ALMOND, Hindostan. The nut is current, 40 to a Pice. See Baddam.
ALTIN, Russian, Silver.
ALTMICHLIC, Turkish, Silver, value 3s., 60 Paras.
ANGEL, English, Gold, value 6s. 8d., bearing St. Michael and Dragon.
ANGELET, English, Gold, the half Angel, value 3s. 4d.

ANGSTER, Swiss, Copper, also Rapp, value half a Rapen. Zurich.
ANKOSEE, Chinsoree, a Rupee of Silver, current in the Deccan.
ANNA, or ANA, Hindostan, Silver, 16 to a Rupee.
APERBIAS, Maltese.
ARCHER, Persian, Gold, the Daric.
ARDITE, Spanish, Copper, ancient and of small value. Catalonia.
ARMOODI, Turkish, Gold.
AS, Roman, Brass, value varied, literally 1 lb. of 12 oz., but reduced, 216
    B. C., to one ounce.
AS LIBRALIS, As GRAVE. Other names for the weighty As.
ASHRUFFY, Hindostan, Gold, value 12s. 6d. Nepaul.
ASPAR, ASPRE, or MINA, Turkish, Silver. 120 to a Piastre.
ASSIGNATS, French notes, first issued April 19th, 1790.
ASSARION, Greek, Brass, rendered farthing.
ATTINE, Polish, Silver, value 5d.
AUGUST D'OR, Saxony, Gold, value 16s. 3d.
AUREUS, Roman, Gold, value 16s. 8d. The Bezant also.
AUTONOMOUS, Coins of Cities in Greece, enjoying their own laws.

B

BAAT, Siamese, Silver, value 2s. 6d., nut shaped.
BACHE, Zurich, Billon, value 1¾d.
BADDAM, Hindostan, the almond of Persia, current on the Malabar
    coast.
BAGATTINO, Venetian, Copper, value half Soldi, ¼d.
BAGOGLEE, Persian, Gold, a ducat. Bajoglee.
BAIOCCO, Papal, Copper, value ½d.
BAIOCHELLO, Papal, Billon, single value 1d., double value 2d.
BAHADRY, Hindostan, Gold, the Star Pagoda, in the Mysore, so called.
BAJOIRE, Genevese, Silver, value 4s. 6d.
BANCO, Genoese, Bank money. The word Bank is derived from the
    Lombards, the Benoh for transacting business.
BAND, African, weight for gold dust, 2 oz.
BANK DOLLAR, Hamburg, Silver,
    In England, the Spanish Dollar, re-stamped and issued, as a Token,
        by the Bank, in 1804.
BARBONE, Luccese, Silver, value 6d. Qu. Bearded head.
BARS, Siamese, Silver, current.
BARS, W. African, Iron, current.
BASARMO, Hindostan, Tin.
BASARUCO, Hindostan, Tin, Malabar coast, value 10 to 1d., see Budge-
    rook.
BATZ, Swiss, Copper silvered, value 1½d., 10 Rappen.
BAWBEE, Scots, Copper, value ½d. Qu. Bas Piece.

BEARD COINS, Russian Copper. Receipt for being shaved.
BEKA, Jewish, Silver. The half Shekel. Baka, divided.
BELL DOLLAR, Brunswick, Silver, D. Augustus 1643, with and without clapper.
BENDA, Ashantee, Gold, value £10 13s. 4d.
BENDIKY, Morocco, Gold, value 9s.
BENER-PENNY, Anglo-Saxon, Silver, given in charity. See Mærra.
BESHLIE, Turkish, Silver, value 3s. 2d.
BESTIC or BESLIC, Turkish, Silver, value 5 aspers, 3d.
BEZANT. The Byzantine ducat, Gold. Also silver Bezantines, Imperial coins from the 5th century after Christ, each value 2s.
BEZZO, Venetian, Copper, value ½d. Bezzi money.
BIA, Siamese, Copper, round and thick, value 200 cowries.
BIGATI, Roman, Silver, the denarius bearing a two-horsed car.
BIGOTA, Chili, Gold. Qu. Mustachio.
BILLON, coins of mixed metal, silver and copper. Bas Billon the worst.
BISTI, Persian, Silver, value 2d.
BIT, the Spanish Real, Silver, in Jamaica: also the Portuguese Testone, there are also Half Bits, silver cut from Dollars.
BLACK DOG, St. Christopher's, Billon. The Cut Dollar, also so called.
BLACK MAIL, Scots protection money.
   Blanque Maille, French, bad Silver.
BLACK MONEY, English, the Bas Billon, denounced, temp. Edward I.
BLACK PEAKE, Indian. Rare shells strung, value 2s. 6d. a cubit.
BLAFFERT, Cologne, a small coin.
BLAMUSER, Westphalia, money of account.
BLANC, French, a silver coin, value 4d.
   The Ecu Blanc, the French crown piece
BLANCA, Spanish, money of account in Malaga.
BLANK, English Billon. The Gros Blanc, Anglo-Gallic, temp. Henry VI.
BLANQUILLE, Barbary, Silver, value 2½d.
BODLE, Scots, Copper, the half Plack. From Bothwell, mint master.
BOHMEN, or Bohemian, Prague, Silver, value 3 Kreutzers.
BOLOGNINO, Luccese, Billon, value 1d. Also at Bologna.
BON-GROS, Hesse-Cassel, Silver, value 2d.
BONNET PIECE, Scots, Gold, temp. K. James I. from the Cap then worn.
BORAGE GROAT, Scots Silver, 1467, value 12d. Qu. From Borax used in it.
BORBI, Egyptian, Copper, value 3 aspers. Qu. Burbi, see Bourbe
BORDHALFPENNY, paid for a stall in a market.
BORJOOKES, Abyssinian, glass beads, current for small money.
BOS. The Greek Didrachm, Silver, bearing an Ox.
BOVELLA, Persian, Silver, value 16s.

BOUGES, African, cowries are so called.
BOURBE, Barbary, money of account at Tunis, value half asper.
BRABANT, English, Base coin temp. K. Edward I.
BRABANT KRONE, Austrian, Silver, value 4s. 6d., 2g. 15k.
BRACTIATE, Roman, and other coins, impressed on one side only, from Bractia, a spangle.
BROAD PIECE, English, Gold, value 20s. The Unit, temp. K. James I.
BUDGEROOK, Hindostan, money of account on the Malabar coast, 6 to a Pice.
BUSHE, Aix-la-Chapelle, Copper, value 4 Hellers.
BUSSORA, Crux, Turkish, Silver, value 16d.

C

CABESQUIS, Persian, Silver, value 1d. Casbesquis, Kasbequis.
CACAO, Mexico, Grains current, 100 to a Medio, 3¼d.
CAGLIARESCO, Sardinian, Copper, value 6 to a Soldi.
CAHAUN, Bengal, Silver, value 7¼d. Cahuse, a quarter Rupee.
CALDERILLA, Spanish, Copper, the Cuarto, value 4 Maravedis.
CANDARINE, Chinese, money of account. 100 to a Tael, value ¾d.
CANTEROY, Hindostan, The Sultany Fanam, so called in the Mysore.
CAPELLONE, Modena, Silver, value 3d.
CARAT, Arabian, a small coin of very base silver at Mocha.
The carat weight for gold, named from the red bean of Abyssinia, the fruit of the Kuara. 4 grains.
CARAGRONCH, Mod. Greece, Silver, value 5s.
CARDECU, French, Silver, the quart D'Ecu, so called in England.
CARIVAL, Bombay, valued 12 Pice.
CARL D'OR, Brunswick, Gold, value 16s. 4d.
CARLINO, Sardinian, Gold, value £1 18s. 10d.
CARLINO, Italian, Silver, value 5d. Coined first in 1490, by King Charles VIII. of France.
CARLO, Lombardy, Silver, value 5s.
CAROBA, Barbary. A coin of Tunis.
CAROLIN D'OR, Bavarian, Gold, value £1 0s. 8d.
CAROLINE, Swedish, Silver, value 1s. 6d.
CAROLUS, English, Gold, value 23s. The Laureat, temp. King Charles II.
CARUBE money of account in Algiers.
CASH, Chinese, Brass, coins for stringing, cast, 1000 Cash, 100 Candarines, 10 Mace=1 Tael. See Tseen.
CASTILLON, Spanish, Gold, probably from bearing the arms of Castile.
CASTELLANO, Spanish, Gold, the ancient coin.
CATI, Chinese, value, 16 Taels, or £5 6s. 8d. Also Catty.
CAVALIER, Swedish, Silver.
CAVALLO, Sardinian, Billon. Cavalli and Cavallucci, Naples.

CAVALLOTTO, Genoese, Billon, value 2d.
CAVEER, Arabian, money of account at Mocha. 40 to a Dollar. Cabeer or Carcar, value 1¼d.
CENT, Dutch, Copper, 100 to a Guilder.
CENT, American, Copper, 100 to a Dollar.
CENTIME, French, Copper, 100 to a Franc; also in Belgium and Ionian Islands.
CENTESIMO, Italian, Copper. Lombardy, value one-twelfth of a penny, 100 to a Lira.
CENTESSIMO, Copper, Uruguay
CENTUSSIS, Roman, 100 As, value in account 40 Sesterces 10 Deniers, or 6s. 3d.
CHAISE, Anglo-Gallic, Gold, temp. K. Edward III.
The French coin of Philip le Bel, the Royal Dur, hard coin.
CHALCUS, Greek, Brass. The earliest of that metal. 431 B.C.
CHALLIES, Ceylon, Copper, value 4 to a farthing. From Chally, Copper.
CHAPPEE, East Indies, Silver. The Rupee, when marked or chopped.
CHAYE, Persian, Silver. The Shaki, value 6d.
CHEDA, Tartary, Tin.
CHEGO, Portuguese, a weight for gold, 4 carats.
CHELON, Polish, Billon.
CHEQUIN, Turkish, Gold, value 9s. 6d.
CHERASIS, Persian, Gold, various value. The Tela, a medal.
CHIDA, Hindu, Tin, when round, value ½d., but if octagonal, value 2d.
CHOUSTACK, Polish, Billon, value 2d.
CHRISTIAN, Danish, Gold, value 16s. 5d.
CHRISTINE, Swedish, Silver, value 1s. 2d.
CINQ FRANCS, French, Silver, value nearly 4s.
CINQUINO Neapolitan.
CISTOPHORUS, Greek, Silver, bearing the Cista, or Chest, of Bacchus. Ancient Cistophori, of cities in Asia. Tri-drachms.
CLACO, Mexican. Elaco.
CLOTH, Abyssinia. Blue Surat cloth, a cubit in length, folded in a three-cornered packet, value half a dollar. See Wadmal.
COAL MONEY, British, found at Kimmeridge, coast of Dorsetshire; it is not quite proven that this was money.
COB, Spanish, Silver, the Duro, or hard Dollar, in Gibraltar, so called.
COCKIEN, Japanese, value £10.
COINS, probably originally tokens given at Temples. The earliest are of religious character in the devices.
COLONATO, Spanish, Silver, the Pillar Dollar is so called.
COLONIAL COINS, Greek money struck for the Roman Colonies; also English, struck for Canada, the Indies, etc.

COLOGNE, the Mark of, Weight, the Standard of Germany, 8 oz. Troy.
COMMASSEE, Arabian, Copper, but contains a little silver. 60 to a dollar at Mocha.
CONDOR, Chili, Gold, 10 Pesos, value £1 17s. 3d.
CONDORIN, Japanese, Copper, value ½d.
CONSTITUTION COINS, Germany, about 1738.
CONSULAR COINS, Roman, Silver, Denarii struck under the Government of Consuls. Family Medals.
CONTO, Portuguese, computation. 1000 Millreis.
CONTORNIATI, Roman, Tickets, not current.
CONVENTION COINS, German, about 1763, also 1818.
COPFSTUCK, Austrian, Silver, value 9d., 20 Kreutzers. Copstick.
COPANG, Japanese, Gold, value £2 4s. 2d. Also Silver, 4s. 6d. Qu. Oubans.
CORNADO, Spanish, Copper, value small. "No vale un Cornado," is, "not worth a farthing."
CORONILLA, Spanish, Gold. Vientin D'Oro, value 20 Reals.
COURONNES DU SOLEIL, French, Gold, 1546, current in England, as Crowns of the Sun, temp. K. Edward VI.
COWRIES, Bengal and Africa, small shells from the Maldives.
COZ, Persian, Copper, value 10 to a Shaki. Coz Bagues.
CRAZIA, Tuscan. value ½d. An old coin.
CREUTZER, or CRUITZER. See Kreutzer.
CRIMBAL, W. Indies, Silver, value 7½d. The Isle du Vent. Bit.
CROAT, Spanish, Silver. The Gros D'Argent of Arragon, origin of English Groat.
CROCARD, English, Base coin, temp. K. Edward I.
CROCIATO, Genoese, Silver, named from the arms. The Croisat, value 4s. 4d.
CROON, Flemish, Silver.
CRORE, Bengal computation, 100 Lacs, or 10 million Rupees.
CROSS, all money bearing a cross. The Cross Dollar, of Spain, bears the Burgundy cross.
CROWN, English, Gold, temp. K. Henry VIII. Crowns of the double rose, Thistle Crowns.
CROWN, English, Silver, temp. K. Edward VI., value 5s.
CRUCIIE, Swiss, Billon, value ½d.
CRUSADO, Portuguese, Gold and Silver, various value, the Crusado Novo, Silver, value 2s. 2d.
CU, thin Brass, bearing a shield; the Ecu, half-farthing.
CUARTA, Spanish, Copper, value 4 Maravedis, the Calderilla.
CUFIC COINS, Arabian, named from Kufa, on the Euphrates.
CUNETTI COINS, Anglo-Saxon, Silver. Pennies struck at Cunctium, Marlborough.

CUT MONEY, Brazilian, Silver. Plata Macuquina.
CZARSONITCH, Russian, Gold, value, 9s. 3d.

D

DAELDER, Dutch, Silver, value, 2s. 6d.
DAEZAJIE, Persian, Silver, value, 5s.
DAHAB, Abyssinian, Silver. See Harf.
DALER, Swedish, the Silver, is Silfermynt; the Copper, Kopparmynt.
DALER RIX, value 3s. 8d. See Dollar.
DAMA, Hindu, Copper. Nepaul.
DANAJO, Lombardy, Copper; or Danajnolo, the smallest money. Danàro.
DANDY PRAT, English, Silver, temp. K. Henry VII. dwarf coin.
DANE MONEY, Roman coins found in Northamptonshire, so called.
DANIM, Arabian, current at Bussora, value, ½d.
DARIC, Persian, Gold, named from Darius. Greek Darics.
DECIME, French, Copper, value, 1d., the tenth of a Franc.
DECIMO, La Plata, Copper, value, ½d., the tenth of a Medio.
DECUPLO, Sicilian, Gold.
DECUSSIS, Roman, Silver, marked X. 10 Asses, same as Denarius.
DENAING, Russian, Copper. Copecs or Pence.
DENAR, Silesia, Copper, the Pfening of Breslau.
DENARIUS, Roman, Silver, marked X. Denos Æres, value, 8d.; it was lowered both in weight and value.
DENARIUS, Anglo-Saxon, as Denarii S. Petri, the Peter Pence, a golden Denarius, temp. K. Henry III.
DENARO, Italian, money of account, value, one 24th of a penny.
DENGA, Russian, Copper, the half Copec. Also Dengop and Denushka.
DEMY, Scots, Gold, like the English half Noble. There are Demi-Pistoles, Louis, and Sequins in Gold.
DENIER, French, Copper, the twelfth part of a Sou. Also Swiss, the Deniers d'Argent, ancient coins, also the Deniers D'Or; The Double Denier, Anglo-Gallic, both of Silver, and Billon.
DENIER DE GROS, Flemish, the Groote, or Penny.
DENUSHKA, Russian, Copper, the half Copec.
DERHEM SEGAR, Barbary, Copper.
DERLINGUE, Venetian, Silver, half the Scudo.
DEVIL'S HEAD MONEY, Chinese, Silver. Spanish Dollars, so called.
DICHALCON, Greek, Silver, the smallest coin.
DICKENS, Swiss, Silver.
DIDRACHM, Greek, Gold, the Stater Aureus, or Philippus.
DIME, American, Silver, value, the tenth of a Dollar, 5d.
DINAR, Arabian, Gold, value, 8s. Denar.
DINERO, Spanish, money of account. "Tener dinero," to be rich.
  DINERAL and DINERADA, a large sum of money.

DINERUELO, Spanish, Copper, current in Arragon.
DIRHEM, Arabian, Silver.
DITTO BOLO, Ionian Islands, Copper.
DIWANI, Abyssinian money.
DOBRAO, Portuguese, Gold, value, £6 14s., the Dobra.
DOBLON, or Doubloon, Spanish, Gold, value, 5 Dollars; the Doblons de Acuatra, and De Ocho, are value, 8 and 16 Dollars.
DOBLON, Mexican, the gold onza, value, £3 4s.
DODEE, Bengal, Copper, the half Pice. Doudou. Dudu.
DODKIN, English, Copper, the small Duyt, once current.
DOG, W. Indies, Copper, value, 3d. The half Dog, value, 1½d.
DOIT, Hindostan, Copper, 120 to a Rupee.
DOLLAR, Spanish, Silver, the Peso Duro, the Piastre, or Piece of Eight, an ounce, value, 4s. 3d.
DOLLAR, American, Silver, value, 4s. 1½d., 10 Dimes, 100 Cents, 1000 Mills.
SPECIE DOLLAR, Norwegian, value, 4s. 6d.
DOLLAR, Swedish, Copper. In 1679, square, the legend and date in a circle, a crown in the corners. The Double Dollar is 9 inches square.
DOOGANEY, Bombay, Copper, a Pice.
DOPPIA, Papal, Gold, value, 13s.
DOPPIETTA, Sardinian, Gold.
DOPPIO, MOEDA, Portuguese, Gold, value, £2 14s. The Double Pistole.
DOREA, Bombay, Copper, value, a farthing.
DORM PENNIES, Roman coins, found in Dorsetshire, so called.
DOS REALES, Mexican, Silver, value 1s. 2 Reals.
DOUBLA, Barbary, value, 4s. 6d. 80 aspers.
DOUBLE, French, Copper, value, 2 Deniers, the Double Denier.
DOUBLE, Guernsey, Copper, value, half farthing,
DOUBLE CROWN, English, Gold, 1604, value, 10s.
DOUBLE DUCAT, various, Gold, value, 18s. 8d.
DOUZAIN, French, Copper, value, 12 Deniers, the Sous.
DRACHM, Greek, Silver, value, 8d., literally a handful, 6 oboles.
DRACHM, Jewish, Silver, the half Shekel, so called by the Greeks.
DRACHMA, Modern Greek, value, 100 Lepta.
DREYER, Silesian, Copper, the half Kreutzer of Breslau.
DREYLING, Danish, Copper, the quarter Skilling.
DRITTEL, Mecklenburgh, Silver, value, 1s., one third of Rix Dollar.
DUBBEL, Batavia, money of account.
DUBBELTJE, Dutch, Copper, value, 2 Stivers.
DUBS, Hindu, Copper. See Dudee, or Dodee.
DUCAT, various, the coin of a Dukedom, first coined at Venice, Gold, value, 9s. 4d., Silver, 3s. 5d.
DUCATELLO, Venetian, Silver.

DUCATO DI BANCO, Neapolitan, Silver, value, 5 Tarins, 3s. 6d.
DUCATONE, Flemish, Silver, the crown; value, 5s. 3d., also, in Parma, the Scudo, value, 4s. 3d.
DUETTO, Italian, Billon, 2 quattrini.
DUMAREE, Hindu, Copper, 12 to a Pice, on the Malabar coast.
DUPONDIUS, Roman, Brass, the double As.
DUTGEN, Dantzic, Silver, value, 3 Groschen.
DURO, Spanish, Silver, the hard Dollar, the Cob.
DUYT, Dutch, Copper, the eighth of a stiver. Doit.

E

EAGLE, English, Silver, Base coin, temp. K. Edward I.
EAGLE, American, Gold, value, 10 Dollars, £2 1s.
ECU, Anglo-Gallic, Gold, temp. K. Edward III. The chaise.
ECU, French, Silver, the Crown, the Ecu Blanc, and Gros Ecu.
EBBOEER, Danish, Silver, value, 14 Skillings. The Justus Judex.
EFFECTIVE, money in Spain and Portugal, so called.
EGISTALER, Hungarian, Silver, the Dollar.
ELECTRUM, coins in metal, partly Silver, and partly Gold.
ESCALIN, Netherlands, base silver; and name for the Bit, in West Indies.
ESCALIN, Liege, Silver, value, 10d. and money of account in Basle.
ESCUDO, Spain, Gold, value, 8s.
ESTERLING, English, Silver, the Anglo-Norman penny, whence Sterling.

F

FALOO, Madras, Copper, value, 5 Cash.
FAMILY COINS, Roman, Silver. Denarii struck under Consuls.
FANAM, Hindu, Silver, value, 1½d. Fanon and Fano. There is
FANAM, Indian, Gold, with alloy, on the Malabar coast, value, 6d.
FARDO, Indian, Silver, value, 2s. 9d. Qu: Pardo.
FARTHING, English, Copper, 1672; some previously of pewter, tokens, value, 960 to the £1.
FARUKI, Hindu, Gold, the quarter Mohur.
FEDERAL MONEY, American and Federation money, German, 1838.
FELDKLIPPE, Netherlands, Silver, a siege piece of William, Duke of Julich, 1543.
FELOUR, Barbary, Copper, value, a farthing.
FENIM, Swiss, money of account.
FETTMANGEN, Flemish, money of account at Cleves.
FEORTHLING, Anglo-Saxon, Silver, literally a fraction, the fourth part of a penny, hence derived farthing.
FERDING, Russian, Silver. Money of account at Libau.
FILLIPO, Italian, Silver. Milan, value, 4s. 11d.

FIORINO, Tuscan, Gold, named from the Fleur-de-Lis, arms of Florence value, 1s. 1¼d.
FISCA, Canary Isles, Silver.
FIVE POUND PIECE, English, Gold, various reigns.
FLINDERKE, Hanoverian, money of account at Emden.
FLINRICH, Bremen, money of account.
FLITTER, Brunswick, Copper, small, literally, a spangle.
FLOOSE, Arabian, value, one twentieth of a penny, money of account at Bussorah, and in Barbary.
Fluce, Flouche.
FLOREN, Flemish, Silver, value, 1s. 8d., the Guilder.
FLORIN, English, Gold, temp. K. Edward III. The gold florin, struck by German States.
FLORIN, English, Silver, 1849, a tenth of the Pound.
FLORIN, Polish, Silver, value, 6d. The Zlot.
FOANG, Siamese, Silver. Fuang, Fouang.
FOLLIS, Roman, Brass, weight, ½oz.
FONDUCLI, Turkish, Gold, value, 7s. 6d.
FORLI, Egyptian, Copper.
FORTY PENCE. Ten groats was a fee for a Lawyer, or Priest.
FOUR ANGEL PIECE, Scots, Gold, temp. K. James IV.
FRANC, French, Silver, value, 9½d. The unit also of Belgium, Switzerland, and Sardinia.
FRANCISCONE, Tuscan, Silver, value, 4s. 4d.
FRANKEN, Swiss, old money of account, value, 1s. 2¼d.
FREDERICK D'OR, Prussian, Gold, value, 16s. 6d.
FUDDAH, Egyptian, Silver. The Para.
FUDDEA, Bombay, Copper. The double Pice, 1d.
FYRKE, Danish, Copper.

G

GALL, Cochin China, Silver, value, 4d.
GASSA, Persian. 20 to a Mamoodi.
GARI, Hindu. About 4000 Rupees.
GAZ, Turkish, Silver. The Para.
GAZZETTA, Venetian, Copper, value, ⅔d.
GENOVINO, Genoese, Silver, value, 4s. 4d. The Scudo.
GENOVINO, Genoese, Gold, value, £3 2s. 8d., 96 Lire, Genovino.
GENEVOISE, Geneva, Silver.
GEORGE D'OR, Hanoverian, value, 16s. 3d.
GEORGINO, Modena, Silver, value, 2½d.
GERAH, Jewish, Silver, the smallest money, 20th of a shekel.
GHERISH, Turkish, Billon, also called Piastre.
GIGLIATO, Tuscan, Gold. The Zequin.

GIULIO, Papal, Silver, value, 6d., as the Paulo, and Leono.
GIUSTINA, Venetian.
GIUSTINIANO, Venetian, Silver.
GOESGEN, Hanoverian, money of account.
GOLCHUTS, Chinese, Gold, in canoe-shaped ingots. The Dutch namo.
GOLD DUST, Africa, current in Tibbar, in the central part.
GOLD LUMPS, Ashantee, current.
GOLD PENNY, English, temp. K. Henry III.
GOURDS, Spanish and Mexican Dollars, are so called in the West Indies
GOZ, Arabian.
GRAIN, Troy weight, the smallest, 24 to a pennyweight; the fourth of a Siliqua, or Carat.
GRANO, Maltese, Copper. Also Neapolitan. Value, one third of a penny.
GRISCIO, Egyptian, Silver, value, 1s. 6d., 30 medini.
GRIWNA, Russian, Silver, value, 10 copecs, 3¼d. Grieve, Grieven.
GROAT, English, Silver, from temp. K. Edward III. Grossum, Greater. Croat, Gros.
 Broadfaced groats, Rex groats, Dominus groats, and Cross Key groats, as well as White groats, so base that a shilling is worth nine of them.
GROOT, Dutch, Copper, value, ½d.
GROS, Flemish, Silver.
GROS, Anglo-Gallic, Billon. Also Gros Blanc.
GROS ECU, Geneva, Silver, value, 4s. 8d.
GROSCHEN, Prussian, Billon, value, 30 to a Thaler, 1½d. Also Russian and Polish.
GROSSETTO, Venetian, money of account.
GROSSO, Luccese, Billon, value, 3d. Mezzo-Grosso, 1½d.
GROTE, Bremen, value, ½d., 96 Grotes to a Specie Rix Dollar, also Flemish, 12 to a Shilling.
GROUCH, Turkish, Silver, the Piastre. Guerche, Goorooch.
GROUPE, Turkish, computation. A bag of money.
CRUESO, Spanish, money of account at Navarre.
GUBBER, Bengal, Gold, the Dutch Ducat, so called. The Sequin.
GUIENNOIS, Anglo-Gallic, Gold, temp. K. Edward III.
GUINEA, English, Gold, 1662, value 20s., afterward 21s. First struck in gold from the Guinea coast.
GUILDER, Flemish, Silver, value, 1s. 8d. The Gulden.
GUILLOT, Brabant, Copper, value, one sixth of a Sou.
GULDEN, Germany, Silver, value, 1s. 8d. 60 Kreutzers, Austrian, Silver Gulden, 2s., Florin.
GUNDA, Bengal, value, 4 cowries.
GUN MONEY, Irish, Brass, temp. K. James II. Made from cannon.
GUT GROSCHE, Prussian, Hanoverian, 24 to a Thaler.

H

HALF-PENNY, English, Silver, from temp. K. Edward I. Also Copper, from temp. King Charles II.
HARD HEAD, Scots, Billon, value, 1½. the Hardie.
HARDI, French, Copper, 1270, the Liard of Philip le Hardi.
HARDIE, English, Billon, temp. K. Edward III.
HARDIT, Anglo-Gallic, Gold, temp. K. Richard II. Double and Half Hardits.
HARF, African. Qu. Haraff. The Dahal.
HARPER, Irish, Silver, value, 9d. A familiar term.
HASER DENARIE, Persian, Silver. Huza Deenar.
HASSHAHSHAH, African, Iron, anchor-shaped. Hashia.
HELFLING, Anglo-Saxon, Silver. The Halfpenny.
HELLER, German, Copper. 4 Hellers—1 Kreutzer, 60 Kreutzers—1 Gulden.
HEMI-DRACHM, Greek, Gold, value, 6 silver Drachmæ, 3s. 9d.
HEMI-OBOLUS, Greek, Silver, the half Obolus, one twelfth of a Drachm. Hemi Drachm, or Triobolum.
HOG, Irish, Silver, the English Shilling, so called.
HOGS PENCE, Roman coins, found in Leicestershire, so called as turned up by swine.
HOON, Madras, Silver. The Pagoda.
HORSE, Danish, Silver, value, 1s. 2d.
HUITIEME, Genoese, Gold, value, 8s. 4d.
HUNA, Hindu, money of account on the Malabar coast. Qu. Anna.
HUZAR DEENAR, Persian, Gold. Haser Denarie.

I

IMPERIAL, Russian, Gold, 10 Rubles, value, £1 12s. 7d., also Flemish, Gold, value, 11s. 3d.
INDEPENDENT DOLLAR, Chili, 1817, Silver.
INDERMILLE, Hindu, Silver, value, 10d. Nepaul.
INFORTIATI, Roman. Senatorian coins of the 12th and 13th centuries.
INGOT, Japan and Burman Empire, current, unwrought, both of Gold and silver.
INGOT, a few were issued by the Bank of England on resuming cash payments, in 1816.
IRON, Angola, now current, in bars. Also Lacedemonian money.
ITAGANNES, Japan, Silver, in lumps.
ITZIB, Japan, Gold, value, 8s. 9d. Bean shaped. Itjib, Itchebo.
IZELOTTE, German, Silver, value, 2s. 9d.

J

JACOBUS, English, Gold, value, 25s. temp. K. James I.
JAGHIRE, Hindu.
JAKU, Jewish, Gold.
JANE, English, Billon. Coins brought from Genoa.
JETON, Flemish, Brass, counter, from Jeter, to cast.
JETTAL, Hindu, Copper, on Malabar coast. Settle. Jetul.
JOANESE, Portuguese, Gold, value, £3 11s. 2d. Commonly termed the Joe.
JULIO, the Papal, and Justiniano, the Venetian, Silver coins. See G.
JUSTINIANO, Venetian, Silver, value, 4s. 11d.
JUX, Turkish, 100,000 Aspers. Juck.

K

KABEAN, Tavoy Hindostan, Copper, value, a farthing. 40 Kabeans—1 Rupee.
KAISER GROSCHE, Bohemian, Silver, value, 1½d.
KALTIS, Lydian, Gold.
KAPANG, Sumatra, Copper, small.
KAZNEH, Egyptian, a Treasury of 1000 Purses, value £5000.
KEES, Egyptian, a Purse of 500 Piastres, £5.
KEFER, Turkish.
KEEPING, Sumatra.
KESITAH, Canaanite, Silver, bearing a lamb.
KHEYREEYEH, Egyptian, Gold, value, 1s. 9d.
KIBEAR, Abyssinian.
KITZE, Turkish Gold. A Bag, value, 30,000 Piastres.
KLIPPINGE, Danish, Silver.
KOBANG, Japanese, Gold, value, 27s. 4d.; it varies.
KODAMA, Japanese, Silver, a globular lump bearing characters.
KOLA, nut, Africa. Current on the Western Coast.
KOMPOW, Chinese, Linen, current in the Philippine Isles.
KOPEK, Russian, Copper, also Copeck and Kopaika, value, three eightns of a penny.
KOPY, Bohemian, money of account.
KOPFSTUCK, Austrian, Silver. 20 Kreutzers.
KOROOMS, Persian, Silver. Keran. Kran.
KORSHUIDE, Danish, Silver.
KRAN, Arabian, also Karaun, 500 equal to 10,000 Piastres.
KREUTZER, Austrian, Copper, value, one third of a penny, from Kreutz, Cross. See Heller.
KRONEN THALER, German, Silver. The Brabant Crown or Dollar, value, 4s. 5d.
KRUMSTERK, Hanoverian. At Emden.

L

LAC, Bengal computation, 100,000 Rupees, etc. Lakh.
LAND MUNTZ, German, Billon, money circulating only in the State where coined.
LARGE BRASS, Roman. The Sestertius, value, about 2d.
LARIN, Arabian, Silver, value, 1s. Laree. Persian.
LAUB THALER, Prussian, Silver. The Dollar with a wreath.
LAUREAT, English, Gold. Temp. K. Jas. I. Laurel, value, 20s.
LAXSAN, Batavian, money of account.
LEADEN COINS, Roman. Nummi plumbei, and current in the Birman Empire, also Tokens English.
LEAM, Chinese, Silver, in Ingots, each value, 6s. 8d.
LEATHER COINS, Roman. Ases Scorteos, and English Tokens.
LEONINE, English, base foreign coin, temp. King Edward I., value, ½d.
LEOPARD, Anglo-Gallic, Gold, temp. K. Edward III.
LEOPOLD, Belgium, Gold, value, 19s. 4½d., when issued 25 Francs, now 24¼ Francs.
LEOPOLDINO, Tuscan, Silver, value, 4s. 5d.
LEPTON, Greek, Copper, ancient; modern Lepta, 100 to a Drachma.
LIARD, French, Copper, value, 3 deniers.
LIBELLA, Roman, Brass. The As of diminished weight.
LIBRA JAQUESA, Spanish, value, 3s. 1d., money of account in Arragon, and Balearic Isles.
LION, Scots, Gold. Le Lion, an early French coin, and Anglo-Gallic in Billon. LION DOLLAR is Dutch.
LIRA, Italian, Silver. Lira Nouva, value, 9½d., Lira Austriaca, value, 8d.
LIRAZZA, Venetian, Silver, base, value, 1s. 3d., 30 Soldi.
LISBONINE, Portuguese, Gold, value, 25s.
LIVONINA, Russian, old coin.
LIVORNINO, Tuscan, Silver, value, 4s. 4d., also Lantern, or Tower Dollar.
LIVRE, Old French computation, value, 10d., 20 sous. Livre Tournois, a coin of Tours.
LOUIS D'OR, French, Gold, value, 18s. 8d.
LOUIS D'ARGENT, French, Silver, value, 60 sous.
LUBS, the money of Lubeck.
LUCULLEA, Roman. Money struck in Greece by Lucullus, by order of Sylla.
LUNGA, the currency of Leghorn, as distinguished from that of Florence.
LUSBURGER, Luxemburg Silver penny, temp. K. Edward I.; forbidden in England, temp. Edward III.
LYANG, Chinese, money of account.

M

MAAMBE, Egyptian, Silver, value, 2 Piastres, 8d.
MACE, Sumatra, Batavia, and China, value, 8d.
MACUQUINA, Brazilian, Silver, the cut money, quina of arms 5 shields Portugal.
MACUTA, Portuguese, Africa, Silver, value, 2¾d., 2000 zimbis or cowries.
MADONINA, Genoese, Silver, value, 1s. 6¾d. The double Lira.
MÆRRA, Anglo-Saxon, Silver. The Bener penny.
MAHBUB, Tripoli, Gold, value, 1s. ½d., also Mahboob.
MAHHBOUL, African, value, 4s. 2d.
MAILE, English, Silver, the Half Sterling, temp. Henry IV.
MAILLE, French, Billon, base coin of smallest value.
MAJORINA PECUNIA, Roman, Brass. Lower Empire.
MALLA, Spanish, Copper, 2 Mallas—1 Denier. The smallest coin at Barcelona.
MALTIER, German, Billon, value, half a Marien Groschen.
MAMOUDA, Arabian, Silver, value, 5½d., 10 Floose—1 Danim, 10 Danims —1 Mamouda. Also Mamoodi.
MANCANZA, Neapolitan, Gold, value 15s., 4 Ducati.
MAMCOUSCH, Arabian, Gold.
MANCUS, Anglo-Saxon, Gold, value, 30 pence. From the Arabian Mancush.
MANEH, Jewish, equal to 50 or 60 Shekels.
MANGAR, Greek, 4 to an asper.
MANILLA, African, Copper, current on western coast, also of Iron and of Tin.
MARABOTIN, Spanish, Silver. Arabic Dirhem.
MARADOE, Chinese, Silver, value, 600 Cash.
MARAVEDI, Spanish, Copper, 34 Maravedis—1 Real, 20 Reals—1 Dollar.
MARC, Danish, Silver, Marc of Currency, value, 4½d., specie Marc, value 1s. 6d., Marc of Hambro and Lubeck, 1s. 6d. Also Mare.
MARC, Norwegian, Silver, specie Marc, value, 10½d., 24 Skillings.
MARCHETTO, Venetian, Billon, value, ½d. Marcucci, the St. Mark.
MARENGO, Lombardy, Gold, value, 14s. 7d. Eridania 1801.
MARIEN GROSCHEN, German, Billon, value, ¾d., 36 to a Thaler, Marien Gulden, at Brunswick.
MARK, English Computation, 13s. 4d. Mearc, Anglo-Saxon, also Danish and Swedish.
MARK, Scots, Silver, 1581.
MARK OF COLOGNE, German weight, 8 oz. Troy.
MARQUE, Mauritius, Copper.

MAS. Qu. Mace, Chinese and Indian Silver, value, 100 Cash. The Masse, 1¼ Rupees.
MASSE, French, Gold, 1314. The Chaise. From the Mace or Scepter.
MATH, Hindoo. Money of account at Rangoon.
MATTAPAN, Venetian, Silver, value, 3d. Coined at Capo Mattapan, 1203.
MATTIER, Hanoverian, Silver. Matthier, Copper.
MAUNDY MONEY, English, Silver. The Silver 1d., 2d., 3d., and 4d., coined for Royal Charity on Maundy Thursday.
MAX D'OR, Bavarian, Gold, value, 13s. 7d , MAXIMILIAN, 1¼ Ducats.
MEDAL, a term for a coin, not struck for currency.
MEDIA ONZO, Mexican, Gold, value, £1 12s. Also Media quarta de Onza.
MEDIAN, Barbary, Gold.
MEDINO, Egyptian, Silver, the Para. The Turkish Medin or Meidein.
MEDIO PESA, Mexican, Silver, value, 2s. 1¼d. The half dollar.
MEDJEDEER, Turkish, Silver, value, 3s. 5d, 20 Piastres.
MEISSNER GULDEN, Saxony. Money of account at Leipsic.
MENIAN, Barbary, Silver, value, 2s. 7d., 50 Aspers.
MERAU, French, Lead. A Token at Religious festivals.
MERIGAL, Barbary, Gold, value, 18s.
MERK, Scots, Silver, value, 1s. 1d.
MESS VALUTA, Tyrol, money of account at Bolsano.
METICAL, Barbary, Gold, value various.
METALLINE, Roman, Copper washed with Silver, so called.
MEZZO SCUDO, Lucca, Silver, half Scudo.
MIDDLE BRASS, Roman. Size of Semis.
MIL, proposed name for the thousandth part of the Pound.
MILL, United States, money of account. 1000 to a Dollar.
MILREA, Portuguese, Gold, value, 4s. 5d.
MILREI, Portuguese, Silver, value, 4s. 5d. 1000 Reis.
MILREI, Brazils, Silver, value, formerly 4s. 5d., now 2s. 1d.
MIMOEDA, Portuguese, Gold, value, 13s. 6d. The half-moidore.
MINCE, Greek, Gold, value, £3 4s. 7d., 100 drachma. Mina, the Turkish Asper.
MINUTA, Anglo-Saxon, Copper. The Styca.
MIOBOLO, Ionian Islands, Copper.
MIRLITOF, French, Gold
MISCAL, Arabian, Gold.
MISSILIA, Roman. Coins scattered at the Games.
MITE, English, Copper, value, one third of a farthing.
MITKUL, Barbary, Gold, value, 9s., 24 Fluces—1 Blankeel, 4 Blankeels—1 Ounce, 10 Ounces—1 Mitkul. Bendiky, Miscal, or Ducat.
MITRE, English, base silver, temp. K. Edward I.

MOBOGS, Hindu, seeds used for weighing gold.
MOCO, W. Indies, Silver, value, £1s. 1¼d. A piece cut from a Dollar.
MOHUR, Hindu, Gold, value, £1 9s. 1d., the Mohur Sicca, 32s. Mohr, Mohar, and Moore.
MOIDORE, Portuguese, Gold, value, 27s. The MOEDA D'ORO.
MONACO, Italian, Silver, value, 4s. 4d. The Monk.
MONZONNAH, Barbary, Silver, value, 1d.
MOSTOSKA, Russian, Copper, 4 to a Kopek.
MOUTON, Anglo-Gallic, Gold. Bearing Agnus Dei.
MUSKET BALLS, American, value, a farthing, current in Massachusetts, 1656.
MURAGLIOLI, Modena, Copper, value, 1d.
MYNET, Anglo-Saxon, whence mint.
MURAJOLA, Bologna.
MUNTZE, German. The small coins.

N

NANDIOGINS, Japanese, Silver. A lump.
NAPOLEON, French, Gold, 1803, value, 15s. 10d., 20 Francs.
NASARA, Tunis, Silver, value, 2¼d.
NAULUM, Greek, money put into mouths of deceased persons. The freight.
NEWEMEEN, Ashantee, Gold, value, £4 5s. 4d. an ounce.
NOBLE, English, Gold, 1344, value, 6s. 8d.; there are George, Rose Nobles, &c.
NUMMUS, Roman, the Sestertius, also the Generic name for money
NOIR, French W. Indies, Billon, 1¼d. the black dog, so called.

O

OBAN, Japan, Gold. Ouban.
OBOLUS, Greek, Brass, also Anglo-Saxon, and English, temp. K. Henry III., base.
OBOLUS, Rhenish, Gold. Also Silver, value, 1s. 2d.
OBOLO, Ionian Islands, Copper.
OBSIDIONAL, money struck during a siege.
OCHAVA, Mexican, Copper, value, ⅜d., 8 Ochavas—1 Rial, 8 Rials—1 Dollar.
OCHAVO, Spanish, Copper, value, ½d. The Chavo and Chovy.
OCHELLO, Venetian, Gold, value, £1 17s. 8d., 4 Zecchino.
OCHOSEN, Spanish. The smallest old coin.
OCTAGON, California. See Slug.
OERTOGS, Swedish, Silver.
ONCETTA, Neapolitan, Gold, value, 10s. 3d., Onza.
ONCIA, Italian, Gold, value, 10s. 3d. in Sicily.

ONZA DE ORO, Mexican, Gold, value, £3 4s. The Doblon.
ONZARO, Papal, Gold, value, 9s. 4d., the Ducat. Ongaro.
OR, Persian, Silver, value, 6s. 8d.
ORA, Anglo-Saxon, computation, an ounce, 20 pennies. Also Danish.
OR, or ORE, Swedish, Copper, and Silver, value, 1d. Koppar Ore, the Rundstyck. Silver, the Styfer.
ORT, Danish, the fourth; as Ort Groschen, fourth of a Groat.
ORTJE, Flemish, Copper.
OSELLA, Venetian, Gold. Oselle, Venetian, Silver, value, 3s. 2d. Osell.
OSTIC, Greek, value, 6d.
OUSTAVA, Portuguese. A division of the Mark.
OWL, Greek, Silver. The Tetradrachm.

P

PADENS, Hindoo, nuts from Persia, current at Surat. The Baddams.
PAGODA, Hindoo, Gold, and also Silver. Star Pagoda, value, 7s. 4d. Arcot Pagoda, value, 4s. 11d.
PAISAH, Hindoo, Copper. Nepaul.
PAOLO, Papal, Silver, value, 5d., 10 Pauli—1 Scudo.
PAPARINA, Roman, coins of 12th and 13th centuries, also called Provisini.
PAPETTO, Papal, Silver, value, 10½d.
PAPIROLO, Sardinian, Billon.
PARA, Turkish, Bilion, 40 Paras to a Piastre. Parat.
PARDO, Barbary, Silver, value, 1s. 3d. Pardao. Also Indian.
PARGO, Portuguese India, Silver, value, 2s. 5d., 4 Tangas.
PARISIS D'OR, French, 1350. And Parisis d'Argent, 1350.
PARPAJOLO, Lombardy, Billon, value, 1d., 8 to a Lira.
PASTEBOARD, Dutch. Siege money at Leyden, 1574.
PATACA, Portuguese and Brazilian, Silver, value, 1s. 5d., Patacao or Sello.
PATACK, Batavian.
PATACON, Spanish, Silver, value, 4s. 3d.
PATAGON, Dutch, Silver, value, 4s. 1d., 50 Stuyver Piece, or Leg Dollar. Swiss, value, 3s. 10d.
PATARD, Flemish, Copper, value, 1d. Patar, the Stiver.
PATTY, Hindoo, inferior coin of Trangania.
PAUNCHEA, Bombay, money of account, value, 5 Rupees.
PAVILLON, Anglo-Gallic, Gold, temp. K. Edward III.
PECCO, Java. Money of account.
PECHA, Tartary, Copper. Pessa, Pice.
PECUNIA, Roman money, from Pecus, cattle.
PENGE, Danish, Pence, money.
PENGUIN, Ashantee, Gold, value, £11 16s. 4d.

PENING, Dutch, Copper, the half-farthing, coin in general in many countries.
PENNY, Anglo-Saxon, Silver; English, Gold, temp. K. Henry III.. also Copper, from temp. K. George III., 240 to a Pound.
PENNY OF SAINT PAUL, Westphalia, Silver, 1260. Munster.
PENNYYARD, Penny, Silver, English coins in heraldry so called. Spence, arms.
PENTADRACHM, Greek, Silver, value, 3s. 6d. 5 Drachmæ.
PERPERO, Ragusa, Silver. Perpera, Greek, Gold, value, 10s.
PESETA, Spanish, Silver, value, 1s. 0½d., 5 Reals; the Mexican quarter dollar.
PESO DURO, Spanish, Silver, value, 4s. 3d. The Hard Dollar.
PESSA, Hindoo, Copper, value, ¼d. Pecha, Pice.
PETERMENGEN, Germany Triers, Billon, value, ¾d.
PETIT FLORIN, Tuscan, Gold, 1340.
PETIT RYAL, French, Gold, 1314.
PEZZA, Tuscan, Silver, value, 3s. 8d. Pezza, Leghorn, Gold, value, 4s., Pezzi Solidi, Piasters.
PFENNIG German, Copper, 12 Pfennings—1 Groschen, 30 Groschen--1 Thaler.
P'HAINUNG, Siamese, weight for gold.
PHILIP, Flemish, Gold. The Ryder. Phillipo, Lombardy, Silver.
PHŒNIX, Mod. Greek, Silver, value, 8d.
PIASTER, Spanish, Silver, the Dollar, value, 4s. 3d.
PIASTRA, a la Rose, Tuscan, Silver. The Neapolitan Dollar.
PIASTRE, Turkish, Silver, value, 3d.
PIATAK, Russian, Copper, value, 5 Kopeks.
PIC, Chinese, value, 100 Catties.
PICE, Hindoo, Copper, 12 Pice—1 Anna, 16 Annas—1 Rupee.
PICCHALEON, Sardinian, Copper. The Centisimo.
PICCOLA, Maltese, Copper, 6 to a Grano, the smallest coin.
PIECE OF EIGHT, Spanish, Silver, value, 4s. 3d., the Dollar, or Piaster formerly 8 Reals, now 20 Reals.
PIED-FORT, French, a standard coin, or Pattern.
PIGNATELLO, Papal, Billon, temp. P. Innocent XII.
PILLAR DOLLAR, Spanish, Silver. The Dollar with the Pillars, value, 4s. 3d.
PINA, Peruvian, Silver Bullion.
PISTAREEN, Spanish, Silver, value, 10d., the fifth of the Dollar, 4 Reals
PISTOLE, Spanish, Gold, value, 16s., formerly 32 Reals, now 80.
PISTOLE, German, various States, Gold, value, 16s. 3d
PISTOLE, Scots, Gold, 1701.
PITIES, Batavian, leaden coins.
PLACK, Scots, Billon, one third of a penny

PLATINUM, Russian, 3 Rouble piece, current value, 8s. 10d, intrinsic value, 6s.
PLAPPART, Swiss, Copper, a Bernese coin, 1458.
PLAPPERT, German, Billon, value, 2d., 4 Albus.
PLAQUETTE, Flemish, Billon.
PLATA, Mexican, Silver money. Plata Macuquina, Brazilian strips.
PLATES, Swedish, Copper. The large coins.
PLOTT, Swedish, Silver, value, 1s. 6d. Plat.
PLUMBEI NUMMI, Roman, leaden coins. Temp. Saturnalia.
POLLARD, English. A Poll head, clipped coin.
POLONAISE, Polish, Gold.
POLTIN, Russian, Silver, value, 1s. 6d., the half Ruble. Polpoltin, the quarter Rouble.
POLTURAT, Hungarian, Copper.
POLUSKA, Russian, Copper. The quarter Kopek.
PONDO, Roman, Brass. The As.
PONE, Tartary, Copper, value, ½d.
PONTE, Sicilian. Money of account.
POOT, Junk, Ceylon, Tin money.
PORCELAIN, a shell, current in W. Indies.
PORTCULLIS, English, Silver, at Bombay, Crown, Half-crown, Shilling, and Sixpence, temp. Q. Elizabeth.
PORTUGALESE, Lubec, Gold.
POTIN, Egyptian, coins of a mixture of lead, copper, and tin.
POUL, Tartary, Copper. Poul e Siaho, Persian, Copper.
POUND, Anglo-Saxon and English, computation, value, 20s.
PROVISINI, Roman, Senatorian coins of the 12th and 13th centuries.
PUBLICO, Neapolitan, Copper.
PUL, Persian, Copper. The general name for coins of that metal.
PULZLATY, Hungarian, Silver, the half Florin.
PUNN, Bengal, value, 20 cowries.
PURSE, Turkish, 500 Piastres.
PYSA, Asiatic, Copper, value, 50th of Mamoud. Qu. Pice.

Q

QUADRANS, Brass, Roman, 4th of the As. Small brass.
QUADRIGATI, Roman, Silver, denarii with four-horse car.
QUADRUPLE, Spanish, Gold, 4 Pistoles, value, £3 4s.
QUADRUPLE, Sardinian, Gold, 80 Lire, value, £3 3s. 4d.
QUADRUSSIS, Roman, Brass, value, 4 Asses. The As Grave.
QUAN, Cochin China, Silver, value, 4s. 6d.
QUART CROWN, Bavarian, Silver, value, 1s. 1d.
QUARTA ONZA, Mexican, Gold, value, 16s. Quarto de Peso, Peruvian, Copper.

QUARENTINO, Modena, Silver, value, 1s. 8d
QUARTER GUINEA, English, Gold, value, 5s. 3d. K. George I. and III.
QUARTILLO, Mexican, Silver. Quarter Real.
QUARTINHO, Portuguese, Gold.
QUARTO, Gibraltar, Copper, value, farthing, 16 Quartos—1 Rial, 12 Rials —1 Dollar, from the Spanish Cuarta.
QUATTRINI, Venetian, Silver, very small.
QUATTRINO, Italian, Copper, value, farthing. Quattrinello.
QUILATE, Spanish. The Carat.
QUINARIUS, Roman, Silver. The half denarius, marked V. Also of Gold.
QUINCUNX, Roman, Brass. 5 Asses. The Quincussis.
QUINTO DI SCUDO, Lucca, Silver, value, 10¼d.
QUINTUPLE, Neapolitan, Gold, 5 Ducati, value, 17s. 1d., 5 Scudi, value, 19s. 2d.

R

RADER FLORIN, German. Money of account at Cologne.
RAGUSINA, Ragusa, Silver.
RAPP, Swiss, Copper, 10 Rappen—1 Batz. Angster.
RATHSPRÆSENTGER, German, Silver, value, 8d. Aix la Chapelle.
RATISBONINA, Ratisbon. Money of account.
RATITI, Roman, Silver. The denarius bearing a Ratis. Raft.
REAL, Spanish, Silver, the Rial, value, 2¼d. 20 Reals—1 Dollar.
REAL, Persian, Silver. The Rupee.
REALE, Sardinian, Silver, value, 4¼d. The Florentine.
RED WOOD, Angola, now current.
REGENSBURGER, Ratisbon. Money of account.
REI, Portuguese, Copper, value, one fifth of a farthing. Rez, Reis, computation, 1000 Reis—1 Millrei.
REICHS GULDEN, Saxony, Silver, value, 1s. 8d. Two thirds of Rix Dollar.
REICHS THALER, Prussian, Silver, value, 2s. 11d.
BESELLADO, Spanish. Money re-coined.
RIAL, English, Gold. The Rose Noble, temp. K. Edward IV.
RIAL, Mexico, Silver, value, 6¼d., 8 Rials—1 Dollar.
RIDDY, Ceylon, Silver, bent wire, value, 7d. Rheedy.
RIDER, Scots, Gold. Temp. K. James IV. Ryder.
RIKS DALER, Danish, Silver, specie value, 4s. 7d. The Rigsbank Dollar, value, 2s. 3d.
RING MONEY, Gold, Silver, Iron, and Tin, Celtic. Now in Africa.
RIX DOLLAR, Hanse Towns, Silver, specie value, 3s. 10½d., and current value, 2s. 11d.
RIX DOLLAR, Sweden, Silver, specie value, 4s. 6d., Rix Dollar Banco, value, 1s 8d.

ROANOKE, Indian shells strung, value, 6d. a cubit, or 18 inches.
ROOKIE, Turkish, Silver, value, 1s. 8d. Qu. Gold.
ROSARIE. A base coin, perhaps Abbey piece.
ROSE NOBLE, English, Gold, value, 6s. 8d., and in temp. K. James I., Rose Royal, value, 30s.
ROSINA, Tuscan, Gold, value, 18s. 3d. Mezza Rosina.
ROUP, Polish, Silver, value, 5d.
RUBIC, Turkish, Gold, value, 1s. 9d. 35 Aspers. Rubich.
RUBLE, Russian, Silver, value, 3s., 100 Copecks. Rouble.
RUNSTYCK, Swedish, Copper, value, one sixth of a farthing. Keppar Ore.
RUPEE, Hindostan, value, 1s. 11d., 16 Annas. Inscription in Oriental characters, the oldest are square.
RUSPONE, Tuscan, Gold, value, £1 8s. 6d., from Ruspo, newly coined.
RYAL, French, Gold. See Rial.
RYDER, Flemish, Gold, value, £1 4s. 9d. Also Silver, value, 5s. 4d. The Ducatoon. See Rider.
RYKSORT, Danish, Silver.

S

SAADEEYEH, Egyptian, Gold, value, 1s.
SAHIB KORAN, Persian, Silver, value, 1s. 2d.
SAIME, Barbary. Money of account at Algiers.
SAINT ANDREW, Scots, Gold.
SAINT JOHN THE BAPTIST, Genoese, Silver.
SAINT MARK, Venetian, Silver. The Crociato, or Scudo.
SAINT THOMAS, Portuguese, Gold, value, 9s. At Goa, in India.
SAINT STEPHEN, Portuguese, Gold, value, 30s. The Milrea.
SALDING, English. Base coin, temp. K. Edward I. Scalding.
SALUNG, Siamese, value, 2 Foangs.
SALUT, Anglo-Gallic, Gold, value, 13s. 4d.
SANNAR, Persian.
SANTA, Chinese computation, 9d. 200 Cash.
SATTALIE, Bencoolen, also Sattellee, money of account, 3 Sattalies—1 Succos, 4 Succos—1 Dollar.
SCARABEI, Egyptian, clay-baked, beetle-shaped, probably current money: also Greek, Gold, and Silver.
SCEATTA, Anglo-Saxon, Silver.
SCHAAF, Hanoverian. Money of account at Emden.
SCHALIN, Dutch, Silver, value, 7d.
SCHELLING, Flemish, Billon.
SCHERFFE, Brunswick. Money of account.
SCHILLING, Hanse Towns, Billon, value, 1d.
SCHLANTE, Swedish, Copper, value, ¼d. Slantar or Lös penningar Copper.

SCHLECH THALER, German. Money of account at Aix-la-Chapelle.
SCHOCK, Saxony, money of account.
SCHUITE, Japanese, Silver, boat-shaped, value, 25s. 3d.
SCHWARE, Bremen, Copper, 5 to the Grote.
SCHWARTZ, Hanse Towns, 5 Schwartzen—1 Grote.
SCORTEOS ASES, Roman, Leather Coins.
SCUDINO, Modena, Gold.
SCUDO, Italian, Silver, value, 4s. 2d., 10 Paoli.
SCUDO D'ORO, Genoese, value, 4s.
SCUTE, English, temp. Q. Elizabeth.
SCYLLINGA, Anglo-Saxon. Computation.
SECHSER, German, Copper, value, 2d., literally a sixer, or Kreutzer Piece.
SECHSLING, Hamburg, Copper.
SECHSTELS, Saxony, Silver, value, 5d., 4 good groschen.
SEGROS, Polish, Billon, value, 4d.
SELAH, Jewish, Silver. 2 Shekels.
SELLO, Brazils, Silver, value, 2s. 9d. See Pataca.
SEMBRELLA, Roman, Brass. Selibra, Semi Libella.
SEMI, Roman, Brass. The Semi As or Semiuncia, and Semi Aureus, Gold.
SENI, Japanese, Copper. The Cas. 600 to a Tael.
SEPECK, Anam Emp. Brass.
SEQUIN, Turkish, Gold, value, 9s. 3d., Chequin or Sultany. Also Italian, Zequin or Zechino.
SERRATA, Roman. Coins with the edges notched.
SESSINO, Parma, Copper. Sesino.
SESTERTIUM, 1000 Sestertii (HS), Roman money of account.
SESTERTIUS, Roman, Silver, 4th of Denarius, also Large Brass.
SESTHALF, Dutch, Silver, value, 5d.
SEVEN SHILLINGS, English, Gold, temp. K. George III.
SEXTANS, Roman, Brass. 6th of the As.
SEXTULA, Roman, Brass.
SHAHEE, Persian, Silver, value, ½d., 4 Shahis—1 Piastre, 5 Piastres—1 Karaun, 10 Karauns—1 Tamaun. Shahi.
SHAKEE, Turkish, Silver, value, 3½d.
SHATREE, Persian, Silver.
SHARI, Kabul, Silver, value, 5d.
SHEKEL, Jewish, Silver, value, 3s. Also in Gold.
SHILLING, English, Silver, 20 to a Pound.
SHOE, Chinese, Gold and Silver Ingots, value various, from one half to 100 Tales. Dutch name, Schuit.
SHOSTACK, German, money of account in Prussia, Poland, etc., Shustack.
SIANI, Syria. Money of account at Aleppo, 24 Siani—1 Aspro.

SICCA, Persian, Gold, at Delhi: means a Die, a Coin.
SICCA Rupee, Bengal, Silver, value, 2s. 1d.; Sicca, a weight.
SICLE, Jewish, Silver. The Shekel.
SIGILLÆ, Roman, Brass, also leaden counters at the Saturnalia.
SILBER GROSCHEN, Prussian, Base metal, value, 1¼d., 30 to a Thaler.
SILIQUA. The Carob Bean. The Carat weight.
SILVER SOVEREIGN, Spanish. The Dollar, so called.
SINGPNAI, Siamese, value, 2 P'hainungs.
SLET DOLLAR, Danish. Schlecht, a 4 Mark Piece.
SLIPS, English, Base money, temp. K. Edward VI., value, 1½d.
SLUG, California, Gold, value, £10 5s. 2d.; 50 Dollars, Octagon.
SMALL BRASS, Roman. The size of the Sextans.
SNAPHANE, Brabant, Silver, 1489.
SOL, Old French, Copper. The Sou.
SOLDO, Italian, Copper.
SOLIDUS, Roman, Gold, value, 12s. Solidus, the Anglo-Saxon shilling.
SOLOTA, Greek, value, 1s.
SOMPAYE, Siamese, Silver.
SOVEREIGN, English, Gold, 1485, value, £1 5s.; 1816, value, £1.
SOVEREIGN, Austrian, Gold, value, £1 7s. 10d., 3 Ducats.
SPINTRIÆ, Roman, Brass, obscene tickets, not current.
SPUR ROYAL, English, Gold, value, 15s. The Spurred Groat, Scots. Silver, value, 16d.
STATER, Greek, Gold, value, about £1 3s., Greek for standard. Early name, Chrysus.
STEPING, English, Base coin, temp. K. Edward I.
STERLING, Anglo-Norman, Silver. Steore, Standard.
STIVER, Flemish, Copper. Stuyver, Dutch, Billon, value, 1d.
STUBER, German, Copper. The Stiver. Styfer, Swedish, Billon.
STYKKER, Danish.
SUCCO, Bencoolen, money of account, quarter dollar.
SUADO, Austrian, Silver, value, 4s. 8d.
SUELDO, Catalonia and Majorca, money of account, 12 Dineros—1 Sueldo, 12 Sueldos—1 Libra, value, 2d.
SUSKIN, English. The diminutive of the French Sou.
SWINE PENNIES, Roman coins found in Lincolnshire, so called.
SYCEE, Chinese, Silver Ingots, canoe-shaped, Chinese standard silver.
SYFERT, Hanoverian, Copper, current at Embden.

T

TAEL, Chinese, Silver, value, 6s. 8d., 1000 Cash. Thail, Japan, Tell.
TAIJA, Spanish, Copper, value the 4th of a Real.
TALARO, Tuscan, Silver, the Dollar, the Thalaro of the Levant, 16 Piastres. Turkey.

TALENT, Hebrew, computation, 60 Shekels.
TALENT, Greek, weight 60 Minæ, the value of the Attic Mina was £4 1s. 3d.
TANGA, Indian, Gold, value, 7½d., 4 Tangas—1 Pargo.
TAOU, Chinese, Knife coins, early brass, cast.
TAR, Silver, Hindoo, value, ½d., current on the coast of Malabar. Tare.
TARIN, Sicilian, Maltese, Silver, value, 20 Grani, 5th of a Ducat.
TARO, Sicilian, Silver, value, 8½d., 5 Tari—1 Ducat; and Malta value, 1¼d.
TELA, Persian. Various value. The Tilla.
TERUNCIUS, Roman, Brass, 3 oz. 4th of Libella.
TESTER, English, Silver. Coin with a head upon it.
TESTON, Italian, Silver, value, 1s. 6d.
TESTONE, Portuguese, Silver, value, 5¾d., 100 Reis.
TETRA DRACHM, Greek, Silver, value, 4 Drachmæ, the Stater Argenteus, value, 3s. 3d.
TETROBOLUS, Greek, Silver, value, 4 Oboli, 6d.
THALER, German, Silver, value, 2s. 11d. First coined in Joachims Thal, a valley in Bohemia.
THIRD OF A GUINEA, English, Gold, value, 7s.
THIRIMSA, Anglo-Saxon. Three fifths of a shilling.
TICAL, Siamese, Silver, nut-shaped. The Baat.
TILLA, Persian, Gold, value, 13s. 4d. The Tela and Tila.
TINFE, Polish, Silver, value, 1s. 3d. Timpfe.
TOKENS, English, Copper, issued by tradesmen in the 16th and 18th centuries; also Silver, English, temp. K. George III.
TOKOO, Ashantee, Silver, value. 8d.
TOMAN, Persian, Gold, value, 10s. 3d., 50 Abassis or Piastres. Touman and Tomaun.
TOMPONG, Malacca.
TONGA, Persian, Silver, value, 7s. 6d.
TORNESE, Neapolitan, Copper. 2 to the Grano.
TOUCH PIECES, English, Silver. Given to persons touched for King's evil. Also Gold.
TOURNAY GROAT, Anglo-Gallic, Silver, temp. K. Henry VIII.
TOWN PIECES, English, Copper, tokens issued by towns.
TRARO, Venetian, Billon, value, 2d., 4 to the Lira Austriaca.
TREMISSIS, Roman, Gold, value, one third of the Solidus, 4s.
TRIDRACHM, Greek, Silver, value, 3 Drachmæ.
TRIENS, Roman. Value, one third of the As.
TRIGROSS, Polish. Value, 2d.
TRIOBOLUS, Greek, Silver. The Hemidrachm, value, 4¼d.
TRIPONDIUS, Roman, Brass, value, 3 Ases.
TSEEN, Chinese, Brass. The Cash.
TURNER, Scots, Copper. A base coin. Qu. Tournois, coined at Tours.

TURNOSE, German, Silver.
TWENTY SHILLING PIECE, English, Silver, temp. K. Charles I.
TWO GUINEA PIECE, English, Gold, from temp. King Charles II
TWO PENNY PIECE, English, Copper, temp. K. George III.
TUNKA, Hindoo, Silver, value, 2s.
TYMFE, Prussia, Silver, value, 8½d, 18 Old Gross.

U

UCHU, Peruvian, species of Capsicum. The Pod, used as a coin.
UDLI, Hindoo, Silver.
UNCIA, Roman Brass. Ounce, 12th of As.
UNICORN, Scots, Gold, temp. K. James III.
UNIT, English, Gold, value, 20s. temp. K. James I. Laureled pieces.
URDEE, Bombay, Copper.
UTA, Batavian. At Java.
VELLON, Spanish, Copper. Or Billon.
VICTORIATUS, Roman, Silver, value, 4d. The Quinarius, with figure of Victory.
VINTEM, Portuguese, Copper, value, 1d., 50 to the Milreis, 20 Reis. Vintin, at Goa; Vintem, Spanish, Gold coin.
VIZ, Bengal, Copper.

W

WAMPAM, Peage, American, shells strung, current in Pennsylvania, 10s. a fathom.
WADMAL, African, woolen, cloth made in Iceland, and current.
WHITE PEAKE, Indian, shens strung, is. a cubit, 18 in.
WILLIAM, Dutch, Gold, value, 16s. 5d., formerly 10 Guilders.
WITTEN, Hanoverian, Silver, 10 Wittens—1 Stiver, current at Embden. Witten Penning, Danish, Silver.
WISSE MUNTZEN, Bavarian, Billon, inferior to current coin.
WOOD, Angola, a red kind from Malemba, current.

X

XERAPHIN, Hindoo, Silver, value, 2s. 1d.
XERIPH, Greece, value, 10s.

Y

YERMEEBESHLEK, Turkish, Gold, value, 12s. 6d.
YUZLIK, Turkish, Billon, value, 2½ Piastres, 3d.

Z

ZAHL PFENNIG, German, Brass, the Jeton, or reckoning penny.
ZARMAHBUB, Greece, Gold, value, 6s. Zermahub, Turkish, Gold, the Sequin.

ZECCHINO, Venetian, Gold, value, 9s. 5d., from Zecca, the mint, the Sequin of Turkey.
ZENZERLI, Turkish. Current in Egypt.
ZIAM, Barbary, Gold, value, 5s. 2d.
ZIMBI, Angola, Shell. The Cowrie.
ZLATY, Hungarian, Silver. The Florin.
ZLOT, Polish, Silver, value, 6d., 30 Groschen, 15 Kopecs.
ZODIAC RUPEES, Hindoo, value, 1s. 11½d., bear the different signs of the Zodiac; there are also Zodiac Mohurs..
ZUZA, Jewish, Silver. 4th of a Shekel.
ZWANZIGER, Austrian, Silver, value, 8d., 20 Kreutzers.
ZWEYDRITTEL, Mecklenburg, Silver, value, 2s. Two thirds of Rix Dollar. Danish, value, 2s. 10d.

THE END.

www.ingramcontent.com/pod-product-compliance
Lightning Source LLC
Chambersburg PA
CBHW030820190426
43197CB00036B/685